Bayview

Bayview

EDUCATIONAL
RECONSTRUCTION

D1733395

RECONSTRUCTING AMERICA
Andrew L. Slap, series editor

Educational Reconstruction

African American Schools in the Urban South, 1865–1890

Hilary Green

FORDHAM UNIVERSITY PRESS
NEW YORK 2016

Fordham University Press has no responsibility for the persistence or accuracy of URLs for external or third-party Internet websites referred to in this publication and does not guarantee that any content on such websites is, or will remain, accurate or appropriate.

Fordham University Press also publishes its books in a variety of electronic formats. Some content that appears in print may not be available in electronic books.

Visit us online at www.fordhampress.com.

Library of Congress Cataloging-in-Publication Data available online at catalog.loc.gov.

Printed in the United States of America

18 17 16   5 4 3 2 1

First edition

Contents

Abbreviations

ADAH	Alabama Department of Archives and History, Montgomery, Alabama
AFUC	American Freedmen's Union Commission, New York
AL-BRFAL-ED	United States Bureau of Refugees, Freedmen, and Abandoned Lands, *Records of the Superintendent of Education for the State of Alabama, Bureau of Refugees, Freedmen, and Abandoned Lands*, National Archives Microfilm Publication, Washington, D.C.
AMA	American Missionary Association Archives, Amistad Research Center, Tulane University, New Orleans
ARC	Amistad Research Center, Tulane University, New Orleans
BRFAL-ED	Records of the Educational Division of the Bureau of Refugees, Freedmen, and Abandoned Lands, National Archives Microfilm Publication, Washington, DC
LVA	Library of Virginia, Richmond, Virginia
MCPSS	Mobile County Public School System, Barton Academy, Mobile, Alabama
MHS	Massachusetts Historical Society, Boston
NEFAS	New England Freedmen's Aid Society, Boston
VA-BRFAL-ED	United States Bureau of Refugees, Freedmen, and Abandoned Lands, *Records of the Superintendent of Education for the State of Virginia, Bureau of Refugees, Freedmen, and Abandoned Lands*, National Archives Microfilm Publication, Washington, D.C.
VHS	Virginia Historical Society, Richmond, Virginia
VSU	Virginia State University, Petersburg, Virginia

EDUCATIONAL
RECONSTRUCTION

Introduction

Wallace Turnage, a former slave from Mobile, Alabama, opened his personal narrative with a plea to readers to ignore its "ungrammatical and desultory" nature.[1] Being "deprived of an education," Turnage explained that the "knowledge I have to present this biography to you, I learnt during that time and since I escapted the clutches of those who held me in slavery."[2] His apology for the lack of literary grace in the narrative of his escape during the 1864 Battle for Mobile Bay served as an indictment against antebellum southern society and its view on African American education. Entrenched antebellum racial and social norms may have denied Wallace Turnage and other African Americans an education, but these societal norms never dampened African Americans' desire to become educated. Like Turnage, urban African Americans acquired literacy and often their freedom whenever opportunity availed it possible. However, these individual examples did not overturn the racial and social obstacles circumscribing African American education. This social and educational revolution occurred only because of the Civil War and Confederate defeat. The fruits of this revolution were apparent to Richmond Colored Normal alumni in 1888.

On June 13, 1888, Professor Daniel Barclay Williams took the opportunity to reflect on the racial progress made since emancipation before an audience of Richmond Colored Normal graduates. "For the last twenty-three years the colored people have made rapid progress in civilization," the Virginia Normal and Collegiate Institute professor informed the audience. "Their intelligence has been wonderfully augmented. Public schools, industrial, normal, professional schools, and colleges have taught millions of children, and educated thousands of teachers, ministers, doctors, lawyers, statesmen, business men, and mechanics." Yet, Williams reminded them, "although much has been done for our people by the powerful influence of intelligence, industry, and morality, much remains to be done."[3]

Despite the work ahead, Williams and his peers could still celebrate their achievements. Education had yielded them success in a variety of professions that might have been viewed by Turnage and other former slaves as impossible before emancipation. Williams, though, recognized that the fight was far from over. He concluded his address by loosely paraphrasing the last two stanzas of Henry Wadsworth Longfellow's "The Building of the Ship," and charged attendees with a mission to "Sail on, O Ship of Education! Sail on, O Normal, hold thy station!" Through the Freedmen's Schools, state-funded public schools, and the insistence of urban African American men, women, and children, Williams and other Richmond Colored Normal graduates benefited from the postwar educational developments that occurred across the entire urban South. It was their duty as the beneficiaries to continue adding to the rich educational legacy.[4]

Turnage, Williams, and Richmond Colored Normal graduates serve as a testament to the expectations and the collaborative efforts of urban African Americans who sought to define the meaning of freedom, citizenship, and the Civil War through education. In viewing education as essential to the transition to freedom, urban African Americans (newly freed and those free before the war) established strategic relationships with individuals and organizations that shared a devotion to education in the postwar period. Yet, competing visions and expectations for African American education often made for uneasy alliances. Power struggles ensued, new partnerships developed, and old relationships were either redefined or ceased. Despite these tensions, a sustainable system of African American education emerged by 1890.

The central question I ask in *Educational Reconstruction* is: how did urban African Americans and their supporters create, develop, and sustain a system of education during the transition from slavery to freedom? Urban African Americans established and fostered educational networks of relationships with individuals and organizations that shared their belief in postwar African American education, including the Freedmen's Bureau, northern missionary associations, and later city and state government officials. Educational Reconstruction, therefore, represents urban African Americans' process of building networks to yield a sustainable system of schools for the largely under- and uneducated masses from emancipation to the failed passage of a federal funding bill in 1890. As in any relationship, internal power struggles ensued and sometimes marred the networks. Even as African Americans witnessed a contested terrain concerning their education on a global, national, and local scale, urban African Americans and their partners experienced educational triumph with the development of the Freedmen's Schools and state-funded public schools. Through Educational Reconstruction, they successfully moved African American education from being a nonentity to a legitimate institution, established a professional class of African

American public schoolteachers, developed educational resources essential to daily school operations, and ensured its continuation for future generations. As partners and circumstances changed over the twenty-five-year period, I argue that urban African Americans never lost sight of their vision of citizenship and freedom in their struggle for educational access and legitimacy, and that they successfully enshrined the African American schoolhouse as the fundamental vehicle for distancing themselves from their slave past.

This vision, moreover, became central to urban African Americans' racially inclusive definition of citizenship in their respective cities and states, and the nation at large. Rather than the war itself, classroom experiences, the partnerships forged therein, participation in literary societies and activism for quality public schools unified urban African Americans around a collective identity and culture reflective of their free status and Confederate defeat. With the adoption of new state constitutional mandates, African Americans maintained the vision but refined their definition of citizenship in a manner that meaningfully incorporated African American education, holding "that all citizens . . . stood equal in rights and protections regardless of race or prior status as slave."[5] The African American schoolhouse, therefore, embodied the participation of urban African Americans, specifically black Richmonders and black Mobilians, in the "recrafting of American citizenship" and transformation of the cultural and physical landscape wrought by Confederate defeat.[6]

As vibrant and contested spaces of educational reform, the cities of Richmond, Virginia, and Mobile, Alabama, provide a window into understanding the process of Educational Reconstruction. The reasons for selecting these cities were threefold. First, these port cities flourished during the antebellum era. Virginia's state capital was a major commercial and industrial center; its political economy and success as an urban center heavily relied on an industrial slave labor force. This enslaved workforce enabled the city's tobacco, manufacturing, flour, iron, and steel industries to thrive. Richmond also maintained extensive national and international trade, transportation, social, and financial networks with major East Coast cities as the terminus of six major railroads and with Europe through its port access to the Atlantic Ocean via the James River. Richmond's role as state capital and commercial center made it one of the most prosperous cities in the nation during the nineteenth century.[7]

Located on Mobile Bay in the old American Southwest, Mobile's importance as an urban center began with its establishment in 1702 as a trading post initially for the French, then the British, and lastly the Spanish. The cotton industry catapulted Mobile into an international and national trading center starting in the

1820s. Cotton exportation connected Mobile to New York and England. Cotton shipped directly from Mobile to Liverpool, England. General freight and goods were transported from Liverpool to New York City. Commerce progressed from New York to Mobile. According to historian Harriet Amos, cotton typically composed 99 percent of the total value of exports from the city. Consequently, cotton strongly influenced the city's infrastructure, including its railroad networks, communication services, and commercial institutions such as banks, insurance agencies, and marketing firms. As in Richmond, an enslaved industrial workforce allowed for Mobile's success as urban center. The enslaved population consequently grew in proportion to the number of cotton bales shipped. "Cotton City" aptly described Mobile during the antebellum period.[8]

Second, white Richmonders and white Mobilians, despite their cosmopolitan nature, shared a common belief about the treatment of African Americans. Such individuals held a status of either free or enslaved. In 1800, Richmond had 2,293 enslaved African Americans and 607 free African Americans. By 1860, 11,699 enslaved African Americans and 2,576 free African Americans resided in the city. While the total African American population increased, the percentage of African Americans decreased from 51 percent to 28 percent because of white migration from other parts of the United States and immigration from Europe. Likewise, Mobile's slave population increased from 1,175 enslaved African Americans and 372 free African American residents in 1830 to 7,587 enslaved African Americans and 817 for the free African American population in 1860. Likewise, the city experienced a decline in the total percentage of the African American population from 48 percent to 29 percent. Rising slave prices, economic competition from whites, immigration, and other factors caused the decline.[9] Regardless of status, the legal system shaped the lives and material conditions of enslaved and free African Americans. The cities' respective state slave codes controlled every aspect of enslaved African Americans' lives, from the ability to be a party in a lawsuit to not being able to legalize their marriages.[10] Considered an anomaly, free African Americans maintained a quasi-free and precarious status in the society. Both cities required the registration of its free African American population and restricted their movement by requiring proof of freedom and even curfews. This racial order shaped the antebellum experiences of enslaved and free African Americans in Mobile and Richmond by emphasizing their exclusion from the body politic.[11]

Moreover, the education of African Americans, free or enslaved, was prohibited and/or limited to a select minority, especially after Nat Turner's Rebellion. Turner's major slave revolt in 1831 created a hostile environment for African

American education in the urban South by influencing the implementation of harsh slave codes that made educating enslaved African Americans illegal in Virginia and Alabama. Fear of another slave rebellion by an educated individual such as Nat Turner motivated these anti-literacy laws.[12] Similarly, the anti-literacy laws also prohibited and severely limited educational opportunities of free African Americans in both cities. A few private schools existed illegally in the residences of literate free African Americans. The Catholic Church in Mobile and Richmond also willingly promoted and provided education as a means of conversion in "places where they had opportunity." Boarding schools as well as relocation to northern states and abroad provided some choice for others. These prohibitions and limitations resulted high rates of illiteracy among free and enslaved African Americans.[13]

Third, Richmond and Mobile were at the forefront of the common school movement in the region with the establishment of a system of public schools prior to the Civil War. Between 1830 and 1860, education and schools became the widely accepted solution to societal ills associated with urbanization, immigration, and industrialization. Common school ideology centered on Protestantism and capitalism, and stressed the virtues of self-control, self-sacrifice, restraint, and industry. Schools, according to proponents, promoted character training, cultural conformity, and discipline in order to influence adult behavior. Reform advocates argued for free schools, better educational facilities, longer school years, better grade-level classification, teacher training, the establishment of state governmental agencies, and other improvements across the nation.[14]

The common school revolution, however, brought little change to enslaved and free African American education. It remained illegal due to both real and imagined fears of instigating another armed rebellion. This reality highlighted the link between education, freedom, and citizenship in Richmond and Mobile. The continued prohibition of African American education after the common school movement merely reinforced African Americans' lack of freedom and their noncitizen status.[15]

The anti-literacy campaigns in Richmond and Mobile did not diminish the communal value of education and literacy, nor did the obstacles deter African Americans from trying to attain an education. Although a small minority of free African Americans attended formal schools outside the cities, most free African Americans also acquired literacy through the same avenues as their enslaved counterparts. They attained an education through literate African American members in their respective communities, religious leaders, slave masters, and/ or individuals in the slave masters' family. Due to the secretive nature of the informal schools, scholars have been unable to accurately estimate the number of slaves who acquired an informal education. Scholars believe that a small percentage of the total slave and free population successfully became educated. Indeed, education and literacy became tools of liberation for the few enslaved and free African Americans who attained it.[16]

Urban African Americans, regardless of status, viewed literacy and education as a means to better their social status and as a benefit of freedom. Their desire to become an educated people would carry over into Educational Reconstruction. Education and literacy symbolized full citizenship in a literate society. Only a revolution would make African American aspirations to education a reality. The Civil War, wartime experimentation, and Confederate defeat served as the catalyst, while antebellum conditions provided the blueprints for urban African Americans' expectations of the postwar educational developments and inclusion as citizens from 1865 to 1890.[17]

This study contributes to the extensive literature on postwar African American education by revealing the dynamic processes by which African Americans developed personal and institutional networks and built an African American educational system from the ground up. Like Heather A. Williams's *Self-Taught* (2005) and Ronald E. Butchart's *Schooling the Freed People* (2010), it examines African Americans and their relationships with varied partners.[18] It also explores the diverse aims, visions, and experiences of different historical actors and organizations in order to explain how a sustainable African American educational system was built in the face of opposition. While the work contributes to a rich historiography on the motivations and experiences of the various educational reformers, the study deviates from this scholarship in terms of the traditional chronology of the closure of the Freedmen's Schools by extending the discussion to include the understudied first two decades of state-funded African American public schools. Rather than presume that urban African Americans' struggle for education ended with the creation of public schools, this study asks how the introduction of local and state government officials as partners changed Educational Reconstruction.

By focusing on the initial years of state-funded African American public schools, this study fills a void in the historiography. A few scholars have critically examined the first two decades of public schools for African Americans, but did so through the lens of African American education during the era of Jim Crow segregation.[19] This backward gaze presumes that the African American education deteriorated immediately following the shift to state-funded public schools and southern Redemption. While white supremacy eventually triumphed over

the African American educational project, it did not occur immediately following the departure of the Freedmen's Bureau. Rather, it was a gradual, two-
decade-long process in which changing white northern attitudes, the failures of
liberal republicanism in fully manifesting itself, and a national economic crisis
decentralized the status of African American education.[20] Moreover, it involved
early educators, urban African Americans, and local government officials who
remained hopeful about the transformative nature of education in the transition
from slavery to freedom. These scholars have missed important opportunities
to engage with the first two decades of public schools through the eyes of the
historical actors who themselves could not have foreseen Jim Crow segregation.
Despite the limits placed on the African American educational project by legal
segregation, the movement succeeded in developing a system of public schools
that could and did survive this later challenge.

State-funded African American public schools, which are the subject of this
study, further complicated Educational Reconstruction in two specific ways.
First, urban African Americans expanded their networks to include new partners. By 1870, city schools boards and state agencies had replaced the Freedmen's Bureau. These new alliances addressed unresolved problems from the
Freedmen's School era as well as new challenges raised by the creation of public
schools. Such an examination illuminates the flexible nature of the networks created by urban African Americans to cope with new challenges while revealing
the continuities and discontinuities between the two periods of Educational Reconstruction. Second, an examination of state-funded public schools offers new
insights into higher education for African Americans during the 1870s and 1880s.
In response to the immense need for public schoolteachers, state educational
boards, northern missionary societies, and urban African Americans established
normal institutions and colleges. The transition to higher education, therefore,
emerged as a response to address the specific needs of the newly created public
schools and was not (as suggested by the existing historiography) merely a natural progression in African American education. In understanding these critical
post–Freedmen's School developments, this study illuminates the complex and
changing nature of Educational Reconstruction in Richmond and Mobile.

This study also contributes to urban history by examining the post–Civil War
experiences of urban African Americans. Some scholars have contended that the
urban South was more closely related to the antebellum plantation than were
their northern counterparts, and in turn, that this relationship would have a direct influence on the benefits of Educational Reconstruction for African Americans. Indeed, antebellum experiences of Richmond and Mobile fit within this

model of the southern city defined by staple-crop agriculture, racial order, and a colonial economy.[21] This study deviates from these scholars' general conclusion that postwar labor systems limited black geographic and socioeconomic mobility.[22] The growth of African American education created new economic opportunities with the creation of a corps of schoolteachers, principals, and administrators. Moreover, it opened opportunities for educated African Americans beyond menial labor to include civil service, journalism, law, bankers, politics, and other middle-class economic positions. Educational Reconstruction created new men and women, but it also established an African American middle class in the urban South.[23]

This study recognizes that not all African Americans escaped to the postwar city or had uniform access to the economic opportunities wrought by advances in African American education. Race still had a role in determining occupational mobility and economic success for African Americans in stagnating cities like Mobile, but it also influenced white New South proponents' acceptance of their African American counterparts in cities like Richmond and Charlotte.[24] Indeed, many African Americans remained in an economy centered on staple-crop agriculture, lived primarily in the rural South, and/or performed unskilled labor in the urban South. Race relations even denied full acceptance of educated African Americans in the new postwar order. Nonetheless, this should not discount urban African Americans who remained committed to the empowering and transformative nature of education as well as the inclusion of the African American schoolhouse as a defining feature of the postwar urban landscape.

This study complements Howard Rabinowitz, Peter Rachleff, Michael Fitzgerald, and other scholars who have attempted to reverse the trend of privileging the rural African American experience.[25] This small but growing scholarship has shown the existence of urban African Americans prior to the twentieth century and that their experiences and activism in labor, politics, and community development influenced the remaking of several postwar southern cities. While each briefly explored urban African Americans' educational efforts, this study provides an in-depth examination. It reveals how urban African Americans' activism had major consequences not only for the their respective cities and states but also encompassed postwar issues regarding labor, politics, taxation, religion, and community development. Black Richmonders' and black Mobilians' refusal to remain slaves and be denied full citizenship any longer permitted the emergence of state-funded public schools, led to development of state normal schools, established a vibrant educator–activist class essential to pre-1945 civil rights activism, and shaped broader regional debates regarding educational funding, administration, and curriculum that continued well into the early twentieth century. Thus the African American schoolhouse becomes the perfect vehicle for understanding postwar urban African American experience and enriches the scholarship.

In short, *Educational Reconstruction* makes four significant historiographical contributions. First, it proposes a new chronology in understanding postwar African American education. The traditional Reconstruction chronology reinforces a declension narrative and fails to fully appreciate the ways urban African Americans challenged and influenced the "Redeemed" southern governments. Second, it addresses the largely ignored early state-funded African American public schools and reveals the significant gains made after the departure of the Freedmen's Bureau. Third, it reevaluates African American higher education in terms of developing a cadre of public school educator–activists. Lastly, it highlights the centrality of urban African American protest in shaping educational decisions and policies in their respective cities and states. As partners and circumstances changed over the twenty-five-year period, I contend that urban African Americans never lost sight of their vision of citizenship and freedom in their struggle for educational access and legitimacy for the African American schoolhouse. Their activism successfully embedded African American education as a state right of citizenship, increased educational access for future generations of African American children, and established educators as middle-class leaders essential for turn-of-the-century activism. By 1890 their vision of freedom, citizenship, and education transformed the postwar South.

Archival research forms the basis of the study. I carefully mined the archives for material, visual, and text sources produced by African Americans. Scouring local, regional, and national African American newspapers yielded the opinions, activities, and organizational efforts of a cross-section of black Richmonders and black Mobilians. I balanced these newspapers with broadsides, speeches, poetry, and other sources in order to retrieve their voices and experiences. Of the sources used, I have faithfully produced them in their original form with virtually no changes to the spelling or grammar. I have occasionally used brackets to indicate the intended word or phrase of the author when the handwriting was not clear. In addition, a close reading of city, county, state, and federal government records revealed urban African Americans' relationships with political officials and allowed me to assess the contours as well as limitations of networks sustaining the African American schools. The rich records of the various northern missionary and secular organizations helped with my understanding of the motivations, nature of the participation, and, more importantly, their interactions with black Richmonders and black Mobilians. Major newspapers and periodicals allowed me to understand the varying popular responses to the African American educational efforts. Lastly, manuscript collections, diaries, and scrapbooks yielded additional commentary on Educational Reconstruction and revealed more African American voices.

Educational Reconstruction is organized into four two-chapter sections and an epilogue. "Envisioning Citizenship and the African American Schoolhouse" examines the first phase of Educational Reconstruction under the Freedmen's Bureau. Through establishing educational partnerships and networks, I argue that black Richmonders' and black Mobilians' vision for the postwar landscape transformed the African American schoolhouse from a temporary, marginalized institution into one enshrined within their respective state constitutions as a fundamental right of citizenship. By examining the various relationships, I demonstrate how the Freedmen's Schools initiated a legacy of collaboration and colleagueship necessary for overcoming obstacles and ensuring the survival of the African American schoolhouse. Without collaboration with their federal, northern philanthropic, and local allies, black Richmonders and black Mobilians would not have been able to realize their vision of state-funded public schools.

"Creating Essential Partnerships and Resources" examines the important development of a corps of African American public schoolteachers through Richmond Colored Normal and Emerson Normal. These institutions addressed the crucial question raised by the creation of public schools in the Reconstruction constitutions regarding who would teach in the African American public schools. I argue that these institutions created not only qualified educators for classrooms across the rural and urban South but also middle-class leaders who refashioned their conception of a useful education outside the classroom to include racial uplift activism. Black Richmonders and black Mobilians greatly relied on this refashioning in their struggle for educational access, legitimacy, and citizenship after the departure of the Freedmen's Bureau. As essential assets, Emerson Normal and Richmond Colored Normal produced a new type of leadership that would be instrumental in late-nineteenth-century struggles for African American education and racial uplift.

"Integrating the African American Schoolhouse" explores how black Richmonders and black Mobilians shifted their activism around the notion of quality schools in order to cope with new partners and challenges posed by the first decade of state-funded public schools. I argue that black Richmonders and black Mobilians embarked on the quality campaigns for a variety of reasons, but that they shared the goal of meaningful integration of the African American public schoolhouse in their respective cities. Over the course of the decade, they achieved success in some areas of their multipronged struggle while encountering setbacks in others. However, black Richmonders and black Mobilians never lost sight of their mission they embarked on in 1865. Their struggle now focused on making the public schools into enduring institutions instrumental in sustaining African American citizenship.

"Perfecting the African American Schoolhouse" explores how black Richmonders and black Mobilians continued to walk "slowly, but surely" in their struggle for quality public schools. Capitalizing on the momentous period of change wrought by the Readjuster movement, I argue, black Richmonders made significant progress in their overall campaign's objectives but still actively sought a resolution to funding challenges. On the other hand, I argue that black Mobilians' unwavering commitment to becoming a literate people in the face of adversity secured increased employment opportunities for nonwhite teachers and newer school facilities, though funding remained the greatest obstacle in obtaining additional gains. By 1890, black Richmonders and black Mobilians came to the shared realization that a renewed partnership with the federal government would overcome the remaining barriers in their quest for quality African American public education.

Lastly, the epilogue reveals the end of the Educational Reconstruction and the opening of another phase in African American education with the failed Blair Education Bill in 1890. Motivated by concern for the plight of the former slaves and inadequately financed public schools for white and black children in the South, Senator Henry W. Blair proposed the bill, which allotted $77 million in federal funds for public schools distributed to states according to their illiteracy rates over several years.[26] If passed, this federal legislation would have demolished the last obstacle in sustaining the public schools for white and African American children. Yet it did not pass. Black Richmonders, black Mobilians, and their remaining allies realized that they could no longer rely on the federal government to intervene on behalf of African American education. The meteoric rise of Booker T. Washington and his industrial education model in the wake of the Blair Education Bill defeat signaled the real closure of Educational Reconstruction. For black Richmonders and black Mobilians, the demise of Educational Reconstruction and emergence of new challenges never overshadowed the triumph of the Freedmen's Schools or the state-funded public schools yielded by their educational networks. They continued to find inspiration in these victories and their recent past.

Although partners changed over the twenty-five-year period, black Richmonders and black Mobilians never lost sight of the larger goal of legitimizing

African American education and providing access for anyone seeking an education. As a result of their insistence to become an educated people, they achieved two significant victories in the Freedmen Schools and African American public schools on their voyage upon the "Ship of Education."[27] Most significantly, black Richmonders and black Mobilians did not end their struggle after obtaining the first major victory. Rather, they transformed their struggle by demanding quality public schools from their new city and state educational partners. Through their demands, they achieved success in securing African American teachers, the creation of normal schools, associations and other auxiliary educational resources, the procuring of additional school facilities, and the promotion of a robust liberal arts curriculum that had enduring effects on later public schools. While they were less successful in terms of funding and securing school board positions, the first twenty-five years of state-funded schools represented a continuation of the gains of the emancipation through the African American schoolhouse in Richmond and Mobile. Notwithstanding the unknown future, urban African Americans had escaped "the clutches of those who held [them] in slavery" through education.[28]

I

ENVISIONING CITIZENSHIP
AND THE AFRICAN
AMERICAN SCHOOLHOUSE

1

Remaking the Former Confederate Capital

Black Richmonders and the Transition to Public Schools, 1865–1870

At a reunion of Richmond Colored Normal graduates, Daniel Webster Davis delivered a poem the message of which the audience wholeheartedly agreed. The 1878 graduate fondly recalled the transformation of "the girls in short dresses, and white pinafores" into respectable women, but also his "quaking with fear . . . 'tis Miss Stratton, whose footsteps I hear." For all the travails, Davis never failed to appreciate his matriculation through the Richmond public schools. He proudly proclaimed in the third stanza:

> My name is still cut on the seat by the door,
> I am trying to cut it much higher, you know,
> But I wonder if fame can e'er give the joy,
> I found at old Normal when I was a boy?

Davis recognized that many opportunities within and outside the classroom afforded the alumni were the direct result of black Richmonders capitalizing on Confederate defeat in April 1865. Without their struggle and the partnerships developed, neither the school system nor the reunion Davis attended would have been possible.[1]

Confederate defeat ushered in a revolution in African American education. Freedom brought new behaviors, new relationships, and new institutions. Schools and the educational relationships that sustained them became a postwar reality. White opposition and internal class strife sometimes tempered black Richmonders' expressions of freedom and entry into the body politic through education. These forces galvanized them. Black Richmonders saw their struggle in much larger terms. It was not merely a fight for access to literacy and education but one for freedom, citizenship, and a new postwar social order.

The Freedmen's School period illustrates the ways black Richmonders defined the meaning of freedom and citizenship through the African American schoolhouse. It proves that internal strife between the educational partners and local white opposition shaped the quest for schools, access, and legitimacy in the post-

war urban South. Through a network of educational partnerships, black Richmonders successfully developed the Freedmen's Schools, legitimized African
American education with new state mandates, and laid the foundation for tax-
supported public schools. By emphasizing the educational relationships formed
by black Richmonders, new insights are offered into how the quest for education
manifested itself on the ground and contributed to the major developments of
Educational Reconstruction—the Freedmen Schools and public schools. The efforts of black Richmonders and their allies, I argue, fundamentally transformed
African American education from a marginalized institution into a state right of
citizenship. Indeed, black Richmonders' postwar vision prevailed in remaking
the former Confederate capital.

Black Richmonders embarked on their post-emancipation quest with the fall
of Richmond on April 3, 1865. Within days of Union troops securing the city, black
Richmonders quickly established schools in churches that still stood amid the ruins of the Confederate capital. This school system immediately attracted Henry
and Augusta A. Hawkins Dixon of Amelia County, Virginia, for their daughter as
well as other African Americans seeking an education for themselves and/or family
members. They enrolled in the various schools where literate black Richmonders
like Peter Matthews diligently instructed those desiring an education. Eager students quickly filled these schools because Confederate defeat enabled their fulfillment of becoming a literate people without any encumbrances. School attendance
symbolized their free status and entry into as citizens in the body politic.[2]

In May 1865, black Richmonders met and officially inaugurated the educational movement. Meeting attendees attempted to unify the various schools into
one system. They consolidated smaller schools into the various churches. They
also appointed teachers, established school hours of operation, and created an
administrative structure overseeing the schools. According to an *Anglo-African*
article, "The project was so far perfected that the schools will be opened at
9 o'clock this morning in all the colored churches of the city." The quest for access
and legitimacy had a great start.[3]

Encouraged by the possibility of remaking the former capital of the Confederacy, northern benevolent societies sent missionaries to educate former slaves.
While black Richmonders did not request assistance, white and African American missionaries representing nine organizations traveled to Richmond as soon
as transportation networks made it possible. Instead of finding a barren educational field, missionaries encountered an existing system of schools. Therefore,
they either established additional schools or co-opted operations within the city's
church system. These various agencies desired the establishment of a permanent

system of schools for African Americans that would ease their transition to freedom.[4] Using these schools, such agencies sought to transform and reconstruct
the region according to their understanding of postwar freedom and citizenship.
Black Richmonders' enthusiasm and the potential of remaking the former Confederate capital invigorated their efforts.

In addition to their shock at finding a system of schools in existence, white
missionaries were also surprised by the number of literate black Richmonders.
Among their 1,075 students, Lucy and Sarah Chase reported that they "found
eighty good readers, two hundred good spellers, and one hundred who had
conquered the alphabet. Of the remaining five or six hundred many had picked
up one or two letters in the secret corner where the negro father kept his trea-
sured book." Another missionary commented, "The colored people of Richmond
are far more intelligent and thrifty than any I have met within the South—and
though the laws against learning have been so strict, many can read and a large
portion know their letters and can spell a little." These remarks demonstrated
that the obstacles against African American literacy never diminished the desire
to become an educated people during the antebellum period. Their clandestine
efforts succeeded. Emancipation merely eliminated some of the obstacles.[5]

Moreover, missionaries marveled at the teaching abilities of some black Richmonders. Peter Matthews's teaching skills impressed Rev. George Stinson, a white
American Missionary Association representative. After witnessing Matthews
instruct a group of young children to read the Bible, Stinson inquired about
Matthews's educational training. Matthews explained that in "his younger years
it was custom of some slaveholders to instruct their slaves so far as to give them
ability to read Gods word but nothing else." Stinson's encounter with Matthews
made him confront assumptions regarding black Richmonders. Sympathetic
slaveholders and clandestine self-education permitted the existence of individuals like Peter Matthews. Instead of viewing Matthews as an object of benevo-
lence, Stinson expressed an interest in retaining him to promote the educational
interests of the American Missionary Association.[6]

Such encounters enabled black Richmonders to establish educational relationships with northern missionary associations. They recognized that these
relationships could benefit their nascent educational movement. Matthews and
others expressed their interest in building relationships with such outside organizations. Based on his conversation with Matthews, Stinson informed American Missionary Association officials of the community's desire for a partnership.
He wrote, "I was told that the colored people would gladly do what they could
to support schools and ministers to labor with them." Hence meetings between

"intelligent colored" persons and missionaries facilitated the growth of a network of educational relationships employed by black Richmonders.[7]

These educational partnerships also secured employment opportunities for some black Richmonders. The New England Freedmen's Aid Society retained Peter H. Woolfolk as a missionary and educator in its Richmond schools. Woolfolk was a light-skinned native of Richmond and a former slave. He taught initially at an independent school located at the Ebenezer Baptist Church before he was reassigned to the school operated by Lucy Haskell as her assistant.[8] Woolfolk's employment forced William L. Coan and other white missionaries to question their racial conceptions of African American intellect and abilities for teaching. Coan, another American Missionary Association representative, depicted Woolfolk as "a perfect Gentleman very light color, very intelligent and although a volunteer is doing much to assist in our great work." Coan's fascination with Woolfolk's personal attributes is significant as he found that neither race nor his former servitude hindered Woolfolk's teaching abilities. His complexion, demeanor, intelligence, and service forced Coan to confront any previous racial assumptions and recognize that the educational partnerships worked. Woolfolk's success as an educator permitted the partnership's continuation, as race could not be used as an obstacle. Through partnerships with Woolfolk, Matthews, and others, Richmond had "five public schools, four private schools, [and] a number of benevolent societies formed" by August 1865. As a result, black Richmonders' became increasingly convinced of both the social and economic benefits derived from their network of relationships.[9]

During the summer of 1865, black Richmonders' educational network expanded to include the Freedmen's Bureau. Established in March 1865, the Bureau of Refugees, Freedmen, and Abandoned Lands was originally designed as a temporary organization mandated by the United States Congress to assist freedmen in their transition from slavery to freedom, deal with wartime abandoned lands possessed by the federal government, and aid displaced refugees. The Freedmen's Bureau Act of 1866 extended the agency's tenure. During its existence the Freedmen's Bureau represented a truly continuous federal presence in the defeated South, and its power affected all southerners. Black Richmonders considered the organization, often staffed with enlisted and veteran military officers, as their government, protector from a hostile white community, and for some, creator of the Freedmen's Schools.[10]

Black Richmonders' found the educational mission of the federal agency conducive to their interests. The strong emphasis on education reflected the attitudes and beliefs of Gen. O. O. Howard, the first and only commissioner of the Freedmen's Bureau. Born in Leeds, Maine, on November 8, 1830, Oliver Otis Howard received his education from Bowdoin College and West Point, where he became a mathematics professor. He served in several eastern Civil War campaigns in the 3rd Maine Infantry before being reassigned to the Army of the Tennessee in July 1864. He marched with Gen. Tecumseh Sherman through Georgia to the sea and in the Carolinas Campaign of early 1865. Owing to his deep concern over the fates of newly emancipated slaves, President Andrew Johnson appointed the "Christian General" as the commissioner of the Freedmen's Bureau. Although the task was fraught with issues, Howard oversaw the federal agency founded on African American education.[11] Howard viewed education as an integral component for remaking the slave society into a free one by encouraging former slaves to develop "the habits, attitudes, and knowledge necessary for free men in a free society." As a result, Howard purposely selected individuals like Ralza Morse Manly, who shared similar beliefs, attitudes, and often Civil War veteran status, to coordinate the agency's efforts in the former Confederate states.[12]

Born in 1822, Ralza Morse Manly, the superintendent of education in Virginia, firmly believed "that the only true form of 'Freedmen's Aid' was education." The white Vermont native served as an educator and principal of several academies and seminaries as well as the editor of the *Vermont Christian Messenger*. Although ordained as a Methodist minister, he devoted much of his energies to teaching prior to the Civil War.[13] In October 1862 he enlisted in the 16th New Hampshire Volunteers and served as the infantry regiment's chaplain.[14] On January 16, 1864, he became the chaplain of the 1st U.S. Colored Calvary and served as an educator among the regiment's African American soldiers until the end of the war.[15] He regarded his "educational labors as a good and necessary work" and consequently found his school overflowing with "men, which are the best specimens of the colored race, eager to learn and quick to comprehend."[16] This success led to his postwar career of creating and sustaining schools that might elevate African Americans in postwar Virginia.

Like other superintendents of education, Manly maintained a supervisory role over the entire state operation and provided the organizational framework for the Freedmen's School system. Unlike other superintendents, Manly had an active role in the day-to-day operations of the Richmond schools. He considered the Richmond system the model for the entire state. Hence he frequently visited the schools, regularly corresponded with members of the African American community, and acted as an agent for the New York and New England branches of the American Freedmen's Union Commission. In short, Manly served as an important advocate for African American education in the city.[17]

These relationships between black Richmonders, northern missionaries, and Manly produced interesting interactions resulting in negotiations over the development and control of the Freedmen's Schools. Each group contended with questions pertaining to the definition of an education most useful in the transition from slavery to freedom, and the role of African Americans in the process. Black Richmonders actively sought more control over the curriculum, the selection of teachers, and the location of new schools than their partners were willing to afford them. While seeking increased autonomy, they worked with their white partners in cementing the African American schoolhouse and African American education into the landscape wrought by Confederate defeat. As they navigated these questions, a more pressing concern of coping with local white hostility inadvertently fostered their cooperation. Within this context, the Freedmen's Bureau, northern societies, and black Richmonders developed and sustained a system of schools.

During the 1865–1866 academic year, black Richmonders and their allies developed a network of schools. The Freedmen's Bureau assisted with the maintenance of day schools for children, night schools for adults, and Sabbath schools. Each school provided rudimentary education, including reading, writing, arithmetic, and geography, but the schools also offered basic industrial and domestic education. Students learned sewing, cleanliness, punctuality, and other skills of self-sufficiency. The schools attracted a large number of African American students. The academic year opened with 1,723 students and concluded with 2,042. Attendance increased dramatically from January to May 1866 and then decreased in June. This fluctuation corresponded with the seasonal labor migrations from rural Virginia to Richmond. Rural migrants came to the city for employment during the agricultural off-season. They took advantage of the urban educational opportunities prior to returning for work during the more intensive agricultural period. The number of schools could not fully quench the thirst for education. Classes were often overcrowded despite continued efforts to secure additional accommodations. By the end of the year, the school system expanded from nineteen to twenty-six schools, of which black Richmonders partially financed a substantial number. During the next year, the school system expanded to thirty-three to begin and concluded with forty-six schools. Black Richmonders financially supported on average sixteen of the schools per month.[18]

Students' scholastic achievement legitimated both black Richmonders' network of partnerships and the resulting school system. Largely illiterate former slaves composed the student body of the initial schools. The newly emancipated and those free black Richmonders unable to attend school before Reconstruction displayed a deep passion for learning. Freedmen's Bureau agents and teachers regularly noted in their monthly reports this passion as well as the rapid progression of their students overall. Both black Richmonders' passion and attendance permitted their northern partners' continued support. For black Richmonders, education became the ultimate vehicle for distancing themselves from slavery and expressing their new status as citizens. Their partnerships enabled the rapid scholastic progression of their children and growth of the school system. Hence scholastic achievement validated their relationship-building efforts and allowed for the network's continuation.[19]

While the educational partners agreed on the role of African Americans as students, disagreement and fierce debate arose over teaching positions for African Americans. These internal questions marred the educational alliances. The resulting questions prompted serious negotiations between the partners to ensure the continuation of the Freedmen's School system.

The school system benefited from dedicated teachers, white and black. Regardless of race, the Freedmen's Bureau expected all of its teachers to be competent. As education was essential to the Freedmen's Bureau efforts, mediocrity was not acceptable. Manly praised African American and white educators equally. He reported to Hannah Stevenson, secretary of the New England Freedmen's Aid Society, "The discipline in Miss M. E. Chase, Miss Angier, and Mr. Woolfolk is without fault, is most excellent, each is entirely and easily master of the situation." In discussing the "skill in the work of instruction," he concluded that "all are excellent. Miss Canedy, Miss Ballard, and Mr. Woolfolk prominently so."[20] Manly retained educators deemed competent and dismissed those who did not meet his standards, regardless of race. For instance, he found a position for Charlotte M. Keith, an African American educator, with another missionary organization in Richmond rather than have her leave the school system. Manly wrote Rev. Woolsey, "I think Miss Keith's merits as a teacher and the strong attachment of the people worshipping at that Church for their teachers are reasons for returning her and send some others in the service of your society." As evidenced by these examples, Manly preferred competent and well-respected teachers such as Peter Woolfolk and Charlotte M. Keith for the Richmond school system. For Manly, competence rather than race aided the quest for legitimating African American education in both Richmond and the state as a whole.[21]

Despite Manly's efforts, racial attitudes and stereotypes influenced the number of African Americans teachers in the schools. The American Missionary Association, the American Baptist Home Mission Society, and other northern religious societies recruited the majority of the teachers. These religious societies and their teachers believed in and practiced a form of evangelical abolitionism. According to this ideology, slavery was a sin against God and humankind and denied African Americans the ability to function as independent moral beings. Thus, to be truly free, African Americans as a race needed liberation from the chains that bound them physically and spiritually. Therefore, education served dual purposes for the "Christian Abolitionists." First, it provided moral and intellectual growth. Second, education permitted racial advancement to the status of an independent moral being. Therefore, evangelical abolitionism assumed that African Americans lacked morality as a result of their enslaved status. Thus the ideology discredited any religious and educational instruction that African Americans, formally or informally, received as slaves.[22]

Unfortunately, these assumptions colored the associations' attitudes in using black Richmonders as teachers. Initially, African Americans served as teachers in the Freedmen's Schools but were slowly replaced by white teachers. According to Bureau reports, white teachers slightly outnumbered African American teachers at first. However, by February 1867 the numerical difference increased. The majority of these teachers maintained a subordinate position to their white counterparts. They were not the principal teachers who wrote the official reports to the Freedmen's Bureau. Often the teachers were listed as aides rather than instructors. Consequently, African American teachers often remained voiceless in the official Freedmen's Bureau monthly school reports.[23]

Despite the racial attitudes of some educational partners, African American educators played a vital role. These teachers took on responsibilities that extended beyond the classroom, as they often served as spokespersons for the community. William D. Harris exemplified how African American educators resisted marginalization. Harris was a freeborn African American from Cleveland, Ohio. In August 1865 he received an appointment as pastor of the African Methodist Episcopal Church in Richmond. As a minister and an American Missionary Association representative, Harris permitted the usage of his church as a day school, a night school, and a Sabbath school. When not fulfilling his pastoral duties, Harris successfully instructed adults in the Lincoln night school. In the classroom, Harris made sure that his adult students read and understood the United States Constitution and news from Congress. He reported to George Whipple, corresponding secretary of the American Missionary Association, that daily exercises consisted of "spelling and defining the words contained in the clause read [of the Constitution] or selections from Congressional proceedings." These daily exercises made the education provided relevant to the lives of his students. As a pastor, administrator, educator, and missionary, Harris demonstrated the commitment and drive of African American missionaries in preventing the confinement of African American education to the classroom. Whether in the classroom, church, or community, racial uplift motivated Harris's refusal to remain voiceless in shaping the transition from slavery to freedom through education.[24]

A few African Americans served as administrators during the initial years of the Freedmen's Schools. They often took the initiative to create and maintain their own schools without the assistance of the Freedmen's Bureau and northern benevolent societies. Since tuition supported these schools, only those who could afford it could attend. Consequently, the schools reinforced class differences between elite, middle-class, and working-class black Richmonders. Manly objected to these schools. He felt that they attracted the best students, created a system in which one's ability to pay tuition determined the quality of education received, and therefore threatened the overall Freedmen's Schools from becoming legitimate. He also objected as they operated outside the direct control of the Bureau, thus depriving him authority over them. Thus the Freedmen's Bureau did not have specific information on the schools except for estimates of the number of schools, teachers, and students enrolled. During the 1865–1866 academic school year, black Richmonders maintained twelve independent schools. The number expanded to as many as twenty-two during the following academic year. As these school operated outside of Bureau control, the few existing sources do not detail the schools' conditions and curriculum. These tuition-based schools demonstrated that black Richmonders remained committed to becoming a literate people but desired more autonomy. Some black Richmonders refused to accept the marginalization of their participation to being merely students and flocked to these schools. Their patronage of the independent schools did not mean that both types of schools could not coexist in the system, as suggested by Manly. Whether "self-taught" or with assistance, the independent schools and Freedmen's Schools fulfilled black Richmonders' quest for education regardless of the opinions held by some partners.[25]

Competition over space, enrollment, and ultimately power in remaking Richmond also revealed the imperfect nature of black Richmonders' network of educational partners. This competition occasionally proved beneficial to black Richmonders. As organizations fought for the Freedmen's minds and souls, they gave incentives in exchange for support. Such incentives ranged from not imposing a fuel charge during the winter months to implementing programs not offered by other organizations, such as an industrial training program offered by the New England Freedmen's Aid Society. Parents, students, and black leaders exploited these incentives. While organizations benefited from increased enrollment, students and their parents achieved educational choice and power in selecting a Freedmen's School. This competition often had more detrimental effects than positive ones. These internal fissures made the educational network less efficient as energies were diverted away from the schools.[26]

The fight over the Winder building, a confiscated Confederate property, exposed the fragile nature of the educational partnerships in the spring of 1866. Known as the Bakery, two factions within the New England Freedmen's Aid Society and the American Missionary Association desired the property for its schools and lodging for its teachers. Andrew Washburn, a white missionary for the New England Freedmen's Aid Society, wanted the property for the schools operated for white children by the organization. Washburn represented both a faction within the New England Freedmen's Aid Society and local whites who would benefit from the proposed schools. Another faction within the New England Freedmen's Aid Society desired the property for its African American schools. This group hired C. Thurston Chase as its agent for securing the property. American Missionary Association officials also wanted the property for expanding its educational efforts. Letters flooded the Freedmen's Bureau. In negotiating for the Bakery, the various groups placed the educational interests of black and white Richmonders in direct competition from late April to July 1866. Each refused to make any concessions on this matter. By making a race a factor, the incident threatened the entire Freedmen's School system.[27]

Ultimately, Gen. Orlando Brown, assistant commissioner for the Freedmen's Bureau in Virginia, ordered that the white schools, under the direction of Andrew Washburn, occupy one of the Bakery buildings. The New England Freedmen's Aid Society retained control over the other Bakery building for their Freedmen's Schools. Embarrassed over the affair, several organizational officials attempted to make amends through meetings and correspondence. Resigning his position, Washburn accepted another commission with the Soldiers' Memorial Society before eventually becoming the first superintendent of Richmond public schools in 1869. Most significantly, this resolution removed race as a factor within the Freedmen's School system and reestablished the amicable coexistence between white and African American schools.[28]

Manly took a more active role in preventing the reoccurrences of such incidents. In 1866 he developed a clear solution to deal with the American Baptist Home Mission Society's departure from primary education for the training of African American ministers.[29] Rather than suffer another Bakery incident,

Manly reorganized the Richmond schools into four districts in order to mini-mize conflict. The district system remade the previous denominational-based system while retaining African American churches as school locations. Manly then designated organizations and community groups to the various districts. This plan not only permitted greater efficiency but also allowed for expansion.[30] In short, Manly averted another territorial crisis. He made the overall educa-tional system more efficient while minimizing the territorial struggles. Most sig-nificantly, Manly restored African American education to the forefront of the educational partners' agenda.

White Richmonders' open hostility effectively brought unity between black Richmonders and their educational partners. Confederate defeat fostered the op-position to black Richmonders' educational pursuits and the entire Freedmen's School project. The mere sight of "crowds of Yankees all over the streets," Julia Porter Read explained in a letter to Harriet Sublett Berry, produced an anger which she "could have knocked one of them with a good grace." Read's senti-ments were not uncommon.[31] While elite white women endured unique chal-lenges as a result of their gender, the trauma of Confederate defeat affected all white Richmonders, to varying degrees. To Read and other white Richmonders, federal troops and Freedmen's Bureau agents symbolized their defeat and a strong federal government's interference in their culture and tradition. Although an actual military occupation by troops was limited and exaggerated, Freedmen's Bureau agents and Freedmen's School teachers, especially white educators, illu-minated the scars of Confederate defeat on a daily basis. These scars made white southerners "a bit defensive about their public image and more than a little anx-ious for reassurance." Hostility directed toward the schools yielded them a degree of such reassurance by making them forget about their defeat.[32]

White Richmonders could not conceive of a world without slavery. They sim-ply lacked precedent in dealing with the new social and racial conditions, which exacerbated their fears of a diminishing white supremacy. As a result, the Freed-men's Schools contributed to the "lamentable state of affairs" felt by Read and other white Richmonders. Education had previously been used as a means of reinforcing black Richmonders' lack of freedom and citizenship. Emancipation inverted the antebellum social order with the extension of education, and in turn citizenship, to black Richmonders. Feeling helpless in preventing the Freedmen's Schools, white Richmonders showed their displeasure through intimidation, ha-rassment, and social ostracism of both students attending the schools and their teachers. Male teachers endured whippings. Female teachers and students often found themselves pelted by rock-throwing white youth while walking the city streets. This behavior provided some white Richmonders with a measure of control in the new society without slavery.[33]

Fears of miscegenation also contributed to white opposition to African American education. For the majority of white Richmonders, white missionaries and Freedmen's Bureau agents displayed a willingness to go outside their race and community by making African Americans their social equals. They equated social equality with miscegenation, and thus the existence of African American schoolhouses and black Richmonders' educational partnerships "fostered a dangerous combination of . . . social equality between blacks and whites." The presence of African Americans and whites in the classroom promoted the elimination of natural racial hierarchies, and ultimately degraded the white race. Thus the Freedmen's Schools undermined white supremacy and white elites' claims to black Richmonders' educational decisions. With the miscegenation claims, white elites sought to delegitimize black Richmonders' claims to freedom and citizenship by controlling their educational decisions.[34]

Newspapers, such as the *Richmond Daily Examiner*, refused to print articles that recognized specific details of the schools and the existence of an increasingly educated African American community. As invisible institutions, this strategy permitted the popular perception that not only were African Americans truly incapable of being educated, but also that African Americans were content with being ignorant. Freedmen "remain slaves in mind" and proved "incapable of intelligently and independently exercising suffrage."[35] Major newspapers, therefore, posited the Freedmen's Schools as northern impositions in which black Richmonders had stepped outside their natural position in the social hierarchy. Furthermore, negative newspaper coverage brings into sharper relief that ways in which white Richmonders resisted. Educators often found themselves arrested, imprisoned, and tried for minor offenses based on the most circumstantial of evidence. Not only did these tactics temporarily close the schools operated by the incarcerated educators, they brought negative publicity to the African American schools. While ignoring evidence of progress, editors featured scathing reports of these incidents in their papers. Black Richmonders and their supporters actively confronted such attacks.[36]

The seduction trial of William Harris exemplified these manifestations. In December 1866 Lomax Smith, an African American barber and Confederate sympathizer, accused Harris of seducing his daughter, Eliza Smith. His accusations prompted the arrest and imprisonment of the popular educator. The white press found the case alluring for its coordinated attack on the Freedmen's

Schools. Harris's alleged seduction fit within several popular narratives of dishonorable Yankee teachers and gullible freedmen. The only "true friend" and protector of freedmen were the former white Richmond elites. This line of attack directly countered the messages imparted to black Richmonders attending the schools, "that the friends of the Union are their friends and that the Union itself is their friend." In the eyes of the white Richmond press, Harris's alleged seduction raised the specter of African American males as sexual brutes. Instead of a white woman, the purity of a black woman deserved white patriarchal protection. Thus the seduction trial of the "Yankee Nigger Preacher" had the potential of irrevocably harming the burgeoning school system.[37]

At the trial, the testimony of Peter Woolfolk and church deacons revealed that Harris counseled Smith's daughter against elopement with William Jennings, a young African American teacher in Richmond. Her father preferred another suitor for her and forced an engagement between them. The broken engagement and Harris's counseling prompted the accusations. The judge acquitted Harris. The white newspapers published articles detailing the acquittal instead of the originally anticipated conviction. White Richmonders failed in using this incident as a means of inflicting irreparable harm to the Freedmen's Schools.[38] They did achieve a minor victory. Since Harris never adequately repaired his reputation, church officials reassigned him to Washington, D.C. False accusations resulted in black Richmonders' loss of an important partner and afforded their opponents a victory, albeit a minor one.[39]

Despite local hostility, the Freedmen's School system succeeded. Opposition only cemented the educational relationships, as the partners resolve to overcome such obstacles. By 1867 a shift in attitude toward the Freedmen's Schools occurred. The challenges never stopped the school system's development and growth, as desired by its opponents. The resolve of black Richmonders impressed some individuals who once were opposed. This resulted in a shift in public opinion toward the Freedmen's Schools from open hostility to general acceptance. However, the system remained vulnerable. As long as black Richmonders lacked suffrage, they remained dependent on sympathetic federal and northern agencies for protection of the school system. Black Richmonders also did not have the full support of the broader white community for African American education as a legitimate right of citizenship. Undeterred and still hopeful, black Richmonders would build on the foundation established during the initial years.

The Reconstruction Acts of 1867 proved to be an important milestone in black Richmonders' struggle for education, freedom, and citizenship. The political significance of the Reconstruction Acts, which outlined the readmission process for the former Confederate states, cannot be denied. However, a narrow focus on their political significance minimizes their effects on education. The Reconstruction Acts fundamentally changed the nature of African American education. Gen. Orlando Brown recognized the significance of the legislation. He commented that the new "military bill" would "give a wholly new character to Freedmen's work." Although acknowledging the political significance, he also recognized that the Freedmen's Bureau would soon end its educational operations with the creation of new state governments and readmission of the former Confederate states into the union. In short, this series of legislation determined the parameters for a new phase in African American education, redefined the Bureau-supported Freedmen's School system, and ensured that black Richmonders would have a political voice in that process.[40]

Virginia, like all other former states of the Confederacy, convened constitutional conventions that met between late 1867 and late 1869. Special state elections determined the convention delegates and included southern African Americans, northern African Americans who had migrated to the region, southern whites, and northern whites that had migrated to the region. Contrary to the sentiment expressed in the white conservative press, the Virginia convention could not be described as being dominated by "Negro supremacy." African Americans represented 22 percent of the convention delegates, northern whites accounted for 18 percent of all delegates, unclassified whites made up 2 percent, and southern whites composed a plurality with 56 percent of the delegation.[41] Lewis Lindsay and John Cox, both African American, represented the city of Richmond at the convention. Despite the actual percentage of African American delegates, the *Richmond Whig* described the gallery of the convention as "opaque enough for an Egyptian, while here and there in the other gallery there was a moderate sprinkling of white men." Although described by conservative white newspapers as depraved, ignorant, and societal outcasts, convention delegates were well-educated, literate, Union Army veterans, business professionals, and/ or educators in the Freedmen's Schools.[42]

A sizeable percentage of white southerners, who were mainly conservative Democrats, opposed the convention on the basis of a lack of representation. The Reconstruction Acts disqualified a majority of these individuals for their previous loyalties to the Confederacy. Others simply refused to participate. This feeling of a lack of a representation created and sustained a hostile environment during the convention proceedings. White southerners often dismissed the white delegates with the pejorative terms of "carpetbaggers" and "scalawags" instead of seeing them as truly representing their community's needs. As a result, they viewed the political gathering as an imposition on the natural order of society and ridiculed it in the press. In addition, white Richmonders convened a rival convention as an expression of defiance to the federally mandated conventions. In their coverage of the counter-convention, the conservative newspapers devoted space to ridiculing the proceedings of the federally mandated convention and reinforced the myths about the delegates' intentions. The *Richmond Enquirer* used "Mongrel Convention," the "Convention of Kangaroos," and the "Black Crook" to describe the Virginia convention. The *Richmond Whig* reported that it preferred "military rule to despotism of an ignorant rabble" when discussing the "so-called convention or whatever it is, sitting in the Capitol."[43] This commentary encapsulated conservatives' anger over their disfranchisement and lack of representation, and their views of the proceedings as being illegal, undemocratic, and unconstitutional. Their attacks and the existence of the counter-conventions set the tone for the convention proceedings and the actions of the delegates.

Amid this hostile climate, delegates created democratic constitutions that featured an expansive state-funded educational system as the centerpiece.[44] The delegates considered the creation of a state-funded educational system a paramount goal from the outset. Most, perhaps even all, of the delegates attending the convention had an awareness of the general enthusiasm for free public education as indicated by the success of the Freedmen's Schools. A resolution establishing a committee whose primary task entailed the creation of a state public school system occurred early in the proceedings. This committee then drafted the constitutional article that called for the creation of a uniform system of public schools and provided the general framework for the new state educational system, which included clauses for the establishment of normal and agricultural schools, the creation of a school fund, and the use of uniform textbooks throughout Virginia. While nearly all clauses passed without amendment, those proposing separate schools and tax funding caused much debate. Ultimately, delegates charged their respective legislature with providing for a uniform system of public free schools, its funding, its composition, and a time frame for its gradual, equal, and full implementation.[45]

Delegates adopted the constitutions with the new educational mandates, which represented the states' first acknowledgment that they had a responsibility to educate children of all races and classes. Virginia was now obligated to financially support African American education as a state right of citizenship. After a somewhat lengthy period between the adoption and ratification of the constitution, Virginia reentered the Union in 1870. Virginians successfully created and fully implemented the state education system by July 1870. Through readmission and implementation of the educational mandates, the state acknowledged its defeat by accepting African American education as part of a postwar definition of freedom.[46]

However, black Richmonders and their allies determined their own path. With city officials as partners, they developed and implemented the framework for racially inclusive public schools prior to the establishment of the statewide system. As with the Freedmen's Schools, they led the way. It was not an easy path, as local responses included fierce resistance, intense negotiations, and accommodation between the various partners in the African American educational networks and the respective white community. In defining what the biracial system could look like in Richmond, white opposition yielded to a reluctant acceptance whereas black Richmonders responded with continued enthusiasm and anxiousness. The varied responses by white and black Richmonders demonstrate that local processes, and not merely state and federal forces, mapped a unique pathway toward public schools and the end of the Freedmen's Schools.

Initially, many white Richmonders opposed the newly created public schools. Their opposition derived from the constitutional convention process that created the schools, the revolutionary shift in attitude toward education by the convention delegates, and a general hostility to the perceived illegitimate Reconstruction government. They expressed their opposition through minor acts of violence directed toward individuals connected with the schools, and editorials in the Richmond newspapers. John A. McDonnell, Freedmen's Bureau agent in Richmond, continually wrote in his monthly reports, "The people are opposed to Free schools." Their efforts proved moot. They could neither prevent the implementation of the new state mandates nor slow the changing momentum of accepting state-funded education as right of white and black Virginians.[47]

Based on the proceedings of the convention, the adoption of a constitution, and the actions of the state legislature, Richmond officials and leaders realized that a tax-funded state educational system would soon become a reality. Rather than prolonging the inevitable, city officials instituted a free public school system for all school-age children, white and black, in 1869, one year before the official start of the state system. The city council determined that the schools were to be separate by race. Unlike the neighboring city of Petersburg, Richmond relied on the existing educational relationships forged by black Richmonders for the operation of the African American schools. By not requiring the end of the alliances, the city council focused its energies on the creation and early development of the public schools for white children while simultaneously collaborating with the Freedmen's Bureau, northern benevolent societies, and black Richmonders. For one year, the Freedmen's Bureau, philanthropic organizations, and black Richmonders provided the school buildings, supplied teachers, and financed a portion of the teachers' salaries, while the city council gave equal allocations of $15,000 to the operations of African American and white schools.[48]

The new biracial city school system directly competed with the independent, tuition-based schools. Since the new city schools were supported by taxes, black Richmonders reassessed their educational options and domestic economies. Many chose to send their children to the free schools. Amid declining economic conditions, the free school system provided a feasible alternative to the tuition-based private schools. The once-vibrant independent school system declined and some schools closed their doors.[49]

Instead of primarily serving elite and middle-class children, some independent schools began serving individuals at the opposite end of the class spectrum, specifically orphans and indigent children. Middle-class women combined their relief work with education because they regarded the orphanage for African American children operated by the Pennsylvania Society of Friends as insufficient. With public schools moving from hope to reality, Mrs. Julia St. Johns led several African American women in establishing a large independent orphanage that included an on-site school for the inhabitants. This school focused on a population not addressed by the public schools. Richmond's school policy did not differ from other cities nationally. By addressing class interests, the private school system served the specific educational needs of black Richmonders that were not being met by the new public schools.[50] Initially viewed as "unnecessary," Manly reluctantly supported the women's efforts because he had "heard nothing against her or the ladies with her, and the appearances at the 'Home' are in their favor." The state eventually incorporated the orphanage school into the public school system in 1872 but maintained the organizational structure established by St. Johns. While incorporation caused a loss of autonomy, the women's class-conscious efforts successfully demonstrate how independent school maneuvered in the new educational landscape and survived by focusing on underrepresented constituencies.[51]

The overwhelming majority of the African American schools continued without much change. Although the Bureau began phasing out its operations, the agency continued coordinating the allocation of funds for schoolroom rentals, teacher salaries, general maintenance, and basic materials for the schools. Manly still required teachers and remaining Freedmen's Bureau agents to submit reports and provide a high standard of education for the freedmen. He found the students continuing to meet his expectations of progress, deportment, and punctuality. According to Manly, the "schools have been the principal cause of hopefulness and patience with which the freemen have endured the hunger, the nakedness, and the unavenged wrongs of their transitional state . . . The schools have also developed self-respect, and a general desire for permanent homes, and the comforts and decencies of social life." Thus the Freedmen's Bureau still regarded its efforts as a total success. The new state educational mandates rejuvenated its operations and spurred the organization to continue its efforts until it had completed the state's transition to a biracial educational system.[52]

Likewise, northern benevolent associations embraced the Richmond School Board as a partner for several reasons. These associations had always believed that education was a responsibility of the state and needed tax revenue support. Officers of the American Missionary Association, for example, hoped that a national system of education for African Americans and southern whites could be created so that the organization could then concentrate on secondary schools and teacher training.[53] Thus the American Missionary Association, the New England Freedmen's Aid Society, the American Freedman's Union Commission, and other northern benevolent societies advocated for and cooperated with the local boards and the state in the creation of public schools. They readily responded to Freedmen's Bureau appeals to continue their financial support and supplying teachers during this transition period.[54] Although they cooperated with city officials, the societies did not relinquish control of their schools since they "strongly believed that southern white teachers could not be trusted with black interests." As a result, the organizations "placed as many northern teachers as possible in southern public schools while blacks were being trained," and even "rented [their] property to local systems only with the stipulation that [their] teachers kept." Mistrust of southern whites justified their partnership with the Richmond School Board and continued operations.[55]

Black Richmonders continued fulfilling their educational quest during the transition period. School attendance and scholastic achievement still exceeded expectations. Lizzie Parsons, a white American Missionary Association educator, discussed her school's continued success and the measures her students took to attend it. Because they lived in neighborhoods inaccessible to the majority of the Freedmen's Schools, Parsons's students traveled great distances for an education. She noted that the distance traveled never impeded her students' attendance, including one gentleman in her night school "who resides five miles out in the county, yet never fails in his place." As evidenced by Parsons's report, the transition to public schools never tempered the communal desire for education.[56]

The transition to public schools, though, produced some angst among black Richmonders. Some feared the premature ending of the Freedmen's Schools before the implementation of public schools was complete. For instance, students and parents expressed this concern to Parsons, as her school was the only Freedmen's School accessible to their neighborhood. As the only option available, they were concerned about its continuation and appealed to Parsons to discuss the matter with her sponsors. Parsons voiced their concerns and urged that the American Missionary Association continue the school for the following year, until free public schools opened. She wrote, "The colored people are very anxious to have it sustained . . . They come to me urging their need." Parsons's assessment of the African American community's anxiety for the continuation of the Freedmen's Schools until the implementation of public schools reflected their desire to become a literate people. An insufficient number of neighborhood schools marred the former system administrators' ability to reach all black Richmonders. Therefore, individuals living near Parsons's school highly valued it due to its proximity to their neighborhood and did not want it to close during this transition period. Parsons was not alone in noting the angst over the transition to public schools by some black Richmonders, but others had a different explanation.[57]

The economy also contributed to the apprehension. Harsh weather during the winter of 1867–68 and extremely dry conditions the following spring resulted in crop failures and incipient famine throughout Virginia. By the winter of 1868–69, these conditions and a poor economic climate in Richmond forced the temporary transfer of several students from Woolfolk's school to the one operated by the Friends. Peter Woolfolk explained the transfer as the consequence of "some parents [being] influenced by the actions of the Friends' society who charge nothing for fuel in their schools this year." Parents took advantage of the lower tuition rates in order to ensure their children's continued education. With the end of winter and the additional fuel surcharge, the parents of the transferred students would most likely return to the Channing School conducted by Woolfolk. In this instance, it was not the quality of the education but the cost guiding their decision. Other teachers noted that their students were "too poor to pay the tax or to buy books," and wished that the northern philanthropists "would send money to expend in books, slates etc." Poorer residents hoped that the free schools would alleviate the immediate economic burden posed by monthly tuition and fuel surcharges collected by the Freedmen's Schools. Thus the new system would make an education available to black Richmonders who simply could not afford to pay for it.[58]

As Manly worked with Richmond's Board of Aldermen and School Board, he met with Dr. William H. Ruffner, Virginia's superintendent of instruction, and representatives of the state legislature. From these meetings, Virginia's uniform system of education was created. While black Richmonders were not always present in these meetings, their long-standing partnership with Manly had established a trust and faith that he would uphold their alliance. He did. The legislature adopted what has become known as the Ruffner plan for the public schools, which included provisions for African American education. It was implemented on July 11, 1870. Twenty days later, the Freedmen's Bureau officially shut down its operations. This closure marked the official end to the Freedmen's Schools but not an end to African American education. State-funded public schools ensured financial support for African American education in Richmond. The new state school system also legitimated the rights of African Americans to become educated as citizens of Virginia and overturned antebellum white sentiments toward African American education. Although black Richmonders lost an ally in the Freedmen's Bureau, they gained new partners in the state and city officials who supported their desire to become an educated people. They would rely on these alliances over the next twenty years.[59]

Confederate defeat initiated black Richmonders' quest for educational access and citizenship that included African Americans in the body politic. They quickly capitalized on the new definitions of freedom, citizenship, and education by establishing schools without outside assistance. Their actions moved African American education from the margins to the forefront of the nation's imagination. Their struggle found national and international support as northern benevolent societies and the Freedmen's Bureau legitimated their claims to citizenship through education by becoming partners in the enterprise. Such partnerships were not always free from problems. As the former capital of the Confederacy, Richmond symbolized the region, the war, and the perceived antebellum ills of southern society. While remaking the former capital of the Confederacy was a top priority, black Richmonders and their educational partners sometimes engaged in power struggles for determining the nature of the school system, teachers, resources, and space. The various manifestations of the opposition forced black Richmonders and their educational partners to overcome any internal division for the sake of the nascent school system's survival. By 1867, African American education was the cornerstone of black Richmonders' postwar reality, though this was not the case for white Richmonders or the state. Expanding the nascent school system and ensuring its permanence became their next priorities.

National and state events, starting in 1867, greatly influenced their struggle. A new state constitution and the creation of state-funded public schools permitted the necessary expansion of educational access desired by black Richmonders. During the transition period, black Richmonders' alliances expanded to include state and local officials. They also secured the gradual acceptance of their postwar vision by white Richmonders. Unlike the city of Mobile, public schools emerged on a firm foundation. Black Richmonders received validation with the new mandates and the transition to public schools. The period demonstrated that their efforts to push African American education to the forefront had not been in vain. By 1870, black Richmonders and their allies felt well prepared to deal with the implementation of the state system. The previous five years revealed to them that the nation and perhaps God had been on their side.

2   No Longer Slaves

*Black Mobilians and the Hard
Struggle for Schools, 1865–1870*

On April 23, 1865, black Mobilians crowded into the State Street Methodist Episcopal Church. Eleven days after Confederate troops surrendered the city, attendees opened the mass meeting, called to discuss their newfound freedom, with the rousing "Song of the Black Republicans." In their rendition, they proudly sang in the second stanza:

> Free workmen in the cotton-field,
>   And in the sugar cane;
> Free children in the common school,
>   With nevermore a chain.
> Then rally, Black Republicans—
>   Aye, rally! We are free!
> We've waited long
> To sing the song—
> The song of liberty.[1]

Black Mobilians proclaimed their freedom with mass meetings, and songs asserting their liberty filled the air of the State Street and Second Presbyterian sanctuaries. A *Black Republican* correspondent reported to his New Orleans readers, "There is at this moment great joy in the hearts of our poor brethren who are just out of slavery." From this joy unleashed by their emancipation they developed common schools. As suggested in the song's lyrics, "free children in the common schools" was a priority and quickly became a reality for black Mobilians.[2]

Three days after Gen. Robert E. Lee's surrender at Appomattox Court House, Union troops captured the city of Mobile on April 12, 1865. The city never experienced the wartime experimentation as other areas did, but black Mobilians quickly established schools as expressions of their freedom when it became feasible. Within days of Union victory, schools emerged in the basements and sanctuaries of the city's African American churches. As black Mobilians expressed their freedom with schools, white citizens in one of the last major Confederate urban strongholds were coming to grips with occupation as well as Confederate defeat. This context profoundly shaped the development of the Freedmen's Schools, the educational partnerships forced, and the obstacles endured. For black Mobilians, it would be a hard struggle for access, legitimacy, and permanency. The perfection of black Mobilians' educational partnerships, intense white opposition, and relations with Creoles of color threatened their goal of becoming a literate people. In overcoming these challenges, black Mobilians proved that they were no longer slaves. By remaining steadfast in purpose, I contend, they remade the postwar landscape to include the African American schoolhouse in Mobile and firmly embedded African American education as a right of citizenship throughout the entire state. Ultimately their postwar vision prevailed.[3]

For black Mobilians, the city of Mobile served as the ideal venue for postwar experimentation in education, freedom, and citizenship for all of Alabama. They recognized the city's position at the forefront of the antebellum common school movement in Alabama and fully expected to expand this educational legacy through the inclusion of new postwar realities of a new social order defined by African American freedom and Confederate defeat.[4] While schools existed within days of Union victory, the Freedmen's School system formally commenced operations on May 11, 1865, at the State Street Methodist Episcopal Church. Dr. C. H. Roe and E. C. Branch, white Northwestern Freedmen's Aid Society of Chicago missionaries, served as the school's principal teachers and quickly saw their enrollments increase from 121 to 510 students by the tenth day of operations. Classes at the Stone Street Colored Baptist Church, the St. Louis Street School, and the Medical College also experienced rapid growth because of the high interest among African Americans to become a literate people. These schools operated until the end of June 1865 and resumed in the fall.[5] With the rapid emergence of these schools, black Mobilians, Dr. Roe, and E. C. Branch embraced the city's pioneer status in public education and cemented its new position at the vanguard of postbellum African American education for the entire state.[6]

Black Mobilians' nascent educational system received a new partner at the beginning of the 1865–1866 academic year. The Freedmen's Bureau concentrated its initial efforts primarily in Mobile and Montgomery in order to develop a strong base for a statewide system. Headquartered in Montgomery, Maj. Gen. Wager Swayne served as assistant commissioner for the state's operations. Born New York City in 1834, Swayne grew up in Columbus, Ohio, the son of a lawyer. He received his undergraduate education at Yale University in 1856 and then obtained a law degree from Cincinnati Law School in 1859. He practiced law with his father in Cincinnati until the start of the Civil War. During the war Swayne initially served as a major in the 43rd Ohio Infantry before moving up the ranks until suffering an injury, which required a leg amputation. While recuperating, O. O. Howard appointed him to become Alabama's assistant commissioner. From the beginning Swayne made justice for black Alabamians his top priority. He oversaw both the educational and noneducational programs and personnel. He worked closely with Rev. Charles W. Buckley, the state's first superintendent of education for the Freedmen's Bureau, in coordinating and supervising the various educational efforts for African Americans.[7]

Rather than hiring educational agents throughout the state, Swayne preferred utilizing individuals directly involved in local African American educational movements as school superintendents. These individuals often had a greater knowledge of local conditions and concerns, but most important, they often had the trust of their local communities. Hence Swayne hoped that hiring individuals directly involved in community efforts would instill trust in the federal agency. The Mobile system reflected this model. Swayne hired E. C. Branch as the superintendent of schools for the district of Mobile in March 1866. Branch reported directly to C. W. Buckley rather than to the Freedmen's Bureau agent located in Mobile. As a result, black Mobilians and their educational partners often deferred to the Freedmen's Bureau headquarters whenever problems arose.[8]

The symbiotic relationship between black Mobilians and the Freedmen's Bureau proved essential in the statewide development of African American schools. The relationship offered legitimacy to black Mobilians' efforts toward education and provided the necessary evidence to convince the broader white community of its merits. It also afforded federal protection of the nascent Mobile school system. Likewise, Montgomery agents benefited from the relationship. As one of the earliest educational systems in Alabama, Montgomery often looked to Mobile as a model for its operations elsewhere in Alabama. By September 1866 the Bureau had established the basic organizational structure, cemented relationships with several northern agencies, and expanded operations throughout the state.[9]

While black Mobilians had fewer northern organizations as partners than did Richmond, the school system quickly developed into an important cultural institution. By January 1866 E. C. Branch reported to the city's African American newspaper that the city's schools had 1,700 students enrolled and 17 teachers employed. At the end of the 1865–1866 academic year, the school system included day, night, and Sabbath schools with 728 enrolled students. The system also included several private schools operated solely by black Mobilians. In addition to maintaining its own operational expenses, the nascent school system regularly made financial contributions to burial societies, an orphan asylum, almshouses, and other relief societies. Through its philanthropic and educational efforts, the school system thrived.[10]

Branch gave several reasons for the system's rapid success. First, Branch cited the school system's policy to admit any interested student, regardless of class or financial circumstances. He proudly proclaimed in his regular report to the city's African American newspaper that "no one is debarred the privileges of the school on account of *color or poverty*." Students paid tuition in relation to what they could afford. As a result, tuition ranged from twenty-five cents to one dollar and twenty-five cents per enrolled student. Second, the school system provided regular structure to the enrolled students' daily routine. The six-hour daily session was highly regimented, as evidenced by the daily exercises at the Medical College. The day began precisely at "fifteen minutes before nine o'clock" for religious services and singing. Afterward, Branch noted that the various "departments return to their respective rooms in military order," where students received rigorous curriculum comparable to any other common school, regardless of race.[11] Third and most significant, the school system benefited from qualified white and African American teachers. These educators employed the latest teaching methods in various subjects and successfully harnessed their students' desire to be educated. Within nine months, Branch described the academic progress made by the majority of as "truly surprising."[12] The rapid success helped to legitimate black Mobilians' project of using the schoolhouse as a vehicle for postwar assertions of freedom and citizenship. Consequently, it quickly became a project worthy of continuation but also protection for future generations.

In addition, black Mobilians established a local newspaper, the *Nationalist*. They viewed sustaining a newspaper as essential to their quest for educational access and legitimacy. Although white American Missionary Association educators served as editors from Montgomery, the *Nationalist* had a trustees' board composed entirely of African Americans and a few Creoles of color. In addition to news coverage, the newspaper placed an emphasis on literacy and citizenship building. John Silsby, the first editor, proclaimed that the advancement of literacy through a newspaper constituted the "new state of things." He also promised that the *Nationalist* would contain "a variety of instructive and interesting matter . . . inculcating the truth that true religion and the virtues that germinate in it, are the only foundations of individual and national happiness." To this end, the newspaper featured a children's section, short stories, poetry, advertisements for literary societies and school events, and coverage of local, state, and national events. The *Nationalist* quickly became an important organ for black Mobilians' educational quest.[13]

Despite the initial success of the Freedmen's Schools, some of the educational partners disapproved of black Mobilians' involvement beyond the role of student. Some viewed the schools operated by African Americans as inferior and led by incompetent educators. State Superintendent Buckley voiced this opinion in a report to Maj. Gen. Wager Swayne: "There are in Mobile several colored schools taught mostly by colored teachers. Some of these teachers are not competent for the position they fill. They need suggestions from experienced teachers . . . and thus bring those of the same degree of advancement into the same school." Buckley also noted that the one operated by E. C. Branch, a white educator, was "flourishing" and had "done a great work for the colored people of the city." Buckley considered the existing educated class of black Mobilians too inexperienced for teaching. He could not overcome the racial assumptions regarding slavery, intellectual acumen, and teaching capabilities. For these reasons, Buckley viewed guidance and supervision by experienced white educators, such as Branch, as necessary during the initial years of the Freedmen's Schools. As a result, he discouraged schools operated by black Mobilians and encouraged those operated and administered by white northern missionary associations.[14]

For black Mobilians, the question over schools operated without white assistance never raised such anxieties. Some preferred independent schools, as evidenced by the students attending these schools instead of the school conducted at the Medical College. However, pragmatism influenced their acceptance of schools operated by the Northwestern Freedmen's Aid Society of Chicago. Individuals often considered factors such as location, cost, and a teacher's experience. Furthermore, black Mobilians generally supported sincere individuals devoted to African American education. For instance, the *Nationalist* noted that E. C. Branch's "constant and faithful labors in this community" received the appreciation of "every loyal citizen." For this appreciation, residents hoped that "he [would] long remain to diffuse among the colored youth that education which will be their best protection." The competition between the independent institutions and schools receiving outside financial support never bothered black Mobilians as it did Buckley.[15]

In short, access mattered more than educational type. Advertisements and articles regarding both types of schools peppered the pages of the *Nationalist*. The various editors praised the work done by both. In its coverage of a school exhibition at the Medical College, the *Nationalist* remarked, "The success of this school reflects great credit upon the efficient corps of teachers, who are devoting their times to the noble work of elevating a depressed race." The newspaper afforded the same level of praise to the work done in the private schools. The newspaper proudly endorsed the school operated by Miss Jeane Ashe, a black Mobilian. In calling attention to the advertisement for her school, the newspaper editors noted, "Her work is a glorious one and we hope that she will be well sustained." For the *Nationalist* and the community, access to an education for all classes mattered most. Independent schools afforded parents choice. They selected the type most beneficial to their family's domestic economy. These schools often provided African American teachers, a similar curriculum offered at the Medical College schools, and a local administration more in tune with the community's dynamics and concerns. Both school types fulfilled black Mobilians' goal of becoming a literate people and therefore could coexist without difficulty.[16]

White Mobilians' intense hostility overshadowed these internal debates over school type. As black Mobilians expressed their freedom, white Mobilians coped with their defeat as a city and a nation through violence directed at the initial schools. They found their greatest advocate in Dr. Josiah C. Nott. Born in Columbia, South Carolina, in 1804, Nott received his degree from South Carolina College in 1824 before obtaining his medical training from the University of Pennsylvania. After touring European hospitals and institutions, he settled in Mobile, Alabama, where he later established the Medical College of Alabama in 1859.[17] Nott received notoriety for his promotion of polygenism, or the belief of multiple origins as a justification of slavery and the repression of African Americans. His 1854 publication titled "Types of Mankind" with George Robins Gliddon formed the scientific defense of slavery prior to the Civil War.[18] Led by the prominent physician and racial theorist, white Mobilians characterized the initial teachers as a "pack of thieves" and "little dirty schoolmasters and schoolmistresses." When federal troops confiscated the property for African American educational purposes in April 1865, Nott publicly declared that he "would rather see the building burned down, than used for its present purposes." His proclamation reverberated among white Mobilians opposed to the Freedmen's School system.[19]

Several individuals acted on Nott's call to action. By the end of the summer 1865, the Methodist Church and Presbyterian Church fell victim to "acts of incendiary violence" because of their connection to the Freedmen's School system. Throughout the 1865–1866 academic year, arson plagued the majority of the churches that housed Freedmen's Schools. According to Maj. Gen. Swayne's report to O. O. Howard, arson even destroyed the Zion Methodist Church in late 1865 "directly after a military order restoring possession to the congregation previously excluded by white Trustees." Many white Mobilians approved of these violent tactics. In March 1866, the *Nationalist* reported the remarks made by a white citizen after the destruction of another church as being "glad of it, and he hoped the Medical college would go next." When pressed further on the futility of such actions, he replied that "when all places of resort for the negroes shall be destroyed, and the troops withdrawn, the whites would be able to manage them."[20] As evidenced by the citizen's remarks, arsonists, and Dr. Nott, a cross-section of white Mobilians sought the swift end to Educational Reconstruction even if it meant the destruction of confiscated property seen as "places of resort for the negroes."[21]

Nott's attack on African American education and the resulting arson, though, never yielded the desired effects. After his initial call for the destruction of the Medical College, Nott made similar arguments to Gen. O. O. Howard. He drafted a more elaborate case against the continued use of the Medical College as a "Negro school" and the overall Freedmen's School system after a fall 1865 meeting with Howard. While extracts of the letter appeared in the local press, the *Popular Magazine of Anthropology*, a London publication, published the entire letter in its July 1866 edition. In the piece titled "The Negro Race," Nott argued, using scientific and historical evidence, that African Americans lacked the intellectual facilities and capabilities necessary for full citizenship and equality with whites. He concluded that the Freedmen's Bureau efforts could not overcome African Americans' natural inferiority, intellectual deficiencies, smaller brain sizes, and lack of history worthy of study. Thus Nott advised Howard to "remove your bureau and the United States troops (particularly blacks) as speedily as possible from our soil, and leave the relations between the races to regulate themselves." In publishing the private correspondence, "The Negro Race" and its variations prompted swift and well-developed intellectual responses from black Mobilians. The nature of their responses directly challenged Nott's characterizations of African American intellectual abilities and their access to an education, citizenship, and equality.[22]

No longer slaves, black Mobilians articulated in the *Nationalist* their critiques of Nott's arguments against their right to education, citizenship, and equality. One letter to the *Nationalist* elaborately debunked the flaws in Nott's arguments, from its racial underpinnings to his failure to acknowledge postwar gains. In ignoring the outcome of the Civil War and emancipation, Nott failed to acknowledge African Americans' rich history and the gains achieved by them in the war's immediate aftermath. However, the unknown author concluded that the reality of Reconstruction and the Freedmen's Schools revealed another reality. Postwar achievements demonstrated that African Americans had not been "consigned to permanent subordination" as suggested by Nott. Instead, they had accepted their rightful place in postwar Mobile as the equals and not the racial subordinates of whites.[23]

In regard to Nott's demand for the removal of the Freedmen's Bureau from Mobile, the state of Alabama, and the entire region, the author reveals black Mobilians' absolute refusal to entertain such a prospect. Maj. Gen. Swayne had proven to be one of their strongest allies in upholding their postwar vision of freedom, citizenship, and education. Acceptance of Nott's proposal would "of course, be made upon the basis of the Dr.'s theory of the permanent inferiority and subordination of the colored people."[24] To this demand the author responded, "We tell the Dr., and all others, that the hope of any such settlement is perfectly visionary. There will be no settlement of matters here but upon the basis of perfect reciprocity of rights and privileges between the two races." The author predicted that there would be "a war of races at hand, compared to which Hayti was mere boy's play," if anyone suppressed their efforts to become an educated people in Mobile or elsewhere in the state.[25] Moreover, he warned that the "guilt and the entire responsibility of the whole thing will be upon the heads of the Dr. and his adjutors." Through his prediction of a race war, the author expressed black Mobilians' nonnegotiable refusal to give up their postwar gains. They would wage another military engagement on the scale of the Civil War first instead of giving up their newly acquired rights. Yet the author still hoped for a peaceful resolution.[26]

Through this nuanced response, the author defined the terms in which participants in Educational Reconstruction would deal with white Mobilian elites. Black Mobilians and their allies maintained the end of the antebellum white elites' infringement on African American citizenship and educational decisions as an inviolable term in postwar relations. In their eyes, emancipation ended black Mobilians' subservience. As full members of the body politic, they justified their freedom and right to claim their citizenship through an education with arguments against Nott and other white elites.[27]

Black Mobilians found in the Freedmen's Bureau a crucial ally against Dr. Josiah Nott. Nott's public denouncements and the resulting arson enraged Maj. Gen. Wager Swayne, who demanded justice from the unreconstructed Confederates. He insisted that the mayor condemn the violence and conduct a thorough investigation of the arson using the local police department.[28] Although no arrests occurred, Swayne's overwhelming support for Educational Reconstruction placed Nott, arsonists, and other hostile white Mobilians on notice. If necessary,

Swayne would use the full weight of the federal government in combating the opposition. Moreover, Swayne's swift response showed that the Freedmen's Bureau fully approved of black Mobilians' expressions of freedom and citizenship through education. The African American schoolhouse embodied the Bureau's overall efforts. They viewed education and not landownership or politics as the best acceptable vehicle in assisting African Americans' transition from slavery to freedom. Hence failure in Mobile was not an option. By not tolerating the actions of arsonists, the partnership between the Freedmen's Bureau and black Mobilians strengthened.[29]

Overall, Nott's proclamation and the resulting arson galvanized black Mobilians' activism. They viewed their fight against Nott and the arsonists in terms of moral warfare. "Ours is a moral war," a March 1866 *Nationalist* article informed readers. "The war simply put down the insurrection of barbarism against civilization, and opened the way for education which is the real liberation. The sword may make the freedman, but only the truth makes the freeman."[30] In defining their plight as a war for education, equality, and a nonracial world, they saw their white partners as essential allies against hostile combatants. These enemies needed to be defeated in order to secure the fruits of their emancipation. Education not only provided individuals with the valuable skills of reading and writing but was essential in preparing them to become freemen upon matriculation. Once they became an educated people, black Mobilians would truly achieve liberation from their slave past and be full citizens in the city, state, and nation. The overwhelming support from their partners reassured black Mobilians that they were not alone in the war. The arson and Nott's proclamations merely increased their resolve and reinforced the importance of their educational partnerships.[31]

Therefore school operations continued. The Medical College remained unscathed by the arsonists' wrath. The school absorbed several of the independent schools destroyed by fire. St. Louis Street School, Methodist Church School on St. Michaels Street, and the Presbyterian Church on Dauphin Street either temporarily or permanently moved into the building. As a result, the Medical College's enrollment increased accordingly.[32] The Medical College also remained a community center for public events, as arson had destroyed several communal meeting spaces. The school hosted Emancipation Day celebrations, public receptions, and the annual end of the academic year closing exercises.[33] These public events held at the Medical College validated the community's continued activism. Neither arson nor other expressions of the local white opposition deterred them. It only spurred them into action.

During the 1866–1867 academic year, a minor shift in organizational alliances occurred. The American Missionary Association took over operations of the schools at the Medical College. The organization forced E. C. Branch out of the school system, as it had done with the African American–operated Savannah Educational Association. While Branch's opinions regarding the American Missionary Association's maneuvering are not clear, it is evident that black Mobilians established ties with the organization.[34] This partnership proved beneficial. Under the American Missionary Association's leadership, the Medical College remained the cornerstone of Mobile's Educational Reconstruction and community services as a result of the missionaries' fund-raising efforts among black, Creole, and white Alabamians. Fund-raising and the continued existence of the Medical College schools cemented black Mobilians' trust in the American Missionary Association. School attendance remained high and public events continued to draw many members of the community. As a result, black Mobilians continued their activism with a new partner.[35]

Ultimately, Nott's proclamation and the resulting arson prevented the return of the confiscated Medical College property to the former school trustees. Dr. Nott petitioned the Freedmen's Bureau for the restoration of the Medical College to the antebellum Board of Trustees. To the dismay of his superiors, Swayne refused the transfer and brokered a sale between the Freedmen's Bureau, black Mobilians, and the American Missionary Association for the property.[36] With black Mobilians provided some funding, negotiations began in earnest after the American Missionary Association received a large donation from Ralph Emerson, Jr., in early 1867. The donation by the son of Rev. Ralph Emerson, a Congregational minister, permitted the opening of Emerson Institute in the former Medical College the next academic year.[37] Whether acting alone or together, black Mobilians' resolve and their educational partnerships strengthened as a result of the local white opposition. Instead of abandoning the cause of African American education, the network successfully resolved the obstacles posed by arson and other expressions of opposition.

Class division, specifically the divide between Creoles of color and black Mobilians, posed another obstacle. Dating from French and Spanish colonial rule, Creoles of color and their descendants claimed an African ancestry mixed with either a French and/or Spanish lineage, often characterized by their light complexion, Catholicism, general acceptance of mixed-race history, and pride in their European heritage. In ceding their land to the United States, French and Spanish colonial officials ensured the continued existence of this group with the

Louisiana Purchase in 1803 and the Adams–Onis Treaty in 1819. The latter treaty had the greatest impact by stipulating that African Americans and their descendants who could claim French or Spanish descent would be recognized as full citizens by the state of Alabama. The treaty guaranteed Creoles of color their civil, social, and legal rights and elevated them into a new social status, widely known as the "treaty population." This treaty and the benefits bestowed on Creoles of color fostered the hostilities between Creoles and black Mobilians.[38]

Creoles of color carved a space within Mobile's antebellum racial order. They represented approximately one-third of the city's population of free persons of color. They ensured the continuation of their rights by regularly invoking the Adams–Onis Treaty. As a result, Creoles enjoyed rights not afforded to free or enslaved African Americans. The nightly curfews and pass system never restricted their mobility as it did for free and enslaved African Americans. They could testify in court. Some Creoles owned slaves in Mobile and the adjacent counties. Others later willingly supported the Confederacy. Economically, Creoles prospered. These social and economic advantages caused the Creole community to "fiercely protect their identities and status" through disassociation and exclusive, by-invitation-only social and civic organizations such as the Creole Fire Company No. 1 and the Creole Social Club. Neither white nor black, Creoles of color actively maintained their unique position in the racial order.[39]

Moreover, Creoles used their access to an education and literacy as a way to distinguish themselves from black Mobilians. While African American education constricted after Nat Turner's Rebellion, Creole education remained legal and expanded from private and parochial schools to city-funded public schools in 1852. The Mobile press deemed these schools as "greatly needed" for Creoles who "had certain of the rights and privileges of American citizens secured to them by the treaty." While the lack of consistent enforcement of anti-literacy laws and the Catholic Church's desire for conversion permitted some black Mobilians to receive an education, the 114 free colored persons reported in the 1860 census as enrolled in the public schools were overwhelmingly Creole. Educational access, therefore, served as a means to reinforce the status of Creoles of color over black Mobilians.[40]

After the Civil War, Creole education remained a source a division. The Creole School was the only nonwhite school recognized by the Mobile school system. It remained outside the Freedmen's School system whose existence Mobile school officials did not recognize. Although the continued recognition and separation reinforced feelings of Creole superiority, black Mobilians attacked the logic of Creole supremacy. "A Subscriber" remarked in a January 1866 letter to the editor of the *Nationalist*, "I rejoice to see the names of scores of our most intelligent citizens enrolled in the glorious enterprise, many of our best informed Creoles falling into the ranks with their less favored brethren, to contend for our rights before the law." This writer and others felt that the postwar development of the Freedmen's Schools invalidated Creoles' claims and they refused to remain silent as done before emancipation. These insults over Creole education resulted in continued ostracism between the communities.[41]

Events following the 1866 annual parade of the Creole Fire Company No. 1 forced a change in relations. In 1819 several Creoles established the Creole Fire Company No. 1. Though the company was founded and staffed by Creoles, Mobile's racial order still dictated that it have a white person serve as its proxy. This proxy gave the company representation in the city's firemen association and legitimated the organization's existence. Like other nineteenth-century fire companies, the Creole Fire Company No. 1 functioned as a fraternal organization. They held social meetings and functions separate from the white fire companies. Social exclusivity also defined the organization's membership. Only Creoles belonged to the organization, and members had to uphold strict guidelines in their day-to-day deportment in the community. The organization even considered fining members for unnecessary fraternization with the members of the free and enslaved African American community. Each year the fire company held a parade. The fireman displayed their equipment for community review and approval, and the company's band provided the music for the event. Creole and white dignitaries delivered speeches at the festivities. This parade annually reaffirmed Creole identity and distinction over the African American community. As a result, the Creole Fire Company No. 1 and its annual parade held a prominent place in the Creole community.[42]

One year after Confederate defeat, the Creole Fire Company No. 1 celebrated its forty-seventh anniversary. As described by the *Mobile Daily Advertiser and Register*, the evening parade opened with a Creole brass band performing "Dixie" and other musical selections. The finely dressed firemen displayed their gleaming fire equipment and the Confederate flag in the procession. The parade concluded with a tribute to five of the organization's surviving founders. In the meeting preceding the torchlight parade, the Creole community relished the official recognition received from the antebellum white elites. Mayor Withers, several white Mobile fire companies, and other white dignitaries toasted the company. Each praised the Creole Fire Company No. 1's patriotism and allegiance to the antebellum social hierarchy in their speeches. The conservative white press also featured two full-length articles on the celebration.[43]

However, not everyone was impressed by the celebration. Black Mobilians attacked Creoles' refusal to accept postwar racial realities through *The Nationalist*. The newspaper rhetorically posited, "Let us ask these Creoles a few questions. Do any of you suppose that the men who partook of your good cheer would, for one moment, advocate the extension to you of the right to vote or hold office?" In response, the newspaper rebuked, "You may toady to white men till doomsday without becoming any whiter, and will only increase the stain by bringing yourselves individually into contempt. There is only thing, which you can do, however, which is both sensible and honorable, and that is elevate your own race."[44] Whereas black Mobilians limited their rebukes to the printed page, a group of young white men showed no such restraint. Enraged by the spectacle, a group of young white males went into interracial crowds viewing the procession. These roving young white males attacked any African American and Creole encountered. The men made no racial distinction between the two groups. In their indiscriminate attacks, the young white men killed a bystander who resisted. Horrified by the events, the mayor ordered the arrest of the white men. Instead of imprisonment, the convicted youth received a fine for their actions.[45]

After the riot a shift occurred. Although the schools remained separated, Creoles and African Americans called for reconciliation. A *Nationalist* article implored readers, "But if the sensible portion of both Creoles and freedmen resolve to rise superior to their prejudice and to cultivate a spirit of amity to work *together* in all good undertakings, their combined efforts secure to both classes the more undisturbed exercise of all the rights of manhood." The author reasoned, "It is to be hoped that the freedmen will do everything in their power to strengthen the fraternizing disposition now beginning to manifest itself, and show a willingness to forget the past of all those who will take a proper position at the present and for the future."[46] While sources remain silent on the details of the behind-the-scenes discussions, it is evident that reconciliation between the communities began within the year. Subsequent Creole Fire Company No. 1 events received positive commentary in the *Nationalist*.[47] When the *Mobile Times* sought an alliance with the Creoles, an unnamed Creole of color explained their refusal: "Since the war, the Creoles have been placed on the same plane as the humbliest freedman. . . . We are all tarred with the same stick—knit together by bonds of common sympathy and suffering, and must rise or fall together."[48] Shared experiences with racism made Creoles align themselves with their African American brethren. Although this cooperation never truly eliminated tensions between the groups, both willingly put them aside. They began seeing their postwar experiences as being shared rather than separate.[49]

By 1867, black Mobilians and their allies successfully established an educational foundation. While fewer partners emerged than in Richmond, the foundation allowed black Mobilians to form more lasting relationships with the Freedmen's Bureau and the northern benevolent societies. It also gave parents options as the Freedmen's Schools developed alongside a well-formed independent black school system. In the process, black Mobilians and their educational partners never failed to remember the system's vulnerability. The extreme rhetorical and violent manifestations of local white hostility convinced black Mobilians that only a strong relationship with federal agencies and suffrage would give the system any possible future. Even the private schools required protection from the Freedmen's Bureau against arsonists. Undeterred, black Mobilians' persevered and continued their struggle for education, freedom, and citizenship. Expanding the nascent school system and ensuring its survival became their next priorities.

Passage of the Reconstruction Acts rejuvenated black Mobilians' struggle for education. The federal legislation afforded them the possibility of enshrining their educational vision in the new constitution while simultaneously expanding African American education. Thus black Mobilians and their partners fully participated in the flurry of political activity. On May 16, 1867, Lawrence S. Berry, William V. Turner, and R. D. Wiggins appealed to the black Mobilian and Creole of color communities of Mobile and members of the state Republican Party in an open letter to the *Nationalist*. The respected African American leaders made two demands for the upcoming state constitutional convention. First, they requested that "no discrimination on account of color" be used in the Republican Party's nomination process for convention delegates. Second and most significantly, they called for the creation of a state-funded public school system that included all citizens regardless of race. "The lack of education which is the consequence of our long servitude, and which so diminishes our powers for good, should not be allowed to characterize our children when they come upon the stage of action," the men passionately pleaded, "and we therefore earnestly call upon every member of the Republican party to demand the establishment of a thorough system of common schools throughout the State, and indeed of the Union, for the well-being of such ensures to the advantage of all." With "education secured to all," Berry, Turner, and Wiggins concluded, "Alabama will commence a career of which she will have just cause to be proud." The men's demands came to fruition in November 1867.[50]

In compliance with the Reconstruction Acts, black, white, and Creole delegates convened in Montgomery, Alabama, to craft a new state constitution in order to be considered for readmission to the Union. John Carraway, former slave, and Ovide Gregory, Creole of color, served as the nonwhite convention delegates from Mobile. As charged by Berry, Turner, Wiggins, and others in their communities, Carraway and Gregory actively advocated that the proposed constitution make no distinctions in terms of race, class, caste, or former servitude, especially in the new educational article. Indeed, the final article addressed their communities' desire for inclusivity. Section 6 specified that Alabama establish "schools at which all children of the State, between the ages of five and twenty-one years, may attend free of charge." Establishing schools for all children, regardless of race, class, caste, or former servitude, was quite revolutionary. State-funded African American public schools would provide the necessary permanency desired by black Mobilians and their partners.[51]

Rather than signaling the demise of African American education, the new state constitution not only ushered in a new phase but also further highlighted that black Mobilians were no longer slaves. Hence the convention, constitution, and new educational mandates produced intense and polarized responses. Internal divisions and attitude shifts within the white, Creole, and African American communities shaped the period beginning with the convention and ending with departure of the Freedmen's Bureau. Both demonstrate that acceptance at the state level did not automatically secure local acceptance of African American education as a legitimate right of citizenship. It required convincing residents. The conservative white community, as represented by the newspapers, vehemently opposed the new constitution and its educational mandates. Their opposition, though, represented a small portion of the white community. Gradually, conservatives lost their hegemonic appeal. Some whites began expressing a viable, alternative vision. The Board of School Commissioners for Mobile County became an outlet for these individuals' ideas and vision. The board actively pursued an alliance with the Freedmen's Bureau for the extension of the city's schools to African American children. The actions of the board represented a major shift in attitudes concerning African American education. These diametrically opposed viewpoints set the stage for the public school implementation. Similarly, black Mobilians' and Creoles' responses included reservation about extending social divisions in the new schools, angst over white conservatives' strengthening their political power, and vindication for the previous educational struggles. These varied reactions to African American education encouraged the development of yet another path toward public schools.

Most white Mobilians vehemently opposed the new constitution and the inclusion of African Americans in the state educational system. The new constitution embodied a postwar vision for the region that threatened their social, political, and economic hegemony. The state constitution was considered a document created by and for individuals deemed their inferiors and thus did not represent white conservatives' self-interests. Utilizing the *Mobile Daily Advertiser and Register* (renamed the *Mobile Daily Register* in early 1868), they launched a campaign to block ratification of the state constitution. Through a barrage of articles and editorials, the newspaper discouraged its readers from participating in the ratification election and thereby forcing its defeat through a failure to obtain the required majority of registered voters. The newspaper editor and staff promoted organizations, like the Constitutional Committee of Mobile, that shared the anti-ratification sentiment. Created for the sole purpose of "defeating the so-called Constitution," these organizations found a forum and willing audience in the newspaper's readership. With the support of the *Mobile Daily Register* and other conservative newspapers, white Mobilians embarked on their campaign.[52]

Anti-ratification campaign organizers also advocated extralegal measures as a tactic. Several *Mobile Daily Register* articles and editorials strongly suggested that economic and social repercussions would occur against any voter who gave electoral support to the constitution. One article recommended that black Mobilians "keep out of the election" and not risk any detrimental consequences. Another article shamed white supporters of the constitution by publishing their names and occupations. This tactic forced the targeted individuals to redeem their honor and reaffirm their southern identity. Two days after a public outing, John Weldon appealed to the *Mobile Daily Register* readers with a letter to the editor. After reaffirming his Democratic political loyalties, Weldon expressed his desire to end military occupation as the reason for his supporting ratification in the election and his general resignation in accepting the new postwar order. The newspaper never detailed any repercussions incurred by Weldon or other supporters of the constitution after such public humiliation. Still, these extralegal measures and the overall campaign proved effective in forcing some to yield to the organizers' vision.[53]

The campaign succeeded in limiting public discourse, discouraging electoral support throughout the state, and briefly blocking ratification. At the time of the election Alabama had approximately 170,000 registered voters; however, only 6,700 white voters and approximately 63,000 African American voters participated in the ratification election.[54] Although the majority of the voters approved ratification, the election failed to receive the 85,000 votes required by the Second Reconstruction Act. This technicality blocked ratification and readmission. The *Mobile Daily Register* hailed their victory with articles, editorials, and letters to the editor. Its celebration, however, was brief, as federal officials intervened. After a congressional intervention, a presidential veto, and a congressional override, the state constitution eventually received recognition and approval for readmission. Readmission made state-funded African American public schools a reality.[55]

While many white Mobilians fought a ratification battle, another viewpoint emerged and steadily gained acceptance by a few white Mobilians. This group began to accept the importance of the Freedmen's Bureau's educational vision and advocated for the creation of African American public schools in Mobile. Despite many obstacles, the Freedmen's Schools succeeded. Their success convinced some white Mobilians that African American education was a postwar reality they must accept on account of their defeat. This change in attitude revealed itself in a proposed alliance between the Board of School Commissioners for Mobile County and Freedmen's Bureau agents in Mobile and Montgomery. This alliance ultimately undermined the efforts of more conservative white Mobilians.

Shortly before the constitutional convention, the Board of School Commissioners for Mobile County approached the Freedmen's Bureau regarding a possible partnership. In an August 1867 letter, C. A. Bradford, secretary of the board, made the request. He wrote that the board received an inquiry from several black Mobilians that asked "whether our system of public instruction can be extended to the colored children of Mobile, and if so, in what manner and by what means such instruction can be most efficiently accomplished." This inquiry directly questioned existing school policy and reflected the petitioners' efforts in amending it. In discussing the inquiry, the board agreed with the petitioners and looked into the feasibility of extending its educational system to include black Mobilians. Funding seemed to be the main obstacle. In the course of the discussion, several school commissioners mentioned that the Bureau had funds appropriated for the creation and operation of African American schools. Bradford inquired, on behalf of the board, to "ascertain what aid it is in the power of the Bureau to give to this object," specifically toward school construction and teacher salaries. The potential alliance would serve both organizations' needs. Access to the Bureau's financial networks would greatly improve the board's overall financial situation. Having the full cooperation and support of the Board of School Commissioners would fulfill the aims of African American education for the Freedmen's Bureau.[56]

Bradford's inquiry purposefully appealed to the Freedmen's Bureau's humanitarian aim of elevating former slaves to full citizens. In building the case for a partnership, Bradford gave a revised history of the Mobile school system. He emphasized the board's education of free Creoles of color before the war: "Indeed, from the re-organization of the system in 1852 to the present time, we have had a School for Creoles in the City and one in the Country, successfully conducted and operating in harmony with the schools for whites." Bradford then reassured State Superintendent Buckley, "There is not the slightest reason to fear that it cannot be indefinitely extended, if the board is put in possession of adequate means." These comments strongly suggested that the existence and acceptance of the Creole School would easily allow for the expanding existing system the African American schoolhouses.[57] His humanitarian depiction actually masked the racial and legal reasons for the Creole schools. Racism and not the lack of finances, as suggested by Bradford in his letter, guided the board's decision to only educate Creoles and not black Mobilians prior to and immediately following the Civil War. Therefore Bradford purposely overlooked the context that made Creole education possible in order to gain access to the agency's financial networks.[58]

The board's apparent about-face piqued State Superintendent Buckley's interest. The proposal fulfilled a crucial aim of the Bureau's educational efforts. The Bureau viewed its job as temporary until local and state officials adopted the postwar definitions of education and citizenship. The creation of a permanent public school system that educated all children, black and white, would put an end to their services for the newly freed. It would also fulfill the aims of the participants with which the Bureau had established working relationships. Bradford's partnership request, therefore, produced great enthusiasm among Buckley and other Bureau agents. In his response to Bradford, Buckley extensively quoted passages from the request that highlighted the agency's aims. The tone of the letter and general remarks, moreover, offered reassurance that a partnership would most likely occur. He wrote that the "cooperation in its expenditure, even though your Board is without funds," would benefit the "colored element of your city." Furthermore, Buckley predicted that Mobile would serve as a model for the rest of the state for its willingness to cooperate with the Bureau and its adoption of a postwar definition of education. He wrote, "Besides your example will hasten the day when an efficient system of public instruction shall be provided for every child of the State." Indeed, Bradford achieved the desired results with the inquiry.[59]

Bradford's inquiry cemented the realization of the Bureau's educational goals for Mobile, the state, and the entire region. Buckley's correspondence with the sub-assistant commissioner as well as his annual report proudly proclaimed the possible partnership. After providing a synopsis of the correspondence generated by Bradford's initial August 1867 letter, Buckley strongly argued, "There is some ground of hope then for the option that the state is willing to accept and support a system of common schools." He predicted that the new system would have as "its foundation upon the principle now almost universally recognized that it is the primary duty of the every community to provide ample means of instruction for every child within its borders." Buckley's elation and bold prediction set the tone for the November 1867 constitutional convention and the future relationship between the school board and the Freedmen's Bureau in the transition to public schools.[60]

As Buckley predicted, Mobile served as a model for Alabama. The delegates from Mobile and Bureau educational officials led the campaign for a state school system at the constitutional convention. As the convention and ratification debate progressed, Buckley resigned, but his successor finalized the details of the Board–Bureau partnership. In his annual report, R. D. Harper, state superintendent of education for the Bureau, alluded to the successful partnership's transformative power on the state level. In noting the successes in both Mobile and the state, Harper remarked, "The future is hopeful. The State, the Bureau, and Northern Associations are now combining their power and concentrating their efforts for the education and elevation of the colored race." Harper then suggested an illustrious future for public education: "Ten years hence the great mass of children of the State will have received a common school education, fitting them for the responsibilities devolving upon them and for acting well their part in all, the relations of life."[61] Harper's annual report and correspondence with local officials, the American Missionary Association, and Bureau officials also illustrated the degree of cooperation occurring during the transition toward public schools with these progress updates. The Board–Bureau partnership, the new state constitution, and the failed ratification campaign further pushed the conservatives to the periphery and elevated the vision of moderate whites in Mobile.[62]

According to the terms of the partnership, the Bureau relinquished direct control over the schools. The organization pledged financial support for the erection of new schoolhouses and for paying rent on the existing schoolhouses. The American Missionary Association agreed to supply the state with qualified teachers, though it was not required to relinquish any of its schools. The state agreed to pay the teachers with monies from the state education fund via the local school boards. The partnership went into effect on January 1, 1869.[63]

Schools not affiliated with the American Missionary Association were incorporated into the local and state educational system. The Stone Street and Zion Schools were the first transferred. Good Shepherd School followed thereafter. St. Peter's School joined the city system at the start of the next academic year. The schools transferred to the board only provided primary education and did not

offer either intermediate or advanced studies. Located in the heart of black Mobilians' neighborhoods, these schools had operated independently of northern
benevolent societies and were either fully self-sufficient or partially funded by
the Bureau. The lack of northern affiliation facilitated the ease of transfer.[64]

It is difficult to ascertain whether this transfer greatly affected the classroom
activities, but one significant consequence definitely occurred—school enrollment increased. On average, approximately 605 students per month attended
the Freedmen's Schools and restored Creole School prior to the new city school
system from 1865 to 1868. By the end of the 1868–1869 scholastic year in June,
919 African American and Creole of color children attended the public schools.
Officials deemed the transfer a success, as evidenced by Dr. Barnas Sears's annual Peabody Education Fund report. Quoting heavily from a progress report
made by the Mobile school board dated September 14, 1869, Dr. Sears wrote,
"More than half of the pupils under instruction in the schools were free. All the
scholars of the primary grade, which embraced the entire number of colored
children, were taught free of charge for tuition." As the initial Bradford inquiry
requested, the Mobile County school board expanded its city's primary schools
to include all classes and racial groups—whites, Creoles, and African Americans.
Additional funding from the Peabody Education Fund and other sources permitted the expansion to include intermediate grades as well. Thus a more moderate white Mobilian vision for African American education proved victorious in
the transition to public schools.[65]

Internal class and social divisions shaped black Mobilians' responses to the
convention, new educational mandates, and the transition to public schools.
Black Mobilians and Creoles worried that existing class differences would affect
access to the public schools, continuation of the Creole School, and the coexistence of private schools with public schools. Addressing these fears was necessary in order to gain acceptance of the new state educational mandates. The
conservative white ratification campaign, however, made a significant difference.
It allowed the black and Creole communities to set aside their differences and
develop a unified political strategy that would save African American and even
Creole education. While the political turmoil sometimes penetrated the classroom, a feeling of fulfillment of an educational vision permeated the schools.
The responses, inside and outside the Freedmen's Schools, profoundly shaped the
transition to public schools.

The *Nationalist* proved instrumental in securing support for the convention
and ratification. The newspaper sought to minimize class divisions among black
Mobilians and Creoles in order to secure their approval for the convention and

during the ratification process. Albert Griffin, the *Nationalist* editor, appealed to the communities prior to the convention by guaranteeing that the new constitution would include provisions for a public school system. However, his assurances did not always eliminate speculation and anxiety. An 1867 letter to the editor charged the newspaper with advocating against the creation of public schools. Griffin refuted these charges by publishing a barrage of articles and editorials dismissing this charge during its coverage of the convention and pre-ratification election.[66] The newspaper also appealed to white Alabamians for their electoral support in the ratification of the new constitution. Griffin stressed that the new educational system was necessary for the state and did not "require both races to attend the same schools." The newspaper's appeal reflected the concern that African American electoral power was not sufficient to achieve the necessary votes for ratification. The efforts, however, were not enough. Opponents successfully blocked ratification; in so doing, white Mobilians prevented the creation of state-funded public schools.[67]

White conservative Mobilians' triumph during the initial ratification election dictated a change in tactics. After the failure to ratify the constitution, the *Nationalist* editor and staff devoted their attentions to alleviating the internal divisions. They posited that their Republican allies in Congress would approve the constitution and allow Alabama's readmission without convening another convention. Thus the editor devoted little coverage to the subsequent ratification debate. The strength of the white conservatives' hegemony provoked the necessity of unity in order to have African American education and other postwar gains remain viable.[68]

The African American and Creole communities proved receptive to the *Nationalist* editor's and state Republicans' vision for inclusivity in the state-funded public schools. Fear of conservative whites' regaining political saliency and power motivated them. Unity between and within the respective communities would prevent the overturning of Reconstruction gains as conservative southern white Democrats regained political power. Intimidation, violence, and other extralegal measures had allowed for the restoration of Democratic Party rule and failure in the ratification election. In an open letter to Mayor Caleb Price, several members of the African American and Creole elite appealed to white Mobilians in order to lessen the violence against them during the congressional ratification debate and 1868 elections. The violent restoration attempts threatened the new constitution. This threat made unity a necessary strategy against the aggressive political adversaries. Solidarity, as historian Michael Fitzgerald demonstrated, allowed for previous factionalism to cease in the city's educational and political advancements. The willingness to put aside class and color differences, Fitzgerald concluded, proved an effective strategy for the next two decades. Although social divisions still existed, the once prevalent Creole and African American divide was minimized in the political realm shortly after the ratification debate.[69]

Inside the classroom, on the other hand, participants in the Freedmen's Schools responded with hope about the convention and new constitution. The creation of state and city educational systems validated their postwar educational efforts and their definition of citizenship in postwar Mobile. Although a coincidental school closing occurred during the convention as a result of a yellow fever epidemic, the students continued to display enthusiasm for education during the ratification debates. Attendance remained high. Between 400 and 780 students per month flocked to the schools during the first half of the 1868–1869 scholastic year. Overall, the Freedmen's Schools thrived before the official transfer. Teachers' reports continued to praise the continued enthusiasm for education and expressed optimism for the newly created state and county public school systems.[70]

The creation of public schools deterred neither black Mobilians nor Creoles from opening and maintaining independent schools. As in Richmond, private schools began addressing the needs of African American orphans. For instance, the Colored Orphan School opened a few months prior to the January 1869 transfer. Sustained by the aid of the Tuscaloosa Scientific and Art Association and the Order of Love Charity, it promised to be "a first-class school, where poor colored children can be educated free of charge." Leading African American and Creole citizens managed the school. It employed one teacher and an assistant and educated the children excluded from the public schools due to their poverty. The school provided another alternative for African American education until the free school system inclusion of orphans became a reality. It also reinforced to black Mobilians and Creoles that public education could coexist with a private tuition-based system. Parents had choice in deciding on the appropriate option for their children. Both options still permitted the fulfillment of black Mobilians' desire to become an educated people, allowed for Creoles to maintain their heritage through education, and alleviated the internal divisions between and within the Creole and African American communities.[71]

The American Missionary Association initially viewed the constitutional convention and new state commitment to African American education with optimism and hoped for a peaceful resolution during the ratification crisis. While black Mobilians and the Freedmen's Bureau contributed some money, the American Missionary Association successfully purchased the Medical College, remodeled and erected buildings, and opened Emerson Institute during the convention proceedings. AMA executives hoped that Emerson Institute would replace some of the deteriorating Freedmen's Schools and put the public schools on a firmer foundation after they were transferred to the city system. Centrally located, Emerson Institute quickly became the crown jewel of the organization's and Bureau's educational efforts in Mobile. Bvt. Gen. James Gillette noted the immediate respect received by "colored school enterprise" and its transformative effects on popular attitudes toward African American public schools. With its opening, Gillette wrote that the "community of Mobile has lately given expression of approval to efforts towards educating the ignorant; poor of all classes, and none speak openly against educating the negro now where much bitterness was manifested a year ago." From its inception, Emerson Institute offered primary, intermediate, and advanced instruction in a multilevel structure and had a separate teacher's home on-site. By late April 1868, black Mobilians, the American Missionary Association, and the Freedmen's Bureau considered the school a "judicious investment" and found conditions inside the school encouraging. Owing to the immediate success of Emerson Institute and the partisan nature of the ratification debate, the organization kept an increasingly skeptical yet still hopeful eye toward city and state political developments.[72]

The embittered ratification debate, though, made some American Missionary Association officials question the future of its Mobile operations. As the debate prolonged, the organization became increasingly uneasy about transferring Emerson Institute to either the Mobile school board or the state due to the political actions of white conservatives. Emerson Institute's newness and the organization's financial investment in the school made the American Missionary Association demand a continued role in school operations while trying to work within the changing nature of African American education in the state. They achieved this by securing several school board positions for local AMA administrators and trusted white and African American allies. They also sought alliances with state educational officials in order to deal with any potential threats. Yet the organization still hoped that the ratification crisis would end in their favor and African American education would prevail.[73]

In January 1869 the Board–Bureau alliance and the American Missionary Association had achieved relatively suitable arrangements for the African American schools. While the American Missionary Association retained control over the daily operations of Emerson Institute, the organization had secured one of its agents and other friends on the newly appointed, Republican-dominated school board for Mobile. Optimism reigned. These sentiments quickly turned to turmoil, however, as two school boards representing the old and new political regimes competed for power and legitimacy. This struggle threatened the new public school system and had the potential to end the progress made in African American education. The crisis resurrected debates over education first raised during the state constitutional convention and ratification process and divided the white, Creole, and African American communities. The fate of African American public schools rested on the strength of the relationships formed by black Mobilians and their allies, and the ability of those parties to broker a suitable resolution.

The Bureau–Board alliance quickly broke down as two school boards vied for control over Mobile County schools and their state appropriations. The "old" school board comprised white conservatives, members of the antebellum school board, and individuals appointed under the administration of moderate Republican mayor Gustavus W. Horton. In an attempt to limit Superintendent George Putnam's control over tax revenues, they "placed themselves in opposition to free schools." However, the "carpetbagger opportunist of questionable probity" appointed a rival "new" school board comprising radical white and black Republicans, Catholic Democrats, and wealthy Creole of color Constantine Perez. Moreover, Putnam secured state legislative approval for the rival board.[74] The "old" board, though, refused to leave office and claimed the title as the legitimate body. Acting against state law and ignoring the duly appointed "new" board, the "old" board still collected taxes, disbursed the monies to the Mobile schools, and charged tuition in the African American schools. As both boards considered themselves the legitimate government agency, a peaceful and timely resolution was not possible.[75]

Dr. N. B. Cloud, superintendent of public instruction for Alabama, brokered a compromise. First, it mandated George Putnam's appointment as superintendent of colored schools and that his orders and directions come directly from the Board of School Commissioners. Second, it required the retention and certification of the American Missionary Association teachers and principals in the county school system. Third, Emerson Institute remained under American Missionary Association control but the Board of School Commissioners oversaw its general management. Embattled school commissioners, the state superintendent of public instruction, and the American Missionary Association agreed to the terms. Employing the *Nationalist*, Cloud assured black Mobilians that the public schools were "ENTIRELY FREE" and existed under the terms of the compromise. Dr. Cloud's reassurance proved fleeting. The "old" board agreed to but never fulfilled the terms of the compromise. Faced with no other option, in June 1869 Dr. Cloud revoked their commissions for violating the Alabama school law. Cloud's intervention unintentionally placed the newly established African American public schools in peril.[76]

In a campaign of words and lawsuits against state and city officials, both boards jockeyed for control. The "old" board leveled slanderous attacks against Putnam and his administration in the city newspapers. Gustavus Horton, former city mayor, renounced his previous support of the partnership between the AMA, the Freedmen's Bureau, and the city, and endorsed the "old" board. Horton and other proponents also flooded the American Missionary Association headquarters and local Bureau office with letters and petitions questioning Putnam's character and suitability for government office. These letters openly challenged the organization's support of the new board as the legitimate agency. Major James Gillette, local Bureau agent, proved ineffective in finding a suitable resolution for all parties. The Freedmen's Bureau adopted a policy that relied on the court system to rectify the situation as a means to "harmonize and avoid conflict of people engaged in the same work." Putnam responded to some of the attacks to American Missionary Association executives but concentrated his energies on the legal challenges.[77]

In October 1869 Judge Elliot offered a resolution. He ruled in favor of the "new" board. However, the "old" board immediately filed an appeal. Instead of resolving the rival school board debate, the Elliot decision only fueled another legal challenge and increased speculation over the fate of the African American public schools. Putnam and his administration now had to address the appeal. Simultaneously, they had to assure black Mobilians that the "new" board was "unanimous in their desire to have the free school in successful operation." The Eliot decision ultimately prolonged the dual school board debate.[78]

This battle prompted a major crisis in the newly created African American public schools. State funds appropriated for Mobile schools were in limbo as only board officials could access the Alabama Educational Fund. State and city funds for teacher's salaries, school materials, and school furniture were temporarily frozen. Teachers and administrators went unpaid. Moreover, the chain of command between teachers, administrators, and school officials was confused. It was unclear to whom teachers and administrators should give their reports or even their allegiance. Should they support the old or new school boards? W. Irving Squire's letter to E. P. Smith expressed the frustration and uncertainty endured by the teachers amid the crisis. The African American educator commented that the "teachers, some of them, are getting impatient" as resolution seemed unattainable.[79] Ultimately the "new" board gained legitimacy from the Alabama State Supreme Court, and African American education survived this major challenge.[80]

However, the dual school board crisis convinced the American Missionary Association to not relinquish control over Emerson Institute to the city. Fearful over the future of African American education, the organization negotiated with the Freedmen's Bureau and black Mobilians. All parties agreed that the American Missionary Association would retain control over the school until black Mobilians could fully sustain and operate it. At this time, according to the agreement, the organization would relinquish control and ownership. Thus Emerson Institute remained outside the Board of School Commissioners' domain. The school board crisis also afforded Emerson Institute a unique position in the city. It was neither a public school nor completely a private school. Its size, location, and prestige made it an affordable alternative for parents and children seeking an education other than that offered by the traditional public and private school systems. Hence Emerson Institute justified the American Missionary Association's decision to remain in Mobile after the Freedmen's Bureau officially left. The organization simply refused to relinquish the school after the rival school board debate.[81]

The dual school board challenge also had financial repercussions. The Peabody Education Fund suspended its financial support of the Mobile schools. The organization viewed the litigation and the entire affair with disdain. Dr. Sears wrote in his annual Peabody Education Fund report, "In Mobile, there has been a litigation about the jurisdiction of the State and city officers, which has had the effect to nullify the agreement previously made by us with the city School Board." Dr. Sears deemed that future financial support, if reinstated, was contingent on reapplication and a stable city as well as state administrative structure "to renew engagement." The loss of an important financial source placed the new free schools for African Americans in an unfavorable position.[82]

As the Freedmen's Bureau officially departed Mobile and the state in July 1870, the situation seemed bleak for African American education. The partial transfer of the Freedmen's Schools and the school board crisis produced major power struggles. The political instability sometimes entered the classroom and had the potential of destroying the new system. Funding concerns remained unresolved. Public schools for African Americans barely survived these early obstacles and entered the next decade on a less than firm foundation. Power struggles over the operation of the new schools between the Board of School Commissioners, state educational officials, black Mobilians, and the American Missionary Association continued during the initial years of the public schools. Furthermore, the role of the independent Emerson Institute in the new struggles remained unclear. It was clear, though, that black Mobilians would continue to fight for education and employ all resources at their disposal. Black Mobilians would leverage Emerson Institute's independence in their fight for teachers, better schools, and better conditions from 1870 to 1890. During this period, Emerson Institute became an effective political tool in black Mobilians' negotiations with the school board and made the survival of African American education possible after the demise of the Freedmen's Schools.

In April 1865, black Mobilians embarked on their long and arduous quest for an education. A vocal white opposition and internal division within the city's black community quickly tempered the initial success. Despite these obstacles, they successfully established an educational foundation based on an extensive network of relationships with the Freedom's Bureau, the American Missionary Association, editors of the *Nationalist*, independent school educators, and Creoles of color. Unity and a strong public front proved essential in combating the concerted opposition led by Dr. Josiah Nott. By 1867, black Mobilians still had more work to do to expand the school system in and beyond Mobile, eradicate the system's vulnerability, and ensure its continuation for future generations.

National and state events greatly aided their cause. The Reconstruction Acts of 1867 and the new Alabama constitution validated and strengthened black Mobilians' resolve. The newly adopted state constitutions provided provisions for a tax-funded educational system for all school-aged children regardless of race and created a more precise link between education and citizenship. As a state right, Alabama now had the obligation to provide a public educational system to all its citizens, white and black. The education provision alone enshrined black Mobilians' vision for postwar Alabama and demonstrated that their efforts had not been in vain. Although it took some time to design and implement the official state system, the embrace of postwar notions of education and citizenship at the state level had broader consequences at the local level. Acceptance of postwar notions of African American education and citizenship did not occur immediately in Mobile. Rather, it remained an arduous process.

Black Mobilians' struggle during the transition period demonstrates how local conditions and responses mediated the impact of federal and state forces. The Reconstruction Acts of 1867 and the fraught transition to public schools forced black Mobilians and their allies to carefully navigate the local terrain in developing a racially inclusive system. With the incorporation of state and local officials, these new partnerships would eventually give the public schools a firm foundation for the next twenty years. However, black Mobilians' struggle for education, citizenship, and freedom remained difficult. Intense white resistance prompted

the elimination of class differences among black Mobilians and improved relations with Creoles of color during the convention and ratification proceedings.
The dual school board crisis threatened the existence of African American public
schools and tested existing relationships between black Mobilians, the Freedmen's Bureau, and the American Missionary Association. With their efforts
proving ineffective, black Mobilians and their allies drew on their relationships
with state officials in order to bring a resolution to the challenge. Although a
solution was eventually found, white opposition did not cease. Undaunted, black
Mobilians forged ahead with new partners as they dealt with new challenges and
unresolved issues of acceptance as full citizens by white Mobilians. No longer
slaves but not quite full citizens, black Mobilians' remained steadfast to their
postwar vision and continued their struggle.

II

CREATING ESSENTIAL
PARTNERSHIPS
AND RESOURCES

3

To "Do That Which Is Best"

Richmond Colored Normal and the Development of Public Schoolteachers

On October 27, 1913, Superintendent J. A. C. Chandler declared a half session of classes for the following day at the African American public schools in Richmond, Virginia. According to his memorandum to the "principals of the Colored Schools," he granted the unexpected time off because the "City of Richmond and the Public Schools in particular have suffered a great loss in the death of D. Webster Davis." His funeral warranted special observance.[1]

Daniel Webster Davis represented many things to white and black Richmonders. Davis was born to slave parents, John and Charlotte Ann Davis, in Caroline County, Virginia, on March 25, 1862. Following his father's death, Charlotte Davis relocated the family to Richmond, where he enrolled and later graduated from the public schools. For over thirty years he was a beloved teacher to city students and administrators at the Navy Hill and Baker schools. He was "Professor Davis" to hundreds of African American schoolteachers who attended the annual summer teachers' institutes across Virginia, North Carolina, and West Virginia. He was "Webster" to his close friends and family. To the majority of attendees at his funeral and later at his memorial service at the First African Baptist Church, Davis was first and foremost a 1878 graduate of the teacher-training program at Richmond Colored Normal and High School.[2]

The sentiments expressed in Chandler's memorandum and white and black Richmonders' reminiscences reflected the shared feeling of debt for Davis's teaching service and the school that produced him. Richmond Colored Normal predominantly helped former slaves, like Davis, and children born after the end of slavery to become teachers, administrators, and leaders within their communities. However, the early release and the subsequent memorial service would not have been possible without the crisis generated by the creation of state-funded public schools.

Richmond Colored Normal demonstrates the ways in which black Richmonders and their educational partners responded to the crucial question raised by the creation of state-funded public schools—who would teach African American students in the new state system? Richmond Colored Normal and the resulting corps of public schoolteachers emerged from black Richmonders' education partnerships and their interpretation of what constituted a useful education. These teachers, in turn, refashioned their education, which benefited black Richmonders' struggle for educational access, legitimacy, and racial equality. The corps of qualified and well-trained Richmond Colored Normal graduates became an essential asset. As a result, they provided the foundation for future struggles by African American educator–activists while ensuring the future of state-funded African American public schools.

Moreover, Richmond Colored Normal and its alumni reveal the expansion and refinement of the educational relationships forged by black Richmonders after the departure of the Freedmen's Bureau. These relationships not only facilitated the creation of crucial resources for African American education but also permitted the continuation of educational opportunities for African Americans whether as students, teachers, or administrators in the new system. Outside the classroom, Richmond Colored Normal graduates considered their training as preparation for middle-class leadership and actively participated in the period's racial uplift organizations. Hence they tailored their education accordingly. Without the training of African American teachers and the strength of the black Richmonders' alliances, state-funded public schools and turn-of-the-century activism would have been greatly impaired in the urban South. In short, Richmond Colored Normal and its graduates were essential resources in black Richmonders' struggle for quality public schools, citizenship, and equality after the departure of the Freedmen's Bureau.

Prior to the establishment of Richmond Colored Normal, the training of African American teachers was a projected goal from the start of the Freedmen's Schools. While black Richmonders, Freedmen's Bureau agents, and northern philanthropic executives shared this common goal, each group differed over the intended purpose and targeted student population for normal training. This major obstacle stalled the formal training of African American teachers.

Black Richmonders sought the simultaneous training of teachers with the general primary education of members of the community but were hindered by the system's focus on illiterate, newly freed African Americans. This resulted in the slow development of advanced classes for the existing class of literate African Americans. Yet African American missionaries and black Richmonders viewed this educated population as useful for the purpose of giving the community greater control over the schools and the information disseminated to their children.³ John W. Cromwell, future editor of *The People's Advocate*, voiced these aims in a letter to *The Anglo-African*, an African American newspaper published in New York City. He believed that schools "supported by the parents, would thrive better under the management of colored teachers, as many of the missionaries, to say nothing of qualifications, were totally indifferent to the progress of their scholars." Cromwell and others reasoned that qualified African American teachers lacked this indifference. Thus they wanted the simultaneous training of literate and illiterate members of the community. This approach would create a class of individuals capable of instructing and managing a school in accordance with common school pedagogical methods. With trained teachers and administrators from their community, black Richmonders desired expanding educational opportunities while eliminating the indifference experienced from some white teachers in the city. Their solution involved the development of a normal school in Richmond for the benefit of the local community. This simultaneous and local approach differed greatly from those preferred by some of their white allies.⁴

Several white educational partners viewed teacher training and African American education in terms of stages. The fulfillment of prerequisites made progress between stages possible. Teacher training could only occur after the creation of primary schools and the development of a sizeable advanced student population. Hence simultaneous development could not occur until these conditions were met. Gen. Orlando Brown, assistant commissioner for the Freedmen's Bureau in Virginia, expressed his preference for this model in his correspondence. Brown felt that the development of teachers would only occur after the emergence of the "most promising pupils" selected from the Freedmen's Schools. His solution involved the removal and isolation of these students from their community as the "first condition towards a proper training of these youth to be good teachers of their race." Brown reasoned in his letter to Gen. O. O. Howard for proposing such an establishment, "They have never seen colored people living respectfully by any enlightened standard. . . . Hence the necessity of removing them from these influences and placing them under such as will develop their higher social and moral qualities." In the minds of these partners, normal graduates would then educate other African Americans throughout the state, specifically in the rural areas. Brown viewed their usefulness as educators outside of Richmond but within Virginia. Rural Virginia needed both schools and qualified teachers to teach African American children. White hostility, violence, and social ostracism toward white missionaries were major hindrances to schools spreading in rural areas like they had in urban ones. Brown and others reasoned that African

American teachers would not have same experience as their white counterparts in rural Virginia.[5]

Rev. G. L. Stockwell similarly viewed the training of African American teachers in terms of stages but had a different rationale for their usefulness. After establishing schools on the outskirts of Richmond and elsewhere, he felt that the students in "these [normal] schools can be educated with the idea that they have a mission to perform and that Africa is to be the great field for them to cultivate, thousands of them will be ready to go there as teachers and missionaries." Stockwell viewed normal graduates' future careers as occurring outside of Richmond and the United States. It seemed inconceivable to him that African Americans could benefit their local or regional communities.[6]

The "stages model" and possible postgraduate benefits espoused by Brown and Stockwell countered the desires of black Richmonders. Neither option permitted the simultaneous grassroots approach, nor did these options provide a concrete timetable for transition between stages. Moreover, the "stages model" illuminated some of the underlying racial assumptions held by some white racial moderates of a useful education and the role of African Americans in the process. Brown and Stockwell reinforced the assumption that slavery kept all African Americans ignorant and that all needed to be made into useful and productive citizens. Upon receiving an education, African Americans had as their principal duty elevating the race. Teacher training facilitated this mission. African Americans, according to Brown and Stockwell, had yet to receive the necessary education and moral training. These administrators, teachers, and philanthropists "were slow to believe that the 'grown-up children' . . . had matured to a point of readiness for adult responsibilities" of teaching and administrating the schools. Thus only white northern teachers were capable of instructing African Americans initially. This worldview held by Stockwell and others, though, purposely overlooked the existing African American teachers and independent schools maintained by African Americans. These racial assumptions hindered the widespread development of formal normal schools prior to the passage of the Reconstruction Acts of 1867.[7]

Despite the reluctance of some white allies, black Richmonders found encouragement in their relationships with Manly and several branches of the American Freedmen's Union Commission (AFUC). These partners believed in the stages model espoused by Brown and Stockwell. However, they also recognized the presence of literate and educated black Richmonders. These individuals had achieved the level of education and moral standards necessary for the transition to the next stage.[8] Manly's letter to the Lyman Abbott, president of the AFUC,

epitomized this sentiment. He wrote, "The only remedy is, at the principal cities of intelligence and influence, to educate the better class of colored youth to
be teachers of their own people." As evidence, he pointed to black Richmonders
and reasoned, "To withhold these advantages would be the worst possible economy." He then assured Abbott that black Richmonders supported the development of a normal school and would "contribute money and labor to the extent of
their ability." Through such appeals, Manly convinced officials of the New York
and New England branches of the American Freedmen's Union Commission to
expand their educational operations with teacher training. Unlike Brown and
Stockwell, Manly and AFUC officials saw the simultaneous educational training as a viable option in Richmond. The existence of a "better class of colored
youth" facilitated the development of formal normal schools prior to the creation
of public schools.[9] Encouraged, black Richmonders drew on their relationships
with Manly and several branches of the American Freedmen's Union Commission and not with Brown or Stockwell.

While fund-raising began during the fall of 1866, the racial assumptions embedded in the stages model hindered their efforts until the passage of the Reconstruction Acts in 1867. The promise of southern Republican governments and new
constitutions with provisions for African American public schools changed the
attitudes of individuals wedded to the stages model. Using Bureau funds, Manly
purchased the Twelfth Street lot. Located on a hill overlooking the Shockoe ra-
vine, the proposed school would have a physical presence in the city. According
to Manly's letter to Robert Murray, the New York and New England branches
of the American Freedmen's Union Commission secured approximately $5,000
for the Richmond school. Black Richmonders, as Manly wrote Murray, "by contributions of labor and money, will prepare the grounds for the foundation, will
erect the outbuildings and fence the whole and I think purchase a bell." The series of federal legislative acts accelerated their fund-raising efforts by initiating a
change in white attitudes regarding the role of African Americans in their education. As a result, Richmond Colored Normal opened in October 1867.[10]

From the beginning, Richmond Colored Normal upheld rigorous academic
standards. Strong letters of recommendation, personal character references, and
prior demonstration of scholarly achievement were prerequisites for admission. Manly, Bessie Canedy, and other school administrators scrutinized every
application and carefully selected students. Only the most promising students
in the Freedmen's Schools and private schools filled the two-story brick building during its inaugural year. Enrolled students received a high-quality education according to the common school standards. Manly served as the school's

principal and occasionally as instructor of the students. Bessie Canedy and other leading AFUC educators taught these students with the most current pedagogical methods. The curriculum included Latin, German, French, algebra, history, geography, cartography, music, government, and a nonsectarian religious course. Students had access to the best school furniture available, a modern science laboratory, and a library containing over five hundred volumes. In addition to classroom training in the evening, students received hands-on experience as assistant teachers in the Freedmen's Schools during the day as part of the curriculum. The rigorous nature of the school program not only persuaded white cynics that African Americans were capable of becoming teachers, but it convinced proponents of the stages model that this educated corps of teachers was vital to the continuation of African American education.[11]

Early students, like James Herndon Bowser, demonstrated the school's utility. Born in 1850 to free African American parents, the Richmond native excelled scholastically in the city's Freedmen's School system. His studious nature and scholarly achievements attracted the attention of Bessie Canedy, Manly, and the New England Freedmen's Aid Society, a branch of the AFUC. As a result, he was admitted into the inaugural class of Richmond Colored Normal.[12] As a normal student, he again impressed his teachers. Canedy made Bowser her assistant in the model primary school. Upon graduation he received a formal teaching commission in his own Freedmen's School at the recommendation of Canedy. In her April 1868 report she noted that Bowser was "teaching very successfully." The New England Freedmen's Aid Society rehired Bowser for another term. He then received a position in the Richmond public school system. Bowser represented the experiences shared by the initial graduates from the school. By 1870 several normal graduates received teaching positions in Richmond and elsewhere.[13]

State officials accepted Richmond Colored Normal into the state education system in 1871. In addition to state funding, incorporation brought new teacher qualification requirements. These new requirements mandated the retraining of previous graduates for employment, including Bowser. As with the inaugural class, the new graduates proved the school's utility. Rosa L. Dixon was one of the initial graduates under the new state program. Dixon was born January 7, 1855, to slave parents, Henry Dixon and Augusta Hawkins Dixon, in Amelia County, Virginia. Her parents relocated to Richmond after the Civil War for employment and educational opportunities for their daughter. Dixon, like the majority of the initial graduates, passed through the Richmond Freedmen's Schools and later public schools. While at Richmond Colored Normal, Dixon impressed not only her instructors and Principal Manly, but also her future husband, James Herndon Bowser. With special training from Manly in the higher mathematics and Latin, Dixon and fourteen other students graduated from the new state program at the conclusion of the 1872–1873 academic year.[14]

Manly recognized that he must convince state officials of its benefits. The future of Richmond public schools and the state system was contingent on the school's ability to train African American educators. The retraining of former graduates never deterred Manly. He viewed it as necessary in gaining public financial support as northern "funding began to grow scarce" and for the future of African American education. In response to a series of questions posed by the state superintendent of public instruction, Manly shared his views on the importance of training future educators at Richmond Colored Normal and other normal schools. "Schools are what we make them. 'As is the teacher, so is the school,' is as true of these schools as of any other," Manly wrote. "I am more than satisfied. I am certain that colored normal schools, properly conducted, will turn out teachers with the scholarship and all other qualifications necessary for first rate success in the profession." Through these annual reports, Manly highlighted the school's benefits for the city, state, and region in order to secure its future.[15]

To achieve "first rate success," Manly understood that he needed evidence and not simply glowing reports. In order to convince skeptics, he addressed three important areas. First, he modified the school's organization to three grades of approximately thirty students each. The new organization now mirrored the one used in the city's white normal school. Second, he maintained a curriculum that followed the pedagogical and instructional offerings of any reputable teaching college of the period. According to the *First Annual Report of the Superintendent of Public Instruction*, the curriculum embraced the common school branches, namely, vocal music, calisthenics, linear drawing, map drawing, object teaching, physiology, civil government, physical geography, botany, natural philosophy, algebra, and the history and philosophy of education. Senior students also received hands-on training in the model primary school attached to the normal school. The school gave students "their first discipline as teachers under the supervision and criticism of their own teachers." This rigorous curriculum demonstrated that enrolled African Americans had the same caliber of training as their white counterparts. Therefore, Richmond Colored Normal graduates met the necessary qualifications for careers in the public schools, which meant that race should not be a factor. Third, Manly continued a highly selective admission process for the tuition-free school. Only the best students from the public schools gained admission. Dr. Barnas Sears noted the existence of a lengthy waitlist for admission to the illustrious school in his annual Peabody Education Fund report. Through the school's organization, the curriculum offered, and the selective admission process, Manly created an image of respectability.[16]

As Manly cultivated the school's image over the next several years, Richmond Colored Normal faculty carefully trained the first generation of teachers in the state system. Under their instruction, they also trained "model citizens" who would be seen and accepted as the best representatives of their race. These citizens would then create the leadership that would promote industry, thrift, and moral character in their community. Admission did not guarantee completion for these early students. Students who met the high standards received praise. For instance, Mary Patterson Manly praised James Hugo Johnston as being "one of the finest pupils I have ever had in my long teaching experience" in a 1933 letter to his daughter. Praise did not come easily, though. Many fell short of the high intellectual and moral standards held by the faculty and principal. Those unable to meet the moral and educational expectations did not complete the program. When comparing the graduates per year to the average of thirty enrolled students per grade listed in the annual reports, it is evident that not everyone completed the program. As the school was a part of the high school, these students simply received a high school diploma. Thus only the "best" students graduated.[17]

Manly's efforts succeeded. State and city officials praised the school. William H. Ruffner, the state's first superintendent of public instruction, regularly commended the school in his annual reports. In discussing the training of African American elementary teachers, Ruffner specifically mentioned Richmond Colored Normal as an exemplar: "There are two excellent colored normal schools in Virginia, which I have often mentioned. The one is in Richmond, and is conducted in a twenty thousand dollar building." By signaling out Richmond Colored Normal, he recognized its importance for the state. Graduates provided "over three hundred colored pupils the very best education they are capable of receiving," and consequently, in Ruffner's estimate, "winning favorable opinions."[18] Even the conservative Richmond *Daily Dispatch* shared Ruffner's assessment and conceded that Richmond Colored Normal benefited the city and state. In 1871 the newspaper acknowledged the school's closing exercises with a brief article on its front page. The paper could not find fault with the exercises or the school's success in the "professional training of young colored people as teachers for our public schools." The newspaper proclaimed that "the attendance of influential citizens . . . as well as parents and friends of the pupils" demonstrated the school's value to the state's educational program. In 1873 the publication featured an article acknowledging that there was "no colored school of higher grade . . . in the State, and we venture to assert there is no school where more pains are taken with instruction than this." As noted by Ruffner and the conservative white Richmond press, Richmond Colored Normal addressed the statewide teacher crisis by creating a corps of African American teachers.[19]

In June 1876 Richmond Colored Normal officially became a part of the Richmond Public Schools. During the first half of the decade Manly attempted negotiations for the sale of the school to the city on behalf of the Richmond Educational Association. However, the city's financial difficulties prevented the sale. Undeterred, Manly did the unthinkable. As president of the Richmond Educational Association, he donated the entire property, the brick building, lot, furniture, and school apparatus, valued at $25,000, to the city. His only condition was its continuation as a normal school for African Americans. The city accepted the generous gift and abided by Manly's conditions. This donation firmly cemented its legitimacy and permanence.[20]

Divergent expectations on the part of administrators, government officials, financial sponsors, and black Richmonders shaped not only Richmond Colored Normal's development but also employment opportunities for its graduates. State and city officials saw this group as essential in spreading the state educational system to African Americans living in the countryside. Rural Virginia lacked adequate schools. Ruffner found clear discrepancies between the rural schools and the urban schools. He attributed the discrepancies in the initial reports to the lack of qualified African American and white educators willing to teach in rural schools. State government officials, local school board commissioners, and the school administrators expected graduates primarily to serve rural Virginia and not urban public schools during the 1870s and early 1880s. Hiring practices reinforced this expectation. Instead of using Richmond Colored Normal graduates in the city schools, school officials employed white teachers whose low examination scores disqualified them for placement in the white public schools. As a result, few graduates found employment as teachers in Richmond from 1870 to 1883. Margaret F. Woolfolk and Rosa L. Dixon received a few of the coveted teaching positions in Richmond during this period. For state and local school officials, the corps of the African American teachers was necessary in the expansion of the statewide system to rural areas. Hence primarily white teachers and a select few African American teachers obtained employment in Richmond and other urban centers. Rural Virginia had the greatest need for African American teachers.[21]

These expectations and hiring practices directly countered the desires of black Richmonders. They wanted African American teachers in the city schools. Richmond Colored Normal graduates joined the community in their struggle with petitions and newspaper articles calling for African American public school-teachers in Richmond. Initially, success was limited to a few schools. From its inception as a public school in 1869 to the 1882–1883 academic year, the Navy Hill School had an all-African American faculty with a white principal. By the 1882–1883 academic year, Richmond Colored Normal graduates filled all fourteen teaching positions available. The school's success instilled hope for the attainment of African American faculties at all of the African American public schools. The newly established East End School also featured an all-African American faculty with a white principal that academic year. Likewise, Richmond Colored Normal graduates composed the entire teaching staff. Both schools evoked a sense of hopefulness and anticipation among black Richmonders that school officials would "see that it is best for all concerned to appoint colored teachers for all of our colored schools." Despite the divergent expectations, Richmond Colored Normal graduates taught, albeit not always in Richmond. As a result, black Virginians found a new ally in the public schools.[22]

Differing expectations of the graduates diminished neither interest nor enrollment at Richmond Colored Normal. Its existence inspired some Richmond public school students to become teachers. For Daniel Webster Davis, the white and few African American Richmond public schoolteachers profoundly influenced his decision to become an educator. He regularly recalled the lasting impressions made by his Richmond Colored Normal teachers in his poetry, lectures, and public speaking engagements. In a 1902 lecture for the Summer Institute at Hampton Institute, for instance, Davis instructed the educators to have role models and use them as guides to live their lives. Davis's role models came directly from his normal teachers: "Let your own life and character be an ideal. I remember Miss Stratton, Miss Patterson, Miss Hadley, Mr. Manly. They were my ideals of what men and women should be." Upon graduating at the age of sixteen, he was too young to teach in the Richmond and state school system. As noted in an early biography, he held a series of menial jobs until he reached eighteen, the city's minimum age requirement for teachers. With Manly's assistance, Davis readily received employment in a Richmond public school in 1880, where he remained until his death in 1913. Davis was one of the 280 who graduated from the incorporated state program between 1873 and 1890. Like Davis, the majority of these later graduates attended the lower grades of the Richmond public schools. The lack of employment in the Richmond schools did not deter these students from aspiring to become teachers or attending Richmond Colored Normal.[23]

Unlike Davis, Richmond Colored Normal graduates typically found teaching employment outside of Richmond or in other fields during the late 1870s and

1880s. Hiring practices simply prevented many from acquiring jobs in Richmond. Graduates, like Marietta Chiles, John Mitchell, Jr., and Wendell Phillip Dabney, received positions initially in nearby cities and counties like Fredericksburg, Petersburg, and Louisa County before landing a position in the Richmond public schools. Some taught primarily in rural Virginia. Many pursued nonteaching careers as postal clerks, merchants, and other professions. This was the reality until 1883, when favorable political conditions made it easier for graduates to find positions in Richmond public schools. This shift made admittance into Richmond Colored Normal for professional teaching careers even more desirable. However, a glut of Richmond Colored Normal graduates and few positions available still made it difficult for all graduates to find a job in Richmond.[24]

Beyond the classroom, the newly trained educators refashioned their useful education in their work for racial uplift. The Richmond Colored Normal–trained educator–activists challenged the racism experienced in their communities through educational-related organizations and activities—specifically teacher training, cultivating a new literate identity through literary societies, and participation in racial uplift organizations.

Richmond Colored Normal graduates assisted with the training of other educators. The state and city school system required continuous education for its teachers. James Binford, Richmond superintendent of public instruction, implemented weekly Saturday teacher's meetings for all Richmond public school educators in 1871. These two-hour meetings served two purposes. First, they kept educators informed of events occurring in the school, such as student suspensions and observations from the superintendent's visits. Second, the meetings provided for the continuous training of the educators. Each meeting focused on methods of teaching phonetics, penmanship, and special subjects assigned for the day, such as the methods of teaching orthography, reading, object teaching, map drawing, history, and vocal music. As the number of Richmond Colored Normal graduates that became educators in Richmond increased, they actively participated in the separate meetings for African Americans. They discussed their teaching strategies and eventually taught some of the special subjects assigned for the meeting. In 1882 they organized with county educators and established the Henrico Teachers' Association of Virginia State Teachers' Association. This organization, with the assistance of the respective schools' principals, took over the administration of the Saturday teachers' meetings. Through their participation, graduates demonstrated that African Americans teachers were equal to their white counterparts in terms of their ability to teach and understand pedagogy.[25]

In addition to the Saturday teachers' meetings, Virginia sponsored several segregated summer teaching institutes throughout the state for existing educators. Subsidized primarily by Peabody Education Fund monies, leading northern and southern African American educators led these six-week summer institutes. In 1880 Mr. and Mrs. Henry P. Montgomery, African American educators from Washington, D.C., instructed the participants at the Lynchburg session "in school organization and discipline, and also in the primary branches as to their subject matter and the best methods of teaching them." The 240 enrolled teachers also learned vocal music, calisthenics, and elocution. Hands-on training occurred as well with "Model Lessons" in an adjoining primary school. In addition, the United States commissioner of education, Virginia superintendent of public instruction, and representatives of the Peabody Educational Fund gave special lectures.[26] By the late 1880s, Richmond Colored Normal graduates served as the principal instructors for these institutes. Albert V. Norrell provided the primary instruction with Professor R. L. Mitchell at the 1888 summer institute in Roanoke, Virginia. Daniel Webster Davis led the 1888 and 1889 institutes held at Richmond. James Hugo Johnston led a full corps of instructors including Rosa Dixon Bowser at the session held at the Lynchburg Institute in 1887 and at Virginia Normal and Collegiate Institute from 1888 to 1890. In his 1888 report to the state superintendent, Johnston recommended the expansion of the summer institutes into a three-year program for African American teachers who never graduated from a formal normal program. He felt that such a program would "result in great improvement to the present teachers of our State." These summer institutes ensured that African American educators remained highly qualified for their teaching positions in the public school system. As a result, the African American public schools benefited.[27]

Richmond Colored Normal graduates' capable administration of the summer institutes aided the community's struggle for black faculty and administrators in the Richmond public schools. The quality of education provided by white faculty concerned black Richmonders. This concern precipitated their struggle for African American faculty in the Richmond schools. Thwarted by state and city school officials, parents and community leaders wanted to shift the usefulness of Richmond Colored Normal graduates from the rural schools to Richmond. The summer institutes bolstered their arguments made to Richmond school officials. African Americans, including Richmond Colored Normal graduates, successfully taught at as well as administered these summer institutes. Like their white counterparts, they demonstrated their qualifications for teaching and administrating the African American public schools, as the *Virginia Star, People's*

Advocate, and community leaders had argued. R. L. Mitchell, correspondent for the *People's Advocate*, responded to disparaging remarks made by George M. Childs in regard to African American normal schools and their goal of African American faculties in the public schools. He proclaimed in a March 1882 news article, "Yes, Mr. Childs, we will have colored professors, colored teachers, and a colored Board of Visitors for the state Normal and Collegiate Institute. The superior race have managed for us and have failed. We can at least do not worse than they." The summer institutes' successful administration increasingly invalidated claims such as the ones made by Childs. Teachers who previously lacked formal training received the necessary credentials to teach in any school district in Virginia and could easily transfer these skills to any other school district in the region. Through professionalization, black Richmonders' acquired respectability for the public schools and dignity for those engaged in education. As a result, they gained more persuasive arguments in their struggle for African American faculties.[28]

Interestingly, black Richmonders never publicly argued for African American teachers at Richmond Colored Normal. With the exception of three positions from 1870 to 1890, the school's staff remained overwhelmingly white. Howard Rabinowitz noted this phenomenon in his comparative study of the urban South. He reasoned that school board members' absolute power over the schools prevented any substantive reform to the school's teaching staff.[29]

By focusing on the relationships between the Richmond Colored Normal staff, graduates, and the community, another explanation emerges. First, Manly, Mary Elizabeth Knowles, Mary Stratton, and others had been devoted to the school and African American education in Richmond since its inception. As strong proponents for the school, they served as mentors to the graduates. Daniel Webster Davis referenced their valuable mentorship in his 1902 lecture on the importance of role models. Daniel B. Williams pursued advanced studies at Worcester Academy and then Brown University at the suggestion of Manly and Knowles. This mentorship afforded graduates with many opportunities inside and outside of the classroom. Without it, Davis would have given such glowing reports of his former teachers and Williams might not have pursued advanced studies at New England schools.[30]

Second and most significantly, Richmond Colored Normal educators provided necessary letters of recommendation for teaching employment inside and outside Richmond. For instance, Manly wrote a glowing recommendation for Rosa Dixon when she left the Richmond schools upon her marriage to James H. Bowser. In his recommendation, Manly described Bowser as "a studious, faithful and intelligent scholar, her character always above criticism, and her deportment marked by a dignity, sobriety and respectfulness not common with girls of her age." Due to her success as a teacher, Manly recommended her for reemployment, if necessary, "with entire confidence that she would do her work not only faithfully, but wisely and with approval of yourself and School Board." Indeed, she used the letter in her return to the Richmond schools after her husband's death. As these examples suggest, claims of white indifference proved harder to make by graduates, parents, and community leaders. It was not their experience with the white Richmond Colored Normal faculty. In fact, their relationships with these key white allies remained essential to the future of the school and its graduates. Thus, challenging the continued presence of white educators at Richmond Colored Normal would have proved detrimental.[31]

As a result, graduates and black Richmonders remained silent on the issue. Instead, the community argued for African American educators in the Richmond public schools and the creation in the state of a "Normal School where our young people may be instructed by those who have their interests at heart." Advances made in these two areas between 1883 and 1888 reinforced the community's silence on the predominantly white faculty at Richmond Colored Normal.[32]

Between 1883 and 1888, parents, community leaders, and Richmond Colored Normal graduates achieved two major victories in the fight for African American faculties in the Richmond public schools. First, the Readjuster regime broke the stalemate on the Richmond school board, which paved the way for African American teaching staffs in all the city's African American public schools, except for Richmond Colored Normal, during the 1883–1884 academic year. The Readjuster-backed Richmond school board also promoted three Richmond Colored Normal graduates to become principals of city schools that same academic year. Albert V. Norrell, James H. Hayes, and James Hugo Johnston became the principals of Navy Hill, Valley, and Baker schools, respectively. Although the men retained the principal positions for one year, African American teachers remained. The monopoly of white teachers ceased as the Richmond school board rejected a petition of displaced white teachers and white community leaders for their reemployment during the 1884–1885 academic year. After the Readjuster revolution, white educators only served in African Americans schools as principals and/or faculty members at Richmond Colored Normal.[33]

The second victory occurred in the training of African American teachers. In addition to changes in the Richmond public schools, the Readjuster regime established a state normal school for African Americans located at Petersburg in 1882. After a lawsuit, the school opened for students in 1883 with John Mercer

Langston as its first president. When Virginia needed a new president at the state normal school for African Americans, state officials turned to a Richmond Colored Normal graduate for the position. James Hugo Johnston, class of 1876, served diligently as the second president of Virginia Normal and Collegiate Institute for Colored Persons in nearby Petersburg from 1888 until his death in 1914. In addition to his presidential duties, he taught mental and moral philosophy. Johnston's administration received continuous praise from state officials. His reports held a prominent place in the annual state superintendent reports. Black Richmonders regarded Johnston's hiring as a victory both for African American education but also for the race as a whole.[34]

Johnston's hiring and the graduates' refashioning of their Richmond Colored Normal education eased the way for all–African American faculties and administrators throughout Virginia. Consequently, black Richmonders and Richmond Colored Normal administrators praised his administration. Through attendance and active training of teachers, graduates refashioned the useful education received for the betterment of the African American education and the broader community. These successes, though, fostered black Richmonders' continued silence on the hiring practices at Richmond Colored Normal.

Richmond Colored Normal graduates also filled the ranks of literary societies. Beginning in the 1870s, Richmond saw the growth of a literate African American middle class. James H. Bowser, Rose L. Dixon, Albert V. Norrell, Margaret F. Woolfolk, and other Richmond Colored Normal graduates joined business entrepreneurs, physicians, lawyers, politicians, and other professionals in this class. These individuals had benefited from the political, economic, and social gains of Reconstruction. In accordance, they adopted the same symbols of middle-class status used by white Americans. One of those symbols was the creation of and participation in literary societies.[35]

In the post-emancipation South, literary societies underwent a major transformation. Postwar African American literary societies, according to historian Elizabeth McHenry, had four objectives. First, literary societies promoted a form of literary study that better prepared African Americans for the demands of citizenship and challenges posed by the postwar world. Second, they promoted a new literate identity that was distinct from the antebellum identity. Third, literary societies sought to transform racist stereotypes regarding African American intellect by demonstrating a capacity for learning and improving. Fourth, they promoted a new type of literacy that sought "effective avenues of public access and ways to voice their demands for full citizenship." Black Richmonders and Richmond Colored Normal graduates established and filled the ranks of the Virginia Educational and Historical Society in the mid-1870s and later the Acme Literary Association in the 1880s.[36]

The Virginia Educational and Historical Society and Acme Literary Association typified the postwar literary societies described by McHenry. The Virginia Educational and Historical Society tended to discuss topics more focused on educational concerns, such as the role of music in public schools and industrial education. On the other hand, the Acme Literary Association used their formal meetings "to consider questions of vital importance to our people," including but not limited to African American education. Both organizations held regular meetings in the city's prominent African American churches. According to published notices and minutes, these meetings typically included musical selections, oratory selections ranging from poetry to dramatic readings of theatrical scenes, and a formal paper on a specific literary work, historical topic, and/or current affair topic. Although meetings were open to the public, the formality of the gatherings and the nature of the discussions often highlighted both class and educational biases. In order to transform racist stereotypes of African American intellect, members of both organizations used the meetings to achieve this goal. As a result, the middle-class African Americans often decided the agenda for each meeting and dominated the open discussions at the expense of working-class, largely undereducated African Americans. Unlike labor organizations, fraternal societies, and ward meetings, literary societies would not be an effective vehicle for working-class African Americans to promote their concerns.[37] Overall, the organizations promoted a literate identity that was far removed from slavery and stressed a new type of literacy necessary for the postwar landscape.

Richmond Colored Normal graduates and other members used the organizations for practical purposes. Literary societies allowed members and meeting attendees to develop strategies "to voice their demands for full citizenship" and equality. In this regard, literary societies served as an important training ground for black middle-class activists.[38] Over the 1870s and 1880s, black Richmonders found themselves under attack. Viewed as uncivilized and uneducated, many white Richmonders employed a white supremacist discourse in order to remove civil and political rights from black Richmonders and decrease their overall influence in shaping society at large. Race had even prevented Richmond Colored Normal graduates from finding gainful employment in the Richmond public schools. Literary societies, specifically the Acme Literary Association, applied their new literate persona in combating the increasing attacks on African American civil and political rights.[39]

By the mid-1880s, the focus of Acme Literary Association meetings moved from more innocuous topics to ones that specifically addressed the emergence of a new racial and political order that excluded African Americans. For instance, literary societies debated specific racial incidents such as the Danville massacre in 1883. Within these meetings, attendees honed their arguments addressing the state Democrat Party's violent campaign to regain political control. Out of these meetings, society members issued public responses in the press. As evidenced by the May 19, 1885, Acme Literary Association gathering, meetings of mid-1880s and 1890s addressed the development of arguments that justified society members' and other middle-class professionals' position to lead civil rights agitation while simultaneously defending the future of civil and political rights of African Americans to white Virginians.[40]

At the May 19, 1885, meeting, Capt. Robert A. Paul addressed the Acme Literary Association. His brief address to primarily Acme members at the Third Street African Methodist Episcopal Church dealt with the internal and external attacks on black Richmonders. After providing the context of African American political rights and leadership, he argued that African Americans could no longer rely on the Republican Party or white politicians. He reminded audience members of the party's betrayal in the contested Hayes–Tilden election that allowed for the restoration of "Bourbon Democratic party" rule. He then reminded the audience that it was a coalition of "liberal Democrats, Republicans, and, . . . the united support of the colored citizens," and not the sole assistance from the national or state Republican Party, that allowed for the triumph of the Readjuster regime in Virginia.[41] Since Republicans had failed to give African Americans their "proper recognition," Paul proposed that African American men and women needed "safe leaders of his own race to advise him." These leaders, according to Paul, "should be selected with great care, because the masses of his people are, from circumstances over which they had no control, ignorant, and hence they are easily deceived by dishonest, trading politicians." Otherwise, racial prejudice would continue and African Americans would lose their rights on account of race and their slave past.[42]

In the address, Paul also sought to resolve the internal community problems in regard to the question of who was qualified to be a "safe leader." In terms of the struggle for future political rights, Paul pointed directly toward literate middle-class African Americans, specifically Acme members and Richmond Colored Normal graduates, as natural leaders. They had achieved both "intelligence and wealth" and had the best interests of all African Americans at heart.

Under their leadership, Paul foretold "that the future prospects of the Negro for acquiring wealth and education, for receiving due recognition and power, are bright and glorious."[43] Paul's arguments and reasoning found a willing audience. Members embodied the individuals that Paul deemed as "representative men." They had benefited from the gains of Reconstruction by obtaining intelligence from Richmond Colored Normal and other similar institutions as well as wealth from middle-class professions. Through literary societies, they developed effective strategies in voicing their demands of citizenship and equality. Using the skills perfected in the meetings, they had successfully challenged some of the external attacks on the African American community from 1876 to 1885. They have proven themselves to be "safe leaders" as a result of their postwar literate persona.[44]

Yet it was evident internally that working-class African Americans challenged their leadership. Paul and other literate middle-class African Americans had to continually justify their power and influence. According to Paul, their leadership was not simply accepted by all. To these ends, Paul made a plea for racial solidarity in the struggle for civil and political rights. Without a unified community, Paul, Richmond Colored Normal graduates, and other Acme members recognized the limitations of their proposed struggle to "do that which is best." However, they firmly believed and maintained that their attainment of higher education and participation in organizations like the Acme Literary Association had better equipped them with the necessary tools to cope with the post-emancipation world compared with some members of their community. Hence their new literate identity could never fully eradicate the internal problem of class and educational bias even by those seeking to "do that which is best."[45]

Normal alumni, especially female graduates, extended their participation in literary societies to join racial uplift organizations. Since the teaching profession was predominantly female, the activism of Richmond Colored Normal female graduates reflected the intersections of race and gender as the organizations addressed the plight of African American women and the entire race more broadly, as described by Glenda Gilmore and Evelyn Brooks Higginbotham. Their role as educators afforded them some leverage in their community activism and allowed them to fight for both gender and racial uplift.[46]

Rosa Dixon's activism revolved around issues relating to education, African American women, and race. She was an active member of the Virginia Educational and Historical Society. Through her participation in literary societies, Dixon developed crucial arguments for increasing employment opportunities for African American teachers, increasing their salaries, and providing financial security with state retirement benefits, especially for African American women who had to leave the profession upon marriage. Like her contemporary Maggie Lena Walker, her 1879 marriage to James H. Bowser never impinged on her activism, but it forced her to leave the Richmond public schools. Within two years, she was forced to use the glowing recommendation from Manly when her husband died from "consumption." As a widowed single mother, Bowser returned full time to Richmond public schools at the start of the 1883–1884 academic year.[47]

Widowhood galvanized Mrs. Rosa D. Bower's activism. It made her more keenly aware of the plight of teachers, especially African American female educators. In 1887 she founded the Virginia Teachers' Reading Circle in which African American educators shared and discussed ideas and teaching styles. This organization was one of the first state organizations for African American teachers. As a widow raising a young son, Bowser was deeply concerned with the financial security of the predominantly female teaching force. Through her activism and the collective efforts of the Virginia Teachers' Reading Circle and other African American teacher associations, Bowser ensured that African American public school teachers, especially those who graduated from Richmond Colored Normal, received pensions from the state. Bowser, Nannie J. (Merriwether) Wynne, Kate G. Randolph, Martha Trice, and Ida Hall would earn pensions for their service. Even though Bowser's activism extended to issues such as antilynching, racial uplift, and the clubwomen's movement, the "Mother of Baker Street Mother's Club" never forgot educated women, like herself, engaged in the teaching profession.[48]

Despite the visible activism of graduates, city and state officials continued praising the school through the late 1870s and 1880s. Richmond Colored Normal provided a reliable stream of qualified teachers. The governor and Richmond school board members attended the commencement exercises, as noted in by the local report of the 1886–1887 scholastic year. The Richmond superintendent of public instruction's annual reports proudly featured the commencement program, course of study, student award winners, and a complete listing of graduates. At the school's twentieth anniversary celebration, the governor, local dignitaries, and illustrious graduates participated as speakers and presenters. The ceremony was widely attended by the African American community, government officials, alumni, and proponents of African American education. Indeed, Richmond Colored Normal represented an integral component of the Richmond public school system.[49]

While state and local officials recognized the importance of Richmond Colored Normal, some white Richmonders, like Rev. Hoge, privately and later publicly complained that its graduates made them unfit for labor and notions of ideal race relations. Rev. Hoge argued that Richmond Colored Normal and High School produced a glut of teachers and other professionals who refused to perform agricultural and industrial labor. As a result, he felt that the "liberal education" as taught in the current system had been a failed experiment and that industrial education was more beneficial. He insisted that the public school system should establish the necessary foundation for African Americans to continue as laborers by changing the curriculum to include industrial education. He felt that this would be most beneficial to race relations in Virginia and the South. Rev. Hoge and other critics increasingly gained traction in the public discourse over Richmond Colored Normal around the turn of the century.[50]

Black Richmonders fought the negative discourse through the creation of a distinct collective memory of Richmond Colored Normal. Like the emancipation collective memory described by David Blight, the collective memory of Richmond Colored Normal had a specific function. The celebratory mode of this collective memory served as a political statement by offering an alternative discourse. It legitimated both African American teachers and African American education, and it encouraged perseverance against critics like Rev. Hoge.[51] Therefore, annual closing exercises, graduations, and reunions were well-organized events that publicly celebrated the growth of African American education, intellectual achievement, and racial progress made since emancipation. These events provided a space for graduates not only to reflect on the shared opportunities and experiences afforded by their graduation from the school but also to have serious discussions of the hiring practices of local and state authorities and other concerns. In essence, the collective memory of Richmond Colored Normal and its graduates provided black Richmonders with an effective image to counter negative portrayals of African American intellectual, social, and racial capabilities in an emerging society based on white supremacy.[52]

Furthermore, the annual closing exercises, reunions, and even memorial services for prominent alumni and administrators illustrate the relationship between remembering and forgetting essential to the development and maintenance of a collective memory. In discussing the relationship between remembrance and forgetting, Marita Sturken argued that "memories are created in tandem with forgetting; to remember everything would amount to being overwhelmed by memory. Forgetting is a necessary component in the construction of memory." Memory construction and forgetting, therefore, are intrinsically linked. The act of forgetting becomes a strategic expression of power by those with the authority to shape the meaning of an event. Memory construction and remembrance also reveals the "stakes held by individuals and institutions attributing meaning to the past." Sturken's explanation of the connection between memory, forgetting, and power reflects black Richmonders' use of collective memory.[53]

The public remembrance and conscious forgetting reaffirmed graduates and community members' past and future commitment to education during the crisis period and provided a strategy to combat any detractors. These commemorations also voiced an alternative memory that recognized African American achievement and the benefits of Reconstruction. This alternative memory directly countered the memory project that romanticized the Confederacy and the "Lost Cause" while disparaging Reconstruction. Instead, they promoted a variation of the "Won Cause." Whereas the Grand Army of the Republic emphasized the centrality of African American military participation and the interracial comradeship of Union veterans, white and black, individuals promoted the interracial collaboration of alumni, postwar reformers, teachers, and administrators as well as the centrality of emancipation in allowing for the existence of Richmond Colored Normal and its collective good to the city, state, region, and nation.[54]

The conscious forgetting of certain aspects of the school's history and the experiences of the students, teachers, and administers served an important function, but it allowed for the existence of major silences. The conscious forgetting of certain aspects of the school's history and the experiences of the students, teachers, and administers aided their struggle against critics. Hence reunions, memorial services for Daniel Webster Davis, James H. Bowser, Manly, and other prominent alumni and administrators, as well as other public commemorations continued to resonate well into the twentieth century as the African American schools and teachers came under increasing attack by white leaders.[55] These events as well as the collective memory of Richmond Colored Normal provided black Richmonders with the necessary tools and cultural imagery to survive as well as agitate in an emerging society dominated by white supremacy.[56]

Richmond Colored Normal fulfilled an important state crisis by training African Americans educators. As the decades progressed, a shift from training teachers for rural Virginia to training them for the Richmond public school occurred only at the insistence of former graduates, black Richmonders' demands for African American teachers in their schools, and the cooperation of Richmond school board officials. By 1890, Richmond Colored Normal graduates diligently served in the public schools throughout Richmond and the state of Virginia. Outside the classroom, normal graduates participated in teacher training, literary societies, and racial uplift organizations that sought improvement of African

American education and, thereby, secured its continuation. As the national and local race relations worsened in the 1880s, graduates, administrators, and black Richmonders promoted a particular memory of the school through reunions, memorial services, and other forums. Richmond Colored Normal and its collective memory later served an important function in Richmond and Virginia during the early Jim Crow period. Until the school's closure in 1909, the educator-activists produced there permitted black Richmonders' continual participation in the decisions of their schools. Their broader activism worked alongside other community activism for racial uplift and civil rights.[57]

4

Remaking Old Blue College

Emerson Normal and Addressing the Need for Public Schoolteachers

In reflecting on the history of the educational work of the American Missionary Association in Alabama, L. B. Moore found much to celebrate. In establishing "industrial schools and normal schools and academies, and even universities in the darkness of this land," the American Missionary Association facilitated the growth of a class of leaders. "Oh, how my people need leaders!" exclaimed the African American missionary from Florence, Alabama. "I can take you to place where the blind are leading the blind and they are both falling into the ditch together." From the organization's work at Burrell Normal School in Florence to Emerson Institute and Normal in Mobile, Moore cheerfully reported that the schools "have sent forth a thousand college-bred men who are going to teach that people; and I tell you the time is coming when that thousand will be increased by another thousand, and the ignorant and oft-times immoral leaders will have to give way before the light which is now rising." For these reasons, Moore concluded that the American Missionary Association needed to continue its educational work. Through obtaining advanced education, the American Missionary Association would help to provide justice "to the slave who toiled for two hundred and fifty years and accumulated the wealth of this nation" by adding a growing class of leadership comprising teachers and other educated professionals.[1]

Most black Mobilians shared Moore's assessment of the American Missionary Association's work in Alabama. Their partnership with the organization aided in legitimating African American primary education but also allowed a select minority to obtain advanced degrees at Emerson Normal. The school was instrumental in permitting former slaves as well as the children born after the end of slavery to become teachers, administrators, and, most important, leaders within their communities. In becoming educated leaders, they prevented the blind from "leading the blind" and created the necessary leadership to carry African Americans out of the darkness.[2]

Emerson Normal represented the expansion and refinement of the educational partnership between black Mobilians and the American Missionary Association after the creation of state-funded public schools. This partnership played a critical role in creating the corps of teachers required for the new public school system. Outside the classroom, graduates employed their preparation for middle-class leadership by actively participating in racial uplift organizations and campaigns. Never viewing their service as limited to the classroom, Emerson Normal graduates became an essential asset for black Mobilians and their slow, arduous struggle for African American public education and racial equality in Mobile. Without the training of African American teachers and a renewed partnership with the American Missionary Association, the public schools and turn-of-the-century racial uplift activism would have been greatly impaired in Mobile.

As in Richmond, racial assumptions on the part of white educational partners thwarted teacher training during the initial years of the Freedmen's Schools. Influential white educational partners often viewed the African American educators in the independent Freedmen's Schools as incompetent and inexperienced. Charles W. Buckley, superintendent of education for the Freedmen's Bureau in Alabama, voiced this opinion in a report to Maj. Gen. Wager Swayne. He wrote, "There are in Mobile several colored schools taught mostly by colored teachers. Some of these teachers are not competent for the position they fill. They need suggestions from experienced teachers . . . and thus bring those of the same degree of advancement into the same school." In the same report, Buckley noted that the school operated by E. C. Branch, a white educator, was "flourishing" and doing "great work for the colored people of the city." For Buckley and other white racial moderates, the existing educated class of African Americans was inadequate for the work at hand. Like his Richmond counterparts, Buckley could not overcome the racial assumptions regarding slavery or the "stages model." He accepted that slavery had prevented this class from attaining the formal education necessary for teaching. Hence Buckley viewed guidance and supervision by experienced white educators, like Branch, as necessary until a sizeable number of African Americans reached the educational achievement for progression to normal training. He also discouraged independent schools with African American faculties and encouraged schools operated and administered by white northern missionary associations.[3]

The Reconstruction Acts of 1867, the purchase of Emerson Institute by the American Missionary Association from the Freedmen's Bureau, and the establishment of public schools in Mobile facilitated a shift in racial attitudes by some white educational partners toward African American teacher training. White

educational partners who once opposed to teacher training now deemed competent African American educators as essential for the future of African American
education. State Superintendent R. D. Harper remarked in a May 1868 report
to O. O. Howard that "obtaining competent teachers" was one of the "chief obstacles to our work." Harper, though, viewed Emerson Institute as a solution to
this problem for Mobile and its county. He found encouraging the American
Missionary Association's implementation of a normal program among its most
advanced students by its current teachers. According to Harper, the principal
selected ten of the "more advanced students, male and female," and met with
them privately regarding "the importance of qualifying themselves for teaching."
These selected students accepted and entered the program. Harper reported that
school officials hoped to train additional teachers "who will be well qualified for
the work of teaching the people of their own color or indeed of any color. This it
seems to me is the way and the only way in which the freedpeople of the South
can be educated." The struggle for control of the school board, though, stopped
the nascent program.[4]

Resolution to partisan school board politics in the early 1870s never addressed
the teacher crisis generated by the creation of public schools. The Mobile County
Board of School Commissioners still faced tremendous pressure to adequately
staff the white, African American, and Creole of color schools with teachers. Political rivalries prevented the state from assisting the board. Thus the board had
several options. First, it could have employed any from growing class of southern
African American teachers who were educated in northern colleges or in normal
programs created under the Freedmen's Bureau. Alabama, according to John Alvord's 1870 report, had five schools and 314 enrolled students. The Mobile County
Board of School Commissioners found this option unacceptable.[5]

Second, the board could have continued the practice of hiring white northern
missionaries and teachers for the African American schools. As discussed in a
previous chapter, the American Missionary Association maintained its control
over Emerson Institute instead of turning over operations to school commissioners after the Freedmen's Bureau departed the city. Rather than working with
the organization, the board decided against an alliance with the American Missionary Association. It based its decision on complaints often mentioned in the
white press pertaining to the invasion of northern outsiders who forced African
American education, morals, and notions of freedom and citizenship onto the
community. These invaders created a hostile environment in Mobile over the
clash of ideas and visions for the postwar city. Therefore, school commissioners
struck down this option.[6]

Instead, school commissioners in Mobile adopted a policy of hiring white teachers as the principal educators in the African American and Creole Schools. The departure of the Freedmen's Bureau and designation of Emerson Institute as a private school gave the Board of School Commissioners full power and control over the public schools. Hence school commissioners exerted their power of who taught in the African American and Creole schools through this strict hiring policy. To be sure, Howard Hall and a few white Freedmen's School educators not directly associated with the American Missionary Association received positions. The hiring policy meant that the board rarely hired African American and Creole teachers. If hired, they often served as assistant teachers, aides, or supernumeraries in the schools and not in the capacity of principal instructors.[7]

Sara Stanley Woodward, former Emerson Institute teacher, was an exception. She found employment as the principal of the St. Louis School from 1871 to 1874. School commissioners were unaware of her racial background and interracial marriage to Freedmen's Saving Bank administrator Charles Woodward. City directories often mistakenly noted her race as white although Woodward publicly proclaimed her race as African American. This lack of awareness on the part of school commissioners spared her from sharing the fate of other African Americans in the public schools.[8]

Black and Creole Mobilians attacked these hiring practices by pursuing several strategies independently. The private and parochial school system was one option. M. H. Leatherman cited the poor quality of the public schools and the teachers as the reason for her and others' decision to send their children to private schools. According to her letter to the American Missionary Association, "There are a great many free schools about the city but as they do not amount to much, the people do not care to send their children, so long as there is any alternative."[9] Withdrawal from the public schools often gave African American and Creole parents more control over who instructed their children. Only a small percentage pursued this option. Demographically, these families belonged to the elite and middle classes in the community or had steady employment to cover the tuition costs. Creoles of color utilized the parochial schools created and maintained for the Creole parishioners by the Mobile archdiocese and Catholic charities. Creoles as well as black Mobilians utilized the private schools that individual educated members of their community operated, often out of their homes. Tuition and other expenses made this option unattainable for the majority of families and children in the public schools. This option, furthermore, never adequately addressed the lack of African American educators in the city public schools.[10]

Black Mobilians also directly appealed to the Board of School Commissioners by holding special mass meetings. From these meetings, they developed a course of action entailing petitioning and later providing the school board with qualified applicants. Petitioning had been a long-standing tactic employed by the community in dealing with the school board. For instance, the Colored Mass Convention of the State of Alabama held at the Stone Street Church in Mobile adopted a series of resolutions on May 2, 1867. One resolution called for the expansion of the Mobile schools and the state system to include African Americans. While the white conservative press viewed these resolutions as "poisonous doctrines," the board's response to this demand led to C. A. Bradford's proposal of partnership with the Freedmen's Bureau in August 1867. As a result, black Mobilians felt that petitioning was an appropriate tactic in their campaign for teachers.[11]

Black Mobilians even encouraged educated members of their community to submit applications the Board of School Commissioners. These candidates had attained an advance education and the majority had completed a normal school curriculum at a reputable institution. On paper, these individuals met the stringent state teaching requirements and were suitable candidates for a teaching position in the school system. However, school commissioners either rejected these qualified candidates or hired them in lesser positions. They defended the policy by arguing that all applicants were equally considered and ultimately based their decision on the applicants' meeting the stringent Alabama qualifications, prior teaching experience, and letters of recommendation. The board deemed white candidates as more qualified than nonwhite applicants. Hence the few nonwhite applicants hired met their standards. Despite its limited success, Rev. E. D. Taylor and other community leaders continued this course of action.[12]

After several consecutive teaching cycles, black Mobilians sought another course of action. They turned to the American Missionary Association for assistance. This decision, though, was not made hastily. The society continued its operations of the Emerson Institute, which offered primary, intermediate, and advanced classes. Students who withdrew from the public schools often flocked to this affordable private school. Yet the organization's handling of several school board crises left many in the community weary. After the dual school board affair, American Missionary Association administrators seriously considered their future in the city. Their contemplation resulted in the inadequate administration of the school and a revolving door of American Missionary Association missionaries and agents. As a result, many black Mobilians lost confidence in the organization. Aware of their frustration, Rev. Edward P. Lord wrote his supervisors, "If anything is ever going to be done in Mobile, Emerson Inst. ought never to deceive the Cold'd people again. We have had uphill work all this year in gaining back the confidence which the Inst. had forfeited." Negative encounters with the Board of School Commissioners caused black Mobilians to overlook any previous frustration and disappointment in their relationship with the organization.[13]

Parents and community leaders approached the organization regarding expanding the existing curriculum to include normal school instruction. They hoped that the proposed program would meet the stringent state teacher certification standards. Program graduates would then provide a pool of qualified applicants for the city to draw on and thereby circumvent any arguments concerning qualifications. Moreover, the location of the school in Mobile would lessen the expenses incurred if a student undertook a program at another institution in the state or region. By their estimation, a local normal school would greatly improve the chances of securing black and Creole public schoolteachers. Black Mobilians had every reason to believe that a normal program would result from their appeals. Enrolled students and their parents previously made requests for additions to the curriculum with much success. As a result of student requests, the curriculum expanded to include Latin, French, vocal music, instrumental music, and courses in higher mathematics. The organization yielded to these requests in order to ensure enrollment and tuition revenues. Although the historical record is silent on the specific requests made for the normal program, it is evident by the principal's correspondence to AMA headquarters that community pressure led to development of Emerson Normal.[14]

A white northern benefactor and a change in leadership made Emerson Normal possible. In 1872 Ralph Emerson, Jr., again provided the necessary financial support for the creation of a normal program at Emerson Institute. Without his generosity and pressure from black Mobilians, the American Missionary Association would not have embarked on fund-raising efforts for an institution considered a preparatory school for Talladega College. Moreover, the presence of Rev. Edward P. Lord, the new energetic principal of Emerson Institute, also aided their struggle. Lord was determined to make a viable normal program at Emerson Institute. In Lord, black Mobilians found a strong advocate. The convergence of community pressure, funding, and a new principal allowed for Emerson Normal to become fully operational by the start of the 1873–1874 academic year. Emerson Normal reinvigorated black Mobilians' relationship with the American Missionary Association. City residents now had access to a local program that could aid their quest for African American teachers in the public schools.[15]

Emerson Normal transformed the nature of Emerson Institute from a feeder school for Talladega College into a normal and preparatory school. Advertisements announcing the opening of the 1873–1874 academic year proudly publicized this new focus: "Special attention given to those who wish to Teach, and those preparing for the Ministry." In order to provide the "best Normal and Academic Institutions in the South," its curriculum included courses typically taught in the public school system and other normal programs such as Latin, geometry, natural philosophy, and physiology. The curriculum also included hands-on training in the primary and intermediate classes conducted at Emerson Institute. Lord and his teaching staff strove to "draw the young people into the earnest Christian influence which we strive to exact upon all of our scholars and send them out again as Christian teachers."[16] Since school administrators considered hands-on training invaluable, they found summer teaching employment for several promising students beginning with the summer of 1874. In addition to the traditional normal program curriculum, the donation of a printing press permitted advanced Emerson Normal students to learn how to operate the machine. Students then employed this skill in the publication of the school's newspaper and materials for the Sabbath schools. William A. Caldwell, Mary Europe, Artemesia Europe, and other students also served on the editorial board for the school's newspaper. The robust curriculum made the initial students qualified for both teaching and administering a student newspaper within their future schools upon graduation. By 1876, Lord reported approximately one hundred students attending the normal program.[17]

In the spring of 1876, Emerson Normal held its first graduation exercises with former slaves composing the graduating class. The Europe sisters, Artemesia and Mary, received their entire education from primary to normal solely at Emerson Institute. Both sisters initially received appointments as educators and administrators in the city's private school systems. Mary Europe Jones, the elder sister, eventually left the private school system and devoted her energies to motherhood. She occasionally operated a private school out of her home in order to supplement her family's income. Artemesia Europe eventually received a teaching position in the Mobile County public school system when school commissioners began hiring African American teachers in earnest.[18]

William Aymar (W. Aymar) Caldwell graduated alongside the Europe sisters. Born on September 22, 1859, Caldwell pursued normal training and Congregationalism against the advice of young African American men living in his neighborhood. According to a letter written by his Emerson Normal teacher, Kate A. Lord, they regarded Caldwell's decision as "sinning against the Holy Ghost." Caldwell dismissed this advice and pursued both. As his instructor recounted, Caldwell knew that his reward would "be everlasting life." Caldwell's drive and academic success garnered the praise and support of his instructors. Like the Europe sisters, Caldwell did not receive a teaching position in the Mobile schools upon graduation. Instead, he enrolled and graduated from Talladega College. As a student at Talladega, though, he remained involved in the community, including their challenges to existing hiring practices.[19]

As Emerson Normal held its first graduation, arsonists struck. The resulting fire destroyed Emerson Institute in April 1876. The school's destruction, though, did not result in the effects desired by the arsonists. The relationship between black Mobilians and the American Missionary Association relationship strengthened rather than weakened. African Americans, in particular, evoked the memory of the destroyed building in their activism. "Remember Old Blue" and "Remember Blue College" became their rallying cry. Plans for rebuilding began quickly.[20]

In December 1877 the community participated in the groundbreaking ceremony at the school's new location. At this ceremony, the reverends William H. Ash, Albert F. Owens, and E. D. Taylor delivered addresses. These African American ministers, specifically Owens and Taylor, commended the partnership while stressing a message of racial uplift through education. Owens's address praised the American Missionary Association for its continued participation in the city's educational efforts. The *American Missionary* noted that Owens "said that ignorance was our greatest enemy, and that the building which was to be erected might be regarded as a fort, from which guns were to be aimed at this inveterate foe, and exhorted the people to sustain the teachers who were leading them in their intellectual and moral warfare." Taylor's remarks focused on the educational achievement of African Americans while commending the rebuilding efforts. In an anecdotal style, the elder minister commented that "he had been taught that the negro race could not be educated—that his brains lay in his heels, etc.; but he was glad to see proof to the contrary in the speeches that had just been made by Mr. Ash and Mr. Owen[s]." In both addresses, Owens and Taylor pointed to the mental and intellectual skills achieved through the useful education. These skills, according to the men, justified the continued partnership in the "warfare" against white resistance. The partnership and rebuilding efforts affirmed their resolve and activism. Thus, normal and primary classes continued in a rented, ill-suited, old store building in the city while work at the new Holley Garden location proceeded. Construction was completed in late April 1878.[21]

Rev. E. D. Taylor's address featured prominently at the school's dedication ceremony in May 1878. His remarks encapsulated the feelings of many black Mobilians. "I have cautiously watched the movements of these teachers and their school work, and I am convinced that they are here for the lifting up of my race, and as I go down the steps of life," Taylor told the audience, "I look back upon this school, and these teachers, with a great deal of pleasure knowing that they are leading my people out from a bondage worse than slavery. I thank God that we have these friends to help us." Taylor's comments illustrated the importance of the educational partnership to the community. While the partnership brought frustration at times, Taylor reminded the overwhelmingly African American audience that the partnership also produced fruitful results. Hence Emerson Normal and the partnership between black Mobilians and the American Missionary Association endured instead of falling apart after the fire. Perseverance and overcoming obstacles had defined black Mobilians' long struggle for African American teachers. The fire was one of many challenges faced. The school's rededication, as Taylor's comments suggest, validated their struggle and enabled their perseverance. Hence the destruction of "Blue College" never deterred them from fulfilling their goal.[22]

Despite its relocation, arson plagued the school again during the winter of 1881–82. This fiery attempt to permanently close the school initially caused sadness. Emerson principal Emma Caughey bemoaned the school's destruction: "Emerson Institute is lying in ruins. For the second time in her history she is smoldering in ashes, and we are in mourning for the destruction of our little church, made dear by so many sacred and hallowed associations, and our beautiful school building in which so many happy hours of toil have been spent and labors of love performed. . . . The enemy approaches again and applies the torch— this time with marvelous success."[23] While Caughey mourned, black Mobilians jumped immediately into action by evoking the memory of "Old Blue College." Rev. Albert F. Owens, pastor of the Third Baptist Church, made his church's basement available. Other ministers followed Owens's lead. As a result of black Mobilians' initiative and resolve, classes resumed within days of the fire. In an article to the *American Missionary*, Caughey reported that the school reopened "on Monday, Jan. 30, with three departments, at the Third Baptist Church, about one mile from the 'Home' and two departments in the basement of the Little Zion Church, about three blocks distant from the Home." Moreover, the new school was rebuilt more quickly. Emerson Normal and Institute reopened in October 1882.[24]

In addition to arson, student poverty and a major yellow fever epidemic affected both graduation rates and overall enrollment. To be sure, the school managed to overcome these obstacles by supplying qualified African American teachers to the city's schools. Yet progress was slow. After the initial graduation, the next graduation did not occur until 1880, in which two students graduated.

Two graduated in 1884, nine in 1887, five in 1889, and two in 1890. Fortunately, the incidence of arson and other extreme acts of violence toward the school declined after the second rebuilding. White extremists were unable to break the resolve of black Mobilians and their American Missionary Association partners; their efforts never permanently shut down the school. Ultimately, the relationship between the American Missionary Association and black Mobilians proved resilient.[25]

Evoking the memory of "Blue College" also resulted in a shift in black Mobilians' struggle for African American public schoolteachers. After the first normal class graduated, hopes for the employment of African American teachers and all-African American teaching staffs were quickly dashed. The Mobile County Board of School Commissioners refused to hire the graduates from the inaugural class. The board's continued resistance dismayed the African American community. In 1878 Rev. E. D. Taylor, the pastor of the Good Hope and Mount Moriah Methodist churches, Rev. Albert F. Owens, and several African American leaders petitioned the board regarding its hiring practices. Petitioners questioned the board's decision in not hiring qualified African American teachers. They demanded transparency by inquiring how the board made its decision before insisting on the hiring of black teachers in the future. The board responded to the petition in its September 18, 1878, meeting. Swayed by the activists and the existence of Emerson Normal, the Mobile County Board of School Commissioners adopted the following resolution:

> The Board of School Commissioners have given our weight to the regard of the petitioners and agree that other things being equal, it would be reasonable to prefer Colored teachers for Colored schools. But in the organization of be found capable of managing them and it the Established policy of this Board to make places for others whether white or Colored, when new Schools are Established or vacancies occur in the Colored Schools, The Claims of Colored applicants to fill the same will receive consideration and when equally competent in Scholarship and ability to govern will have the preference in selection.

After this resolution, William A. Caldwell found employment as the principal of the Good Hope School during the 1878–1879 academic year and then from 1881 to 1887.[26]

Caldwell's hiring made possible the employment of other Emerson Normal graduates. Black Mobilians deemed Caldwell's hiring as a victory. They resumed their efforts for additional teachers by submitting qualified applicants for the board's consideration, petitioning school commissioners directly, and even threatening a boycott. Community pressure, the success of Caldwell, and the presence of Emerson Normal eventually led to an increase in the number of African Americans teachers employed by the mid-1880s. Artemesia Europe permanently moved from the private to public school system in 1887 after taking a midyear appointment in 1885. Non–Emerson Normal graduates also received teaching positions, especially those who had attended Emerson Institute as students. For instance, William R. Gleason worked alongside William A. Caldwell as a teacher at the Good Hope School from 1884 to 1887. Other Emerson Institute graduates, including Annie Ewing, Mattie Ewing, and Theresa Page, received teaching positions during the 1880s. Without the presence of these local schools and continued community pressure, the struggle for African American teachers and better conditions may have continued much longer.[27]

Emerson Normal graduates also sought reform to the hiring practices of the American Missionary Association. William A. Caldwell and other First Congregational Church congregants began to question the organization's failure to hire African American educators and ministers who had graduated from their higher educational institutions. They initially voiced their concerns in several conservations with J. D. Smith. American Missionary Association officials hired this advanced theological student at Talladega College for its religious efforts while the regular ministry vacationed during the summer of 1877. In a letter to American Missionary Association administrators, Smith outlined their demands: "I have had men say to me, 'Smith if a colored minister would come here and show to the people that he is *true to his principles; not suffering himself to be led astray* in five or six months, he would soon be the means of leading the more intelligent class without much difficulty.'" He concurred with their reasoning and recommended, on their behalf, the hiring of the "young men . . . being trained up in our Schools and Colleges." Congregants had valid concerns. While the organization hired advanced students from Talladega and other American Missionary Association colleges during the summer months, the organization relied predominantly on white northern missionaries as educators at the school and church during the academic year. American Missionary Association officials responded by transferring Rev. William H. Ash from Providence, Rhode Island, to Mobile in 1878.[28]

Rev. William Henry Ash was born in Charleston, South Carolina, in 1847. Although little is known about his early years, he graduated from Lincoln University in southern Chester County, Pennsylvania, in 1873. This renowned historical black college fully prepared Ash for his entry into the theological school of Boston University. Shortly after obtaining his A.B. in sacred theology, Ash was ordained at the Central Church in Providence in 1877. Mobile represented his first major post since being ordained in the Congregational Church.[29]

Caldwell, church members, and community leaders considered the hiring of Ash as a victory, signaling to them a possible change in the organization's hiring practices that had the potential of extending to Emerson Normal and Institute. Appreciative of Ash's hiring, Caldwell drafted a letter to the AMA on behalf of the congregants. The letter opened, "Dear sir, we the undersigned members of the 1st Congregation Church of Mobile Alabama take this method of showing you our appreciation of our worthy pastor Rev. W. H. Ash, whom you have sent amongst us." Caldwell and the eight other signers felt that Ash exerted "a powerful influence for good in our community." Caldwell and the other petitioners reasoned, "He is just man the colored people of Mobile need." In detailing their appreciation, church members noted the early results from increased membership among young people and the educated middle class to the elevation of the public opinion of Congregationalism. Indeed, Ash's transfer sparked much enthusiasm in Mobile.[30]

His establishment of the Aristotle Literary Club justified their enthusiasm. This literary society attracted church members, Emerson Normal graduates, and other "true representatives—or rather, the best representatives—of the colored population in our city." The club organized public programs consisting of literary discussions, musical entertainment, and debates. Like other period literary societies, the Aristotle Literary Club promoted a new literate identity. As a result, the participation of Emerson Normal graduates increased. Ash recognized the success of his efforts resulted from "his peculiar relation and identification with my race [which gave him an] advantage over them [the white Emerson teachers]." Unlike his white predecessors, Ash better integrated himself into the community. Black Mobilians found an ally to combat the racism within the American Missionary Association.[31]

Unfortunately, racism within the American Missionary Association precipitated Ash's removal. Missionaries purposely excluded Ash from the educational efforts. B. F. Koons justified this exclusion by claiming that Ash lacked the knowledge of properly leading a Sabbath school and a church. She also claimed that the "colored population" had more faith in her, a white northern missionary, than in Ash, an African American. Koons's assessment convinced American Missionary Association administrators to contemplate and eventually remove Rev. Ash to Florence, Alabama, where he remained until his death of kidney disease in 1882.[32]

The decision shocked and dismayed Caldwell and other black Mobilians. They had previously voiced their approval of Ash's hiring to the organization and could not understand his removal. Caldwell actively participated in the special meetings demanding Ash's reinstatement. Drafting one of the numerous petitions sent to the American Missionary Association executives, Caldwell argued for retaining Ash based on his position as an educational and moral leader. The American Missionary Association regarded the development of African American leadership as a major organizational aim. Missionaries prepared their students for entry into the middle class and for becoming moral leaders in their respective communities. As an Emerson Normal graduate, Caldwell appealed to this fundamental organizational aim. He wrote, "Since he has been here, he has accomplished a great amount of good by his influence and example both for the church and the community. His ability as a scholar and his model deportment as a minister of the gospel has won for him the respect and admiration of both white and colored in our city. He has certainly rendered faithful and efficient service in the cause of education and Christianity." By citing Ash's personal character and leadership abilities, Caldwell hoped to show that he both lived and instilled the values promoted by organization at Emerson Normal and the church. Through his example, Ash inspired others.[33]

Caldwell even discussed the educational programs implemented under Ash's administration. Since 1865 the American Missionary Association stressed religion and education as the best means to achieve the transition from slavery to freedom and focused their efforts on black Mobilians' moral and intellectual development. Caldwell's keen awareness of this broader mission guided the concluding section. He felt that Ash instilled these values. "He has especially interested himself in the young people here, and one grand result of his efforts in that direction may be seen in the 'Aristotle Literary Club,' the only successful organization of its kind ever before established among our people here," Caldwell reminded them. Through this literary society, Caldwell contended that a "greater thirst for knowledge and improvement has been created among them than has ever been seen before." After outlining his reasons for reinstating Ash, Caldwell ended the petition with the following demand: "Hence we feel that his removal from here just now would be really detrimental to the cause of religion, morality and education. Impelled by the highest motives and a deep solicitude for the welfare of my people I pen you these few lines." His petition, however, never swayed administrators who were committed to Ash's removal. In this instance, Caldwell's efforts failed.[34]

While Emerson Normal graduates continued to question the organization's practices, they remained devoted to the school. Internal questioning and reform efforts never overshadowed the broader struggle for teacher training and employment of African American teachers in the public schools. Graduates understood the limits of the partnership. Undaunted by failure and frustration, graduates sustained the association. Their Emerson Normal training and their sense of obligation to the African American community drove their activism within and outside the classroom for the benefit of the entire community.

The resiliency of black Mobilians' educational relationships and determination made the Mobile County Board of School Commissioners reconsider its position regarding African American teacher training. In 1887 Broad Street Academy opened as the first public normal and high school for African Americans in the city. The school drew from an educated African American ministry, Emerson Normal graduates, and Emerson Institute graduates for its all-black faculty. School commissioners appointed William A. Caldwell for the position of principal. Artemesia Europe represented the other Emerson Normal graduate hired. In addition to Europe and Caldwell, the faculty featured William R. Gleason, Miss Mattie Ewing, Rev. Albert F. Owens, and Theresa E. Page as teachers and Kate Parkis and Luella B. Thomas as assistants. The curriculum mirrored Emerson Normal and other normal schools, and featured both classroom and hands-on training in the model school attached to the program.[35] Emerson Normal graduates and other educators refashioned the education received in the training of future African American teachers. Caldwell, Europe, and others instilled racial pride and the rhetoric of racial progress via education to their students through their lessons and continued activism within Mobile. As a former student recalled, Caldwell "ran the school with discipline and never tolerated any foolishness of any kind on campus. If there was ever any kind of trouble with a pupil it would be dealt with that day with the parents' involvement." The school's inaugural graduating class of thirteen students reflected the school's focus of academic achievement and discipline. Henry Europe Jones, one of the two male graduates, continued the educational legacy established by pioneer Emerson Normal students Mary Europe Jones and Artemesia Europe. Without perseverance and black Mobilians' activism, Broad Street Academy would not have been possible.[36]

Broad Street Academy coexisted with Emerson Normal. Both schools provided choice in normal education and represented major victories for black Mobilians and their allies. The schools' respective graduates built up a corps of African American teachers on which Mobile, Mobile County, and the surrounding Gulf region could draw for their public schools. Each school resulted from the continued activism and collective determination of the African American community to fulfill their communal desire to become an educated and literate people. Broad Street Academy, though, permitted the training of future African American teachers by qualified African American educators using public funds. Thus the school's existence marked a major achievement in racial progress through education. Until the school's closure due to a suspicious fire in 1947, Broad Street Academy remained a source of pride among black Mobilians.[37]

Emerson Normal reflected the communal desire and determination for the training and hiring of African American teachers in Mobile. Relying on their diverse educational relationships, black Mobilians achieved success. By 1890 two normal schools existed, one public and one private. The corps of teachers established by the schools filled faculties of the African American public schools. In the public normal school, Emerson Normal graduates trained future generations of African American teachers. The long and arduous struggle reinforced in the minds of black Mobilians the need for perseverance and alliances. Both proved essential to the future of African American education in Mobile.

The divergent experiences of black Mobilians and their counterparts in Richmond, though, must not overshadow two important similarities. First, educational alliances were essential to the creation of a corps of African American teachers. In each urban center, the respective communities drew on their relationships with other proponents of African American education. Of these relationships, those with government officials proved critical. Government support provided access to money and other resources. While not ideal, these relationships aided in legitimizing and realizing the communal desire for African American teachers in the public schools. With the creation of a corps of African American public schoolteachers, the respective communities had an important ally within the school system. These educators strove for the betterment of the schools and greater access to an education and citizenship in their communities. In many instances, their education and post-graduation expectations revealed that African Americans were as capable, and perhaps even more capable, than their white counterparts in the instruction and occasionally the administration of the African American public schools. Therefore, relationships forged by urban African Americans proved beneficial.

Second, and most important, this corps of teachers served an important role beyond the classroom in the fight for racial uplift. The educators challenged the racism in their community, from the discriminatory hiring practices in the public schools to the racism within the American Missionary Association. Their participation, as evidenced in petitions, publications, and racial uplift organizations, evoked and sustained a particular collective memory of their normal school. By inspiring hope and perseverance, this memory proved essential in the broader civil rights struggle. Thus Emerson Normal and Richmond Colored Normal represented a major victory by developing a new type of leadership that would be instrumental in the future struggles for African American education.

III

INTEGRATING THE AFRICAN AMERICAN SCHOOLHOUSE

5

Shifting Strategies

Black Richmonders' Quest for Quality Public Schools

At the close of the 1879–1880 academic year, Richmond school board members received a petition from a delegation of prominent black Richmonders. Like other petitions sent prior to the July 9, 1880, meeting, the petitioners' demands centered on improving the overall quality of African American public schools. In this instance, they requested that "we, the colored citizens and tax-payers of Richmond, in mass-meeting assembled, do most respectfully petition your honorable board to appoint colored teachers in all colored public schools of this city and to raise the grade of the same to a level with that of the white schools." By making these improvements, the petitioners felt they would finally attain quality public schools that built on the educational legacy of the Freedmen's Schools. Thus they appealed to the conscience of the Richmond School Board members. "Is it just in the sight of God and humanity to treat us thus? We cannot think so," the petitioners rhetorically answered, ". . . and knowing that, sooner or later by you or by others chosen to fill your places, this wrong must be corrected." Through petitions, such as the above, black Richmonders insisted that Richmond school board members correct the perceived ills of the school system. In so doing, black Richmonders demanded that the Richmond school board and state educational officials continue to build on the educational progress achieved under the Freedmen's Schools and uphold their status as tax-paying citizens by providing quality public schools.[1]

For black Richmonders, the departure of the Freedmen's Bureau in 1870 and the initial uncertainty of the new educational partners did not stop them from pursuing their goals of educational access, legitimacy of African American education, and citizenship. As evidenced in the aforementioned petition, the first decade of public schools merely inaugurated a shift in but not the end to their struggle. They prodded and cajoled their new educational partners to uphold the promises of freedom by insisting on quality public schools. According to the above petition sent by black Richmonders, quality public schools ensured that African American children could "pursue identically the same course of instruction, without omissions or breaks, which the white children of this city take in the white public schools." They realized that without quality schools, the gains made since emancipation would be in jeopardy. New partners and the emergence of new challenges after the departure of the Freedmen's Bureau, therefore, required adaptation and shifting strategies by black Richmonders.[2]

To this end, black Richmonders redefined their activism beyond mere access and legitimacy with a series of campaigns centered on improving the overall quality of the schools. This multipronged struggle encompassed four objectives. The first objective entailed securing local government positions, whether as school board members or as aldermen, through electoral politics. This objective ensured that black Richmonders had a voice in the decisions made regarding the schools. Second, black Richmonders sought the expansion of the school system while maintaining high standards in the schools' physical and material conditions. Third, black Richmonders insisted on the employment of African American teachers as a means of ensuring high levels of instruction to their children. They viewed these educators, especially those who graduated from Richmond Colored Normal, as essential allies in making the schools an enduring institution. Fourth, black Richmonders fought for adequate and equitable school funding. Through these objectives, they pushed the parameters of Educational Reconstruction through new partnerships with local and state government officials in order to make quality schools a reality.

Black Richmonders embarked on the quality campaigns for a variety of reasons, achieving success in some areas while encountering setbacks in others over the course of the decade. Throughout, they never lost sight of their mission for educational access and legitimacy that began in 1865. Their struggle now focused on making the public schools into lasting institutions instrumental for sustaining African American citizenship. By shifting strategies, black Richmonders merely expanded and refined their educational networks in order cope with new partners and new challenges resulting from local, national, and transnational debates. As a result, "Redemption," as typically defined by scholars, resulted in the expansion rather than the demise of the African American schoolhouse in both Richmond and the entire state.

Black Richmonders entered the first decade of public schools on a high note. The departure of the Freedmen's Bureau occurred without much fanfare, as the transition period went smoothly. As city officials pledged to sustain the public schools, black Richmonders transformed their educational networks in order to accommodate the new partners, and they established new roles for old partners. Hence the networks remained viable. Moreover, local officials and the broader Richmond community recognized the validity of African American claims to citizenship and freedom through education. By the end of the transition from the Freedmen's Schools to public schools, African American public schools had become an essential part of the Richmond public school system. Therefore the schools vindicated the efforts of black Richmonders and their partners in African American education.

Neither this feeling of vindication nor the benefits of public education was shared equally by all. The schools were far from perfect. Several school issues, specifically school accommodations and employment of African American teachers, plagued only certain neighborhoods. On the other hand, school board representation and funding affected the entire African American community. Thus several campaigns began as a struggle to resolve local neighborhood concerns before coalescing into larger community concerns, while others began as a larger community struggle. Over the course of the decade, the various quality campaigns evolved into a unified struggle for the overall improvement of the African American public schools. With these campaigns, black Richmonders sought quality public schools that would survive for future generations. In other words, they sought perfection and would be satisfied with nothing less.

The departure of the Freedmen's Bureau and the majority of northern benevolent societies prompted some feelings of uncertainty among black Richmonders regarding their new educational partners. While city and state officials pledged their support of African American public schools, it remained unclear whether they would rescind their support after the return of local rule. It was also uncertain whether these educational partners would address black Richmonders' educational interests, or whether they would view African Americans as equal partners in making decisions regarding the schools. Hence the 1870–1871 academic year was an important one, as the events of that year set the tone for the various quality campaigns undertaken in Richmond.

It quickly became apparent that black Richmonders had an ally in the school superintendent James Binford. He supported the African American schools because he viewed them as models for the entire state. Binford and other school officials made regular inspections of African American as well as white schools. Binford used the information gathered during these unannounced visits as evidence in a public relations campaign designed to convince white Richmonders of the merits of the African American public schools. Through his actions, Binford eased some of the lingering anxieties over the departure of previous educational partners.[3]

Moreover, Binford's active promotion of the Richmond schools as models for the entire urban South served to convince skeptics of the benefits of African

American public education. He regularly invited and hosted visitors from across the region, nation, and foreign countries. In November 1870 Binford hosted the Maryland superintendent of public instruction and superintendent of the Baltimore public schools. During this visit, the Maryland delegation only viewed the African American schools conducted by African American teachers. Like earlier visitors to the Freedmen's Schools, the Maryland visitors as well as representatives of the Richmond press were impressed by what they saw. They first visited the schools conducted by Otway M. Stewart and Miss Frances E. Clark on Seventeenth Street. As a result of "competent instructors and thorough discipline," the visitors noted that the students "answered every question promptly, and gave abundant evidence of their acquaintance with the lessons upon which they were engaged." For the guests, Binford's claims had been show to possibly have some merit. Yet these visitors needed some more evidence in order to be fully convinced.[4]

The Maryland delegation then toured three schools conducted at the Bakery. While in John W. Cromwell's school, they were "amused" by the students' "stentorian yet accurate recital of the list of capitals of the United States, with the rivers upon which they stand, sung to familiar tunes." They felt that Cromwell had effectively instructed them "in every department in [which] they are examined." The group then questioned the students of Elizabeth V. Dixon to their satisfaction before concluding their visit to the intermediate and primary schools conducted by Peter H. Woolfolk and his sister Margaret Woolfolk. These schools left an indelible mark upon the group. "Here half an hour was pleasantly spent, and some very intelligent colored boys and girls were made to show their progress in the pursuit of knowledge," according to the *Dispatch* article. "They showed that they not only knew their lessons by heart, but were well informed as to *principles*." Overall, Binford's claims had proven true as the visitors remarked on their tour at the dinner held for them that evening. They left believing that Richmond could be viewed as a model school system for African American children across the urban South.[5]

The impressions made by the African American students and teachers on the regional, international, and local visitors assisted in broadening public support for the schools. The competency and intellectual capabilities displayed by African American teachers and students mystified curious visitors. While it may have been degrading to the students, these visitations exemplified city school officials' support and their willingness to convince skeptics of the merits of African American education. In 1872 several school board members remarked that their inspections of Richmond Colored Normal and other schools allowed guests to

witness "a sight which will wholly relieve any [unsure] case of skepticism in regard to the susceptibility of the negro to receive a good education." Indeed, these
visits from white southerners as well as "distinguished persons from the North
and from foreign countries" had created a "sensation." This sensation resulted in
increased local interest and support of the schools by all classes in Richmond,
white and black. Within a short period, white and black Richmonders embraced
the public schools as a model system worthy of their support.[6]

Though outsiders deemed them model schools, Richmond newspaper editors reversed their policy regarding the African American public schools. Under
the Freedmen's School system, editors refused to print articles that recognized
specific details of the schools. "Our schools" only referred to schools for white
children. With the return of local rule, the Freedmen's Bureau departure, and
Binford's efforts, editors began recognizing as well as offering praise of the African American public schools in Richmond. Discussions of "our schools" were
no longer exclusive to the white public schools and now included the African
American public schools. The *Daily Dispatch* regularly featured articles ranging
from the hiring of teachers to visits by state officials and outsiders. But the coverage of the annual end-of-the-year examinations and closing exercises best exemplified the newspaper's reversal of its previous policy. The newspaper featured
front-page articles noting specific details of the ceremonies and listing the names
of the students by teacher and grade who had received scholastic and attendance
awards. The newspaper even extended its coverage to the exercises of Richmond
Colored Normal, a private school until 1876. Furthermore, the newspaper listed
the names of the African American children who were promoted alongside the
names of white children who were promoted. This media coverage had previously been exclusive to the white schools. Now, as a result of the return to local
Democratic rule and Binford's efforts, major city newspapers fully embraced the
African American public schools as "our schools."[7]

Through black Richmonders' strategic partnership with Binford, they also secured the support of the state superintendent of public instruction. William H.
Ruffner viewed the Richmond public schools favorably. He based his opinions
on the reports received from Binford as well as personal observations. In his first
annual report, Ruffner devoted a special section to the history of the Richmond
school system and praised city officials' foresight for developing its school system
prior to the creation of the state system. He also ensured that the city received its
share of the state school funds. Thus the financial and nonfinancial rewards of
state recognition permitted the shoring up of African American education for its
continuation during the decade.[8]

However, white recognition of the African American public schools affected the development of the quality campaigns in Richmond. Black Richmonders had to tread carefully in making their demands for improving the public schools. They wanted to maintain white recognition as well as financial appropriations. Hence black Richmonders adopted less aggressive strategies and tactics. They resorted to petitions and meetings with school officials rather than boycotts and other more militant tactics. Moreover, the tone of their appeals employed a specific form. Petitions and meetings started with statements in which individuals thanked school officials for their generosity in sustaining the public schools before listing their demands. Whether addressing the issue of teachers or school accommodations, they could not risk losing their white allies. As a result, more aggressive strategies and increased militancy for better school conditions would not occur until the next decade. In limiting public discourse, white recognition of the schools profoundly influenced the development of a unified campaign for quality public schools.[9]

Furthermore, white recognition provides an explanation of why the various campaigns for school board representation, school accommodations, teachers, and funding took particular paths before coalescing into a unified campaign for quality public schools. As certain issues only affected a segment of African Americans living within the city, black Richmonders had to make sure their demands for better conditions did not result in retaliation on the other schools. Therefore, white recognition, while embedding African American education as an essential component of the city school system, had adverse consequences for the quality campaigns.

School board representation was one concern addressed by the quality campaigns. During the 1870s, the issue of school board representation involved the entire community in a struggle for the right to shape any decisions pertaining to the schools. As black Richmonders lacked direct representation, they heavily relied on their networks with white allies during the course of the decade. Through these relationships, black Richmonders secured a voice in shaping decisions pertaining to school operations. Yet they still sought more agency.

In addition to the support from Superintendent Binford, black Richmonders benefited from having R. M. Manly as an ally on the Richmond school board. The former superintendent of education for the Freedmen's Bureau had been a longtime supporter of African American education. As a liaison between the community and the school board, Manly ensured that their concerns and petitions received the board's full attention rather than being dismissed outright. He also attended the majority of the functions held at or on behalf of the African

American schools.[10] Lastly, Manly served as the principal of Richmond Colored Normal. Using his reputation, he elevated the school from a private school to a Richmond public school by donating the entire property worth approximately $25,000 to city officials in 1876. His actions, while controversial, secured city appropriations and established the option of a normal school as well as a high school for future generations of African American children. For that reason, black Richmonders and white public school supporters equally bemoaned Manly's departure from the school board for the city council.[11]

While black Richmonders had the support of prominent officials, they held school officials accountable for their decisions. Through petitions and letters to the *Dispatch*, black Richmonders critiqued unpopular decisions. For instance, several African American religious leaders openly challenged the school board's decision to not have representatives from local African Americans churches on a special committee regarding the use of the Bible in the public schools. As a result of the "peculiar composition of the Board," one letter to the editors of the *Dispatch* contended that the "rights and wishes of twenty thousand people are about to be overridden and left to the mercies of three thousand whose opinions and principles are not only opposed but absolutely hostile to what they entertain and live for." Hence the unsigned letter demanded that one or more additional committee members representing the African American congregations be added to the board's discussions of excluding the "Bible from our schools." The author reasoned that black Richmonders had the right to be a part of any decision made regarding their schools and suggested that their white allies could not adequately address their interests. In representing the "views of a large majority of the people of Richmond," the author argued, "we have a right to demand that this evil be corrected. We have a right to demand of the Council that the Board be entirely reorganized, and that our people, and our whole people, be fairly represented in it, as they should be." If not, the letter warned that the school board would be "held severely answerable in the future." In this instance, school officials eventually solicited advice from African American religious leaders. But the lack of direct representation hindered black Richmonders' efforts to shape the decisions regarding the public schools.[12]

Overall, black Richmonders proved less successful in obtaining school board positions during the first decade. Racial fears on part of white Richmonders blocked any of their efforts. For white Richmonders, it proved too much to have African Americans, especially African American males, in control of decisions pertaining to the education of white children, the employment of white teachers, and the distribution of white taxpayers' contributions to public schools. As a result, black Richmonders were forced to rely on their white allies on the school board and on petitioning. Furthermore, they used their vote to secure more racial progressive school officials until political conditions proved more advantageous. Unfortunately, significant progress would not be made until the 1880s.[13]

School accommodations represented another quality campaign objective. The campaign sought redress for the insufficient number of schools to accommodate the city's African American school-age population. During the 1870–1871 academic year, 1,573 African Americans enrolled in the city schools, and the schools had an average attendance of 1,330. Enrollments were much lower than the number of school-age children living in Richmond according to both federal and city censuses. The 1870 federal census reported 3,665 African Americans between the ages of ten and twenty-one who could not write. Since these individuals were unable to write, presumably they did not attend the public schools. Throughout the decade, average school attendance reflected 17 percent of school census population as determined by city officials, and by the end of the decade, 21 percent. While some parents enrolled their children in private schools, the Richmond public schools simply could not handle the number of school-age children living in Richmond.[14]

To be sure, private schools offered an alternative to the public schools. During the 1870s, ministers, married female educators, and even public schoolteachers wishing to supplement their household incomes operated schools out of their homes or local churches. The schools operated by Rev. Anthony Binga, Jr., Daniel Barclay Williams, and others thrived as parents sought less crowded school accommodations and African American teachers.[15] Tuition costs, though, hindered many from utilizing this option, as evidenced by an 1876 city superintendent report. Binford reported 449 (226 male and 223 female) students enrolled in private primary schools and thirty-one (six male and twenty-five female) students attending a private high school. He reported twenty-one teachers who instructed these students. As these figures suggest, private school attendance represented a significant number of students opting out of the public school system compared to the total enrolled students of 1,836 students during the academic year. Private school attendance, though, accounted for a small percentage of school-age children living in Richmond who were not enrolled in the public schools. The majority of school-age children were not taking advantage of either the public or private school systems. Thus private schools remained inaccessible to the majority of African Americans not enrolled in the public schools.[16]

John W. Cromwell, parents, and community leaders recognized the limits of private schools in addressing the school accommodation issue. Private schools could not address the needs of the majority. Instead, they pointed to these schools as indicative of the city's negligence in providing school accommodations. If the city furnished a sufficient number of schools, they reasoned that the private schools would no longer be viewed as necessary and public school enrollment would increase. Rather than thwarting their efforts, black Richmonders used the private schools in their arguments for expanding and improving the overall conditions of the public schools.[17]

Inadequate school board policies also influenced the campaign. By the 1871–1872 academic year, school officials phased out the use of African American churches as public schools. Ebenezer Church, Asbury Chapel, and other churches ceased as the sites of public school education. Instead, school officials converted older school buildings that had been formerly used for the education of white children for African American children. For instance, the Lancasterian School became the Valley School for African American children in October 1871. Opening December 1, 1871, the Baker School became the first school built by Richmond for African American children. In the early 1870s, school officials also rented before purchasing from the Richmond Educational Association the buildings that composed the Navy Hill School. In 1876 the public schools expanded with the incorporation of Richmond Colored Normal. This school elevated Richmond into a class above other southern cities. Few southern cities and towns offered a public high school for African Americans. With the addition of Richmond Colored Normal, Richmond now had both a high school and a normal school within its public offerings for African Americans. However, these efforts never alleviated the problem. Classrooms overflowed with students as existing buildings barely accommodated the African American students who regularly attended. This reality forced administrators to turn away new students due to the lack of suitable accommodations.[18]

Furthermore, the use of older accommodations posed several problems. Older facilities were located in neighborhoods that were not always accessible to the targeted populations. The buildings also had a set limit on the number of students who could possibly enroll. The problems associated with the use of older accommodations influenced the activism of black Richmonders living in the Moore Street neighborhood, the East End neighborhood, and the neighborhoods accessible to the Valley School.

At the start of the decade, residents of the Moore Street neighborhood lacked an accessible public school. Interested students traveled great distances for an education, but often the distance proved too great. They either used the private school system or went uneducated. As a result, residents began petitioning the

school board for a school established within or easily accessible to their neighborhood. When their petitions went unfulfilled, residents established a school
sustained by tuition and community funds.[19]

John Oliver spearheaded the Moore Street school movement. The Virginia
native came to Richmond from Boston in 1865 as an observer of postwar conditions but remained in order to organize African American workers. In the spring
of 1875, the former president of the Colored National Labor Union mobilized the
residents into purchasing land to be held in trust by the Moore Street Industrial
Society. The society's purpose was to "promote the instruction of colored youth
in practiced and useful trades" and to raise monies for appropriate equipment.
It maintained a fund in which Moore Street residents as well other Richmonders
donated money via subscription. During his national fund-raising campaign,
Oliver promoted the importance of a vocational education. Before an audience
at an 1877 educational convention in Charlottesville, Virginia, Oliver professed
his firm belief in vocational training. "Our children, therefore, must not only
have the education which books afford, but their hands must be educated also,"
Oliver argued. "Parents should observe the bent of their children's mind and have
them learn trades for which they are fitted; for it is evident you cannot make a
silver-smith out of a boy who is inclined to be a huckster; nor can you make a
successful farmer out of a boy who was born to follow the sea." Through these
efforts, Moore Street residents received a school.[20]

The Moore Street community-based school began in earnest during the late
1870s. Moore Street Baptist Mission began offering afternoon classes in printing
and carpentry for boys and sewing for girls from 1876 to 1877. These afternoon
classes quickly expanded into a full-day program of vocational and common
school classes, with the Moore Street Industrial School officially opening in 1878.
John Oliver and other residents served as teachers at the school. School trustees
also drew on the neighborhood residents as a resource. In addition to Oliver,
school trustees included Rev. Richard C. Hobson, a cupper and leecher; James
Hugo Johnston, a public schoolteacher; Mortimer Bowler, a shoemaker; Temple A. Miles, a teacher and Richmond Colored Normal graduate; and William H.
Carter, a shoemaker. Hence the school, its teachers, its trustees, and its curriculum addressed the needs espoused by residents. The Moore Street neighborhood
now had a school that was sustained by community funds and taught by community members, and that provided an education deemed beneficial to residents.[21]

Middle-class black Richmonders commended the Moore Street residents' initiative. For these individuals, the Moore Street Industrial School represented a
victory in terms of educational access for all segments of the community but also

a victory for industrial education. In June 1876 the Virginia Educational and Historical Society discussed the issue of industrial education at its second meeting as an organization. John W. Cromwell and other members felt that the Moore Street residents fit within the organization's larger aim of reforming African American public schools across Virginia. Its curriculum addressed the education of a growing class of uneducated, working-class African Americans who were "poorly prepared to instruct the youth who are now coming out of the schools and into manhood." Thus the society passed a resolution praising the Moore Street Industrial School. "Looking to the demands of the industrial future and the up building of our people so far as our humble efforts can be conducted to that end, we, your committee on Trades beg to recommend to the favorable consideration of the friends of the youth of the Moore Street Industrial School," the resolution read. "Therefore, resolved that we commend the Moore Street Industrial Society to the confidence of the community as affording an opportunity of training the idle youth of this community in trades, mechanical, and manufacturing pursuits. That the public who are interested in skilled labor for the colored race should rally to the support of this enterprise." With their support, Moore Street residents moved their plight from a neighborhood struggle to a larger community struggle. Residents now employed the society's resources, including Cromwell's newspaper, the *People's Advocate*, for assistance in pressuring the Richmond school board to either establish an accessible school or incorporate the Moore Street Industrial School into the school system.[22]

The plight of the Moore Street residents found support among East End residents. They also lacked an accessible public school but proved unsuccessful in creating a community-sponsored school. They petitioned as well as made public appeals before the school board, with similar results as the Moore Street residents. For instance, representatives from the East End neighborhood appeared before the school board at the meeting held on February 28, 1878. Led by Otway M. Stewart, the delegation presented a petition signed by more than two hundred residents requesting a public school. The board promptly tabled it because of a lack of funds for such an enterprise. Instead, Anthony M. Keiley recommended the possibility of supplying a teacher if the residents supplied their own school accommodations. Keiley's suggestion, though, revealed that the board members did not truly consider the prior demands of the Moore Street residents. The residents had created their own neighborhood school, but the board never supplied them with a teacher. In recommending that East End residents supply their own school, the board effectively dismissed their petition, as it had no intention of supplying East End residents with school accommodations. If it had, the Moore

Street Industrial School would have been supplied with a teacher and incorporated into the city system. But neither occurred. The lack of meaningful results,
however, never deterred the Moore Street residents and East End residents in
their struggle for accessible school accommodations.[23]

Residents served by the Valley School embarked on a school accommodation campaign, though for different reasons. Unlike the Moore Street and East
End residents, they had a school. While remodeled and refitted, the former Lancasterian School proved too small from its inception as an African American
public school. In his 1871–1872 annual report, Binford noted that a "much larger
number of scholars applied for admission into the primary grades of this group
than could be accommodated." He recommended its enlargement "by extending the wing and removing the partitions in the basement." But even after these
repairs, Valley remained unable to accommodate all the interested students living in the surrounding neighborhoods. Consequently, school officials regularly
turned away students; enrolled students endured overcrowded conditions. Under these circumstances, parents and community leaders began petitioning the
school board for the expansion of Valley. Their demands soon became a pressing
concern for the school board.[24]

School board officials responded to their demands, but not satisfactorily. In
1875, officials expanded Valley by merging it with the Twelfth and Leigh Street
and Springfield Hall schools. This expansion, though, could not keep up with
demand, and the school quickly became overcrowded. By 1878, residents began
petitioning the school board for the construction of new schools in the Church
Hill and Rocketts neighborhoods. They felt this would alleviate the continual
problem at Valley. Unfortunately, the city's financial situation hindered the
board's response. Consequently the board tabled their petitions. As the community demands continued, the board promised another expansion of Valley. This
proposal prompted a flood of petitions that were critical of the board's decision
and much discussion at the board meetings in March 1880, June 1880, September
1880, and October 1880. As previous enlargements never resolved the problem,
petitioners stated their case for new schools. Unfortunately, the city's financial
situation prevented any resolution. Residents would not achieve any meaningful
successes until the start of the 1881–1882 academic year.[25]

Initially, the struggle for school accommodations was limited to specific
neighborhoods, such as the Moore Street, East End, and Valley School district.
The national economic crisis of the 1870s transformed the campaign from neighborhood struggles to a larger community one. The 1873 collapse of Jay Cooke and
Company spurred an economic depression that would continue with periods

of "intermittent recovery" until the turn of the nineteenth century. As a result, the city of Richmond's population increased. Seeking jobs, social services, and a thriving school system, rural African Americans migrated to Richmond. The population influx as well as parents' inability to afford private schools resulted in an increase in school enrollment. Already overcrowded, the existing schools could not sustain the increase.[26]

The school board adopted several measures in order to cope with community pressure and the lack of physical space for all individuals seeking a public school education. School officials tried a restrictive enrollment policy of new students across the system and not simply in specific neighborhoods, causing other neighborhoods to join the residents of Moore Street, East End, and Valley in their struggle for school accommodations. New schools would end the restrictive enrollment policy. Since financial difficulties prevented the board from constructing new accommodations, residents received promises for the addition of buildings formerly occupied by the white schools while the white schools received new facilities.[27]

School officials then adopted half-day sessions for the entire school system. This measure was designed to increase access and offer some resolution to the overcrowded school system. "For the past two years we have not been able to accommodate all that have applied for admission into the schools; in fact, quite a large number have been refused for want of seats," Superintendent Peay explained in his annual report. "I have assigned each teacher as many pupils as she could possibly teach with the hope of success . . . Last session there were 300 applicants that could not be received, and I feel quite certain that the number will be at least 1000 at the opening of the next session." As a direct result of the lack of accommodations for prospective and existing students, the school board shortened the overall grading system by one year and created two sections per grade. The system now consisted of seven grades in the primary and grammar schools, and three in the high school. According to the changed course of study, each grade was "divided into two half sessions named respectively A and B sections, the work of one section being a half session in advance of the work of the other." Superintendent Peay and other school officials justified the new organization as making the system more efficient.[28]

While Superintendent Peay found the new organization "well arranged and working smoothly," half-day sessions further pushed the issue of school accommodations into a broader community concern. The solution affected all students enrolled in the public schools. To be sure, it allowed more students the opportunity to secure an education, but the changed curriculum never addressed the inadequate number of African American public schools. Moore Street and East End residents still lacked public schools. The capacity of Valley and other schools remained inadequate. Enrolled public school students now endured a shortened school day as well as overcrowded conditions. Hence African Americans across the city remained unsatisfied. The fight for school accommodations moved from a neighborhood struggle into a citywide quality campaign by the start of the next decade.[29]

The employment of African American teachers represented a third topic addressed by the quality campaigns. This issue arose out of specific hiring practices. Initiated during the 1870–1871 academic year, the school board required that all applicants, regardless of race, take a placement exam. Instead of hiring qualified African Americans, the board filled the majority of the schools with white applicants whose test scores disqualified them for a position in a white public school. Qualified African Americans then competed for a few positions at Navy Hill. This policy made race, rather than testing aptitude, the main prerequisite for teaching in the public schools. While African Americans educators were regularly praised as valued employees, their service never swayed the board in changing its hiring practices. Throughout, the school board maintained a degree of transparency in the process by publishing announcements regarding the annual examinations, the lists of selected candidates, and the final appointments in the major newspapers. Thus the school board never hid its hiring practices.[30]

This policy had several consequences. The city employed fewer African American educators during the decade than it had during the transition year to public schools. African Americans represented 36.3 percent of the positions in the African American public schools in the year immediately following the departure of the Freedmen's Bureau. After this year, African Americans represented on average 25 percent of the teachers employed during the decade. This figure slightly increased to 30.3 percent during 1873–1874 and decreased to a low of 22.8 percent during the 1875–1876 academic year.[31] Many of the early African American teachers lost their jobs due to the employment restrictions. Since the school board rehired former employees without requiring another examination, openings rarely occurred. Death, the marriage of female educators, and voluntary resignations during and at the end of the school year yielded some opportunities for the hiring of additional African American teachers. For instance, the deaths of Ann F. Smith and Amy Dotson in 1877, the marriage of Rosa Dixon in 1879, and the poor health and subsequent death of Alberta M. Brooks created openings for several African American educators. For the majority of African

American children attending the public schools, these hiring practices meant that they were more likely to be educated by a white teacher instead of an African American instructor.[32]

Moreover, the policy influenced public discourse among black Richmonders. Activism was initially restricted to specific schools and neighborhoods and then expanded to a larger community struggle. For the neighborhoods served by the Navy Hill School, parents and community leaders had few complaints. The children attending the school had Mary Elizabeth Knowles as their principal. The Worcester, Massachusetts, native was a respected white woman who had served as a Freedmen's School educator in the city since 1865. Children received instruction from African American educators who often instilled racial pride in their students. Between 1870 and 1877, the neighborhoods surrounding the Navy Hill School benefited from the city's hiring practices.[33]

In some schools, the placement of effective white teachers did not immediately draw the ire of parents and community leaders. While these individuals may not have been racial progressives, they took their job seriously in order to obtain subsequent placement in a white public school. For instance, Maggie Lena Walker attended Valley for the majority of her primary education. She also attended the Navy Hill School for two years before entering Richmond Colored Normal. Since her only exposure to African American teachers occurred at Navy Hill, Walker later praised both her white teachers at Valley and Richmond Colored Normal as well as her African American teachers at Navy Hill. While she never found her education to be lacking at either Valley or Richmond Colored Normal, Walker fondly recalled Otway M. Stewart and other Navy Hill faculty who "created within our youthful souls an unquenchable search for knowledge, an undying ambition to be something, and to do something." For these students, parents, and community leaders, they had few complaints over the hiring practices but they still desired African American teachers.[34]

Many children, parents, and community leaders endured inferior teachers like M. C. S. Bennett. She successfully petitioned the school board for a position in the African American public schools in 1876 after her test scores failed to gain her a position in the white public schools. The board complied by giving her a position at Valley. The employment of such teachers affected test scores as well as promotion rates for the schools. Navy Hill students typically outperformed their peers during the annual examinations. They also were promoted at a higher percentage. During the year in which Bennett found employment, though, Valley outperformed the other schools on the semiannual exams, but Navy Hill still

maintained a higher percentage of students promoted. Employment of less qualified teachers, such as Bennett, made parents and community leaders desire African American public schoolteachers.[35]

Students and parents also experienced individuals like Hubbard G. Carlton
who deemed their employment in the African American public schools as degrading. Carlton's employment at Navy Hill embroiled these neighborhoods in
the teacher campaign. Carlton replaced Mary E. Knowles at Navy Hill when she
became the principal of Richmond Colored Normal during the 1876–1877 academic year. As he was "not relishing the prospect of a colored school," Carlton
switched with the principal of the Clay Street School. When his replacement
was dismissed in May 1877, Superintendent Peay forced Carlton to take over his
original position at Navy Hill "with the promise of the first vacancy in a white
school." After taking charge, Carlton's racial attitudes never changed. At a 1925
conference, he could not recall any remarkable event, student, and/or experience
from his time as principal at Navy Hill. He simply stated that "there was little of
interest to note." Unfortunately, for students, parents, and teachers at Navy Hill,
Carlton remained in this position, with one brief interruption, for ten years. As
Carlton recalled that his transfer "was a long, long time coming," African American students, teachers, and parents most likely celebrated it. Carlton's employment as well as that of inferior teachers formed the basis for the community's
African American teacher campaign.[36]

Initially, campaign participants desired the removal of inferior teachers
within certain schools but not the entire system. City hiring practices meant that
many white teachers whose qualifications were "lower than heretofore enumer-
ated" found employment over more qualified African American applicants. In
June 1875 black Richmonders held a mass meeting in which they elected four
prominent African American men to state their case for African American public schoolteachers in lieu of incompetent white teachers. These men appeared before the school board and presented member with a petition signed by meeting
attendees. The delegation began by "profusely thanking the board for maintaining public schools" and then demanded "more colored teachers in the colored
schools." They stated "of the thirty-three colored schools [classes] of the city of
Richmond only seven are instructed by colored teachers while there is not one
colored principle in the entire city." They concluded, "It does not appear to us
that there is any valid reason for this small proportion of colored teachers in
colored schools, we, therefore kindly petition you, as a matter of justice to us, as
citizens of this Commonwealth to give us a more equitable proportion of teachers and principals in the colored schools of the city of Richmond." Their pleas

went unheeded. By 1876 these individuals secured the support of the Virginia Education and Historical Association. Together, they argued that the employment of the inferior teachers resulted in poor enrollment, lower test scores, and a feeling that education was not a necessity. However, the school board remained obstinate by not acquiescing to their demands.[37]

Richmond Colored Normal aided their activism. Established 1867, the school had trained African Americans to become primary public schoolteachers. Its existence gave community activists an important resource in their fight for African American teachers. Insufficient numbers of trained African American teachers had been an argument made against the hiring of African American teachers in the public schools. Richmond Colored Normal provided community leaders and parents of children in the public schools with a counterargument. They pointed to this qualified corps of teachers as a reason for changing school board policies. In a September 1876 address, John W. Cromwell argued that African American public schoolteachers "would awaken the proper interest in parents and pupils and furnish a report more favorable to the cause of education." With African American teachers, Cromwell concluded that they would improve overall enrollment of African Americans in Richmond and across the state. Parents and community leaders increasingly turned to this growing corps of qualified teachers for their campaign.[38]

Black Richmonders as well as school administrators strongly encouraged Richmond Colored Normal graduates to apply for teaching positions. Few found employment in Richmond. Although meaningful results would not occur until the next decade, African American parents, community leaders, public schoolteachers, and Richmond Colored Normal graduates laid the foundation for African American teachers in the Richmond public schools. Indeed, the majority of the African American educators who found employment in the city schools had received their education at Richmond Colored Normal. With these allies and a local normal school, black Richmonders found crucial partners in their overall struggle for quality public schools. The benefits of these new partnerships and resources would fully manifest itself in the next decade.[39]

Funding represented a final aspect of the quality campaigns. Black Richmonders and their white allies recognized the importance of funding to the success of the public schools as well as the quality campaigns. Inadequate funding often thwarted black Richmonders' efforts in securing new schools, improved school conditions, and African American teachers. Funding, therefore, was essential to the success of the public schools as well as the various campaigns. Yet black Richmonders had the least control over this issue as local, national, and international forces often impinged on their efforts. As a result, they sought as much money as possible for the schools and equity in the distribution of said school funds. Ultimately, the financial difficulties of the 1870s posed the greatest obstacle to their efforts.

Like the majority of southern cities, Richmond suffered from a lack of funding necessary to adequately support the public schools. School board officials did their best to fund the schools. Richmond typically spent between $32,000 and $53,900 in addition to the monies received from the state school fund. The majority of these supplemental monies came from taxation, creative fiscal policies, the Peabody Fund, and bank interest. Thus Richmond school officials funded the public schools to the best of their abilities.[40]

The return of local rule did not inaugurate the immediate underfunding of African American education. Instead of directing substantially more funds to white public schools, Binford and city officials allocated funds in proportion to the number of students documented in the annual school census. This policy ensured as equitable a distribution of the limited funds as possible to the white and African American public schools. Race was never the sole factor. Since the school census never took into account actual usage, absenteeism and private school attendance had no real direct influence on the allocations. However, the policy had an unintended negative consequence. As black Richmonders attended the public schools at a higher percentage than white students, the actual amount of money spent per student was inadvertently less. Thus the rate per student spent was lower for African American students than for white students. This discrepancy of funds resulted from black Richmonders' firm belief in education and not from specific race-based policies targeting the African American schools. But some black Richmonders, such as John W. Cromwell, desired that the school board address this discrepancy. While they understood the difficulties faced by the school board, they wanted more money appropriated, but settled for fairness.[41]

The Panic of 1873 precipitated a national economic depression that unsettled the foundations of postwar industrial capitalism. Across the nation, individuals openly questioned notions of progress, free-market ideology, labor, and the national political agenda. Most significant, these frank national discussions extended to the entire Educational Reconstruction project.[42] Some white Richmonders renewed their opposition of African American public education as a result of the crippling effects of the panic in Richmond and the state. Rev. Robert L. Dabney, a prominent minister who taught at the Union Theological Seminary in Richmond, questioned the necessity of funding public schools for all children amid the economic crisis, but narrowed his focus on the schools for African

American children. He used a series of articles on African American public education in the *Southern Planter and Farmer* to issue a scathing attack on the city's African American public schools but also on the overall state school system.[43]

Dabney's critique opened the April 1876 publication. Titled "The Negro and the Common School," Dabney's piece strongly argued against the state's financing of African American education and the public schools in general. Through observations made in Richmond and other large urban centers, his main objection centered on the perceived benefits of the system primarily for African Americans at the expense of the schools for white Virginians. In raising the specter of "Negro Rule," he wrote, "To one of them only, I would add my voice: the unrighteousness of expending vast sums, wrung by a grinding taxation from our oppressed people, upon a pretended education of freed slaves, when the State can neither pay its debts, nor attend to its own legitimate interests." Dabney also felt that the state system caused more problems in terms of race relations by promoting African American suffrage, encouraging miscegenation, and depriving the state of a labor force. Instead, he concluded that the state should not be "a universal creator and sustainer of schools," and proposed a return to the antebellum state educational system. In so doing, the tax burden would lessen for white Virginians and the state coffers while simultaneously marginalizing African American education to its antebellum status.[44]

Although the editor of the *Southern Planter and Farmer* wholeheartedly endorsed Dabney's remarks, State Superintendent Ruffner objected. He publicly defended the state school system and the city's African American public schools over the course of four days in the *Daily Dispatch* and *Richmond Enquirer* before having his remarks published in pamphlet form. He began by addressing the emotional nature of Dabney's attack in his response. He argued that Dabney chose to use an emotional plea for a specific purpose. His language invoked "the sentiment that education and other privileges are suited to the few and not to the many; it panders in language full of scorn and disgust to the common aversion felt for the negroes; and it strives to lash into fury all the most violent passions of the war." However, Ruffner felt that such language overlooked the necessity of a state-funded educational system as a right for all citizens, regardless of race. He wrote, "As to raising a question between the public debt and the public schools, what could be more unwise . . . We can educate and we can pay! . . . Will the body politic be preserved whilst gangrene is eating deeper and deeper?" Without the public school system, Ruffner concluded that the state could not survive.[45]

Second and most significant, Ruffner succinctly debunked Dabney's claims that African Americans continued to receive access to public education because of a perceived guilt over slavery. He felt that Dabney had misread "the history of emancipation in the past, but without drawing the lessons they ought to have taught them." As taxpaying citizens African Americans had equal access to a state-funded education, but that equal access did not equate to integration. Ruffner argued, "We find negroes in our churches, our theatres, our courthouses . . . our halls of legislation, but there is one place where no negro enters, and that is a *white public school house*." As state law "separates the races in education, and in nothing else," Ruffner reasoned that the "effect of the separation enters into the educational thought and training of the young and establishes the habits and etiquette of society with a firmness that nothing else is doing, or could do." By debunking Dabney's arguments as baseless, Ruffner defended African Americans' right to an education supported by city and state funds.[46]

Ruffner's elaborate response revealed how educational partnerships between black Richmonders and state government officials functioned. At the time of the crisis, as in the case of Dabney's critique, black Richmonders could rely on their high-ranking partners for support. Ruffner's intimate knowledge of the city and state public schools and his relationships with black Richmonders allowed for his passionate response. The passion shown in his defense reassured them that they could count on their white allies. Furthermore, Ruffner's response demonstrated that the creation of African American public schools had become firmly rooted in the state's definition of the body politic. Ruffner's defensive response, therefore, showed that the Department of Public Instruction saw African American education as a vital part of state citizenship and worthy of state resources as well as state protection.

While they had Ruffner's support, black Richmonders refused to allow their white allies to solely speak on their behalf. Through the press and racial uplift organizations, they responded to Dabney. John W. Cromwell responded on behalf of black Virginians against "a most dangerous warfare [that] is being made upon the free school system." Published in the *People's Advocate*, Cromwell's critique first addressed the use of school funds to pay the state's debt. He contended, "The first blow in this direction was the misappropriation of half a million of dollars of the public school funds by the authority of the State, to the payment of interest on the public debt." This decision by the "friends of the cause of free education" instigated Reverend Dabney's war on the public schools. He then reminded his readers that they had fought before against "a religious fanatic and lunatic" who had been enlisted to aid "the destruction of African American education." Cromwell implored black Virginians, urban and rural, to rally against such individuals.

He concluded, "It would be criminal in us to remain silent in the face these rant-ers. We propose to meet them boldly, and handle them fearlessly, because we feel that every consideration of duty and patriotism demands it of us." Through the pages of the *People's Advocate* and the Virginia Educational and Historical As-sociation, Cromwell and other black Richmonders mobilized African American citizens "all over the State, in cities, towns and villages," into immediate action.[47]

Public school students also entered the debate. As the criticism directly af-fected the quality of education received, students attending Richmond Colored Normal and High School deemed it necessary to comment. Two months after the publication of Dabney's original remarks, James Hugo Johnston made a com-pelling argument to his peers. "The professor says: *Public school education has given the masses a smattering of learning, which has been to them the opening of Pandora's box. It has launched them on an ocean which they are incompetent to navigate,*" Johnston informed his audience. "Every manufactory intoxicate their minds with the most licentious vagaries of opinions upon every funda-mental subject of politics and religion. They have only knowledge enough to run into danger." In clarifying Dabney's words, Johnston pondered that if "so much learning as the public schools give is a 'Pandora's box,' a fountain of evil," then "why doesn't the police put a stop to it?" But unlike Ruffner and Cromwell, Johnston went to the crux of the matter for students. Dabney's questioning of the public schools directly challenged the very education obtained by Johnston and his peers. It was their education, their intellectual advancement as well as their intellectual abilities that were being dismissed by the prominent theologian. Through gaining knowledge, according to Dabney's argument, Johnston and his public school comrades had been intoxicated. But for Johnston and his peers, they knew that the "Pandora's box" could not be closed regardless of the efforts of Rev. R. L. Dabney. For their intellectual corruption, Johnston, on behalf of his peers, offered words of forgiveness to their teachers and various educational partners, since "they did not mean us any harm."[48]

As evidenced by Johnston's address, students astutely recognized the conse-quences of Dabney's critique. They would have been the greatest losers if Dab-ney and other detractors successfully removed African American public educa-tion from city and state resources. As a result, they entered the debate rather than have their parents, community leaders, and white allies speak for them. However, they maintained faith in the educational partnerships forged by black Richmonders. They found reassurance when officials continued to appropriate between $49,000 and $53,000 per annum in addition to state and outside fund-

ing received. School officials remained committed to African American education despite the financial difficulties and attacks. Johnston, Cromwell, and others
could breathe a sigh of relief.[49]

However, Dabney's critique made public school funding one of the primary
issues debated in subsequent city elections. During the 1878 election, the *Dispatch* obtained each city councilman candidate's opinion of school funding with
the following question: "Are you in favor of maintaining the public schools in un-
impaired efficiency and would you vote necessary money therefore?" All of the
candidates pledged support of the schools. It would have been political suicide to
do otherwise. Some candidates, such as W. H. Haxall, promised the maintenance
of school funding while enacting fiscal responsibility and efficiency. Others, such
as J. Taylor Ellyson, gave their unequivocal support of the public schools and
promised to allocate any necessary funds that ensured their continuation.[50] Responses to these questions featured prominently in the *Dispatch* as well as in
African American newspapers, such as the *Virginia Star*. For the Jackson Ward
Republicans and other African American political groups, the issue of public
schools and school funding played a pivotal role in their candidate endorse-
ments. After Dabney's critique, city officials could not be elected without providing some comment on school funding. Since the fate of the public schools rested
on elected officials' fiscal policies, black Richmonders used the ballot to secure
the election of individuals who accepted equitable funding of their schools.[51]

The funding crisis never abated. Fiscal policies reached a turning point in
1878. School board officials enacted a mandatory 30 percent cut in teachers' salaries and delayed all projects. While school conditions deteriorated, this measure
allowed the schools to remain open. When promised appropriations failed to
materialize, cuts to teachers' salaries and project funding continued for the re-
mainder of the decade. Despite the school board's financial difficulties, African
American public schools weathered the storm as a result of the insistence of black
Richmonders and their white allies. While not perfect, the public schools never
closed because black Richmonders, even students, successfully argued that the
schools were their fundamental rights as citizens. As long as they could convince
individuals like William H. Ruffner and dismiss detractors, black Richmonders
achieved success.[52]

Although black Richmonders secured favorable white support of the public
schools, they still faced a major struggle for quality public schools. Rather than
mounting a unified campaign, black Richmonders remained divided, as the benefits of the public schools were not shared equally. As a result, individual neighborhood struggles often characterized the initial improvement campaigns before

coalescing into a broader, community-wide struggle. National, state, and city financial crises greatly assisted this transformation. Once unified, black Richmonders' activism, combined with the relationships with high-ranking white officials, permitted the survival of the schools while making some improvements to the school system's quality. In so doing, they also laid the foundation for the quality school campaigns in the next decade and would benefit from the fruits of that labor.

6   Rethinking Partners

*Black Mobilians' Struggle for Quality
Public Schools*

On July 19, 1870, white Mobilians celebrated the departure of the Freedmen's Bureau with discussions of its legacy for their city, state, and region. The *Mobile Daily Register* summed up the discussions with the following conclusion: "The Freedman's Bureau has finished its work, and passed into history. No institution was ever more bitterly opposed, and at the same time, more warmly defended. No act of legislature in the history of the world, has resulted in so much good, to so great a number, in so short a time, and at so little cost as that which gave existence to the 'Bureau of Refugees, Freedmen and Abandoned Lands.'" In focusing on the agency's educational legacy for black Mobilians, the unknown author hoped that "the Freedmen learned these lessons and learned them well, thousands of school houses, and the general law and order which prevail in the south, wherever the white law and order which prevail in the south, wherever the white Democratic Ku Klux do not disturb them, prove conclusively." While the Bureau's educational legacy left an indelible mark on white Mobilians, it was unclear for black Mobilians whether local school officials would continue to build on the educational progress achieved under the Freedmen's Schools.[1]

Like their Richmond counterparts, the first decade of public schools merely signaled a new phase in black Mobilians' struggle for education, freedom, and citizenship. They shifted their activism with the quality school campaigns, but for different reasons than did black Richmonders. Partisan politics would thrust black Mobilians into the quality campaigns. As new educational partners jockeyed for administrative control of the schools, the new political reality forced black Mobilians to look inward and reflect on their goals for the public schools. This introspection made them draw more on their internal networks, reevaluate old partnerships, and, whenever possible, rely less on their white educational partners for success. The quality campaigns, therefore, represented a fight for the very survival of the public schools for their children. They realized that quality public schools under the direction of African American and Creole teachers would prevent previous educational victories from becoming moot. Over the course of the decade they achieved nominal success. Despite experiencing more setbacks than success, black Mobilians never lost sight on their mission for education, freedom, and citizenship. Their struggle now entailed making the public schools into enduring institutions, sustaining African American citizenship through education, and fostering strategic partnerships inside and outside the classroom in order to weather the political and racial storm. Indeed, the quality school campaigns represented a community struggle for education, freedom, and citizenship.

Without the Freedmen's Bureau to serve as a mediator, power struggles among school officials escalated by the start of the 1870–1871 academic year. Residual effects of the dual school board debate dominated school affairs. George L. Putnam remained in his position as the superintendent of schools for Mobile city and the surrounding county. Highly divided, school commissioners viewed the one another's actions as a personal and political affront. James M. Lomery and Charles A. Woodward tried to mediate between the members, but their efforts proved futile. Democrats and conservatives quickly joined forces in targeting the actions of George L. Putnam and other more radical members in order to force their removal. By November 1870, politics prevented the school board from effectively administrating the Mobile public schools.[2]

State officials again attempted mediation. At the urging of the Alabama state superintendent of public instruction, the legislature intervened. Approved in November 1870, the body enacted legislation with three components. First, it reaffirmed Putnam's position as superintendent of public schools. Second, it required new elections for the superintendent of schools and school commissioners to be held in March 1871. This election mandate specifically addressed the claims made by several school commissioners regarding Putnam's legitimacy as superintendent. State officials concluded that elections would legitimate the school board by providing school officials who had been duly elected by the people. Third, it also designated the superintendent of education as the only individual who could withdraw monies from the state education fund. With this legislative act, the state superintendent of public instruction and the Alabama legislature sought a resolution to another crisis.[3]

State intervention provided disgruntled school commissioners with an unexpected boon. Intervention exposed Putnam's ineffectiveness as an administrator because he could not resolve internal problems. In December 1870 they capitalized on the situation by staging a bloodless coup d'état. They convinced Joseph Hodgson, state superintendent of public instruction, to suspend George L. Putnam and to appoint Maj. W. T. Walthall as interim superintendent until the March 1871 elections. Putnam responded to his suspension with a lawsuit against the interim superintendent. Ultimately, the prolonged court battle forced Walthall's resignation, but not Putnam's return. When the city, county, and state judiciaries questioned the legality of Putnam's suspension, Hodgson officially removed Putnam on the basis of "malfeasance in office." He appointed John R. Tompkins as the new interim superintendent and insisted that elections continue as scheduled.[4]

Most white Mobilians openly acknowledged their support of the coup. On Christmas Day 1870 the *Mobile Daily Register* congratulated the school board for the "change which has at last been effected to their great relief." The newspaper hoped that Putnam's removal would "be the inauguration of a new era in our school system." The article concluded with encouraging words pertaining to the upcoming school board election: "Now, the only battle to be fought in March next will be simply a fair, and we hope, courteous contest between friends of the old and new systems." Similarly, letters to the editor praised the coup and the events precipitated by Putnam's replacement. One published letter encouraged students, white and black, to force Putnam out of the schools if he returned to office. In conclusion, the author praised the present board for doing its "duty to the county . . . [in the defense of the citizens'] sacred rights." Other letters to the editor weighed in on the legal proceedings that could permit Putnam's return. Throughout, they expressed frustration at the legal system for issuing an injunction that permitted teachers to go unpaid and impeded the board from moving forward. This overwhelming support effectively silenced individuals who may have opposed the board's actions.[5]

Harnessing white Mobilians' support, Democrats and Conservatives continued their alliance during the campaign. As in the 1868 state constitution ratification debate, articles, editorials, letters to the editor, and notices flooded the *Mobile Daily Register*. Evoking white fears of "Negro Rule," newspaper editors and strategists in the Democratic–Conservative Party employed the proven race-baiting strategy in order to eliminate white apathy in the school board electoral campaign. For instance, "This Day's Election" informed potential white voters that Putnam had "humbugged" black Mobilians. The author argued, "The lamentable truth is that a Yankee–carpetbagger can stuff any nonsense and absurdity into their heads, while they will not believe an oath of the most respectable white citizen of the community." By allowing themselves to be persuaded by "nonsense and absurdity," as the author suggested, black Mobilians lacked the intellectual facilities to make decisions pertaining to school board politics. Since Putnam had the support of the majority of black Mobile voters, the author concluded that only white voters could resolve the situation. The author implored readers to "turn them from the field with the solid arguments of ballots. Turn out and do it, men of Mobile." If not, he warned that "bitter regret and remorse will follow your neglect." This warning forced white Mobilians to take a stand politically on the school board issue as they had previously done with ratification. Only E. R. Dickson, Putnam's challenger, and the Democrat–Conservative ticket could redeem the schools.[6]

These polarizing political events catapulted black Mobilians into the quality campaign. The campaign made the community increasingly aware of the need for direct representation on the school board. They first turned to a cadre of local African American politicos, but they suffered a major setback during the campaign: in February 1871 Lawrence S. Berry committed suicide. The ardent Republican had been a crucial ally for the community since emancipation in 1863 and African American enfranchisement in 1867. As an alderman under Mayor Harrington's administration, Berry "distinguished himself as an advocate for aggressive measures to benefit black constituents, especially poorer ones." Moreover, he fully supported George Putnam on the issue of free public schools. His suicide made many black Mobilians rally behind the People's Free School ticket. This political coalition nominated Putnam for the superintendent of schools and nine candidates for school commissioners. These candidates canvassed the black Mobile community, specifically through mass political meetings held in the local churches. To the dismay of the editors of the *Mobile Daily Register*, Democrats, and conservatives, these meetings, held in the "hot-houses for political incendiarism and plots against the welfare of society in the matter of judicious and honest suffrage," resulted in a large black Mobilian turnout on Election Day.[7]

Ultimately, the Democrat–Conservative coalition ticket won the superintendent of education position and the majority of school commissioner positions. However, this victory was not a landslide. A postelection *Mobile Daily Register* editorial remarked, "The wiley Putnam, taking advantage of it, and counting also on absentees among the fireman, ran a muck by way of a surprise which came near being successful." The editorialist rhetorically asked, "Will the white people of this county never learn not to forget that there is a dangerous inflammable element of black suffrage here that is ever on the alert for mischief, that they cannot safely ignore, and that needs always to be vigilantly watched." Indeed, black Mobilians' participation resulted in the addition of three school board members who promised their allegiance to the black community. They achieved some representation amid the political upheaval.[8]

As a result of the contentious election, some black Mobilians feared retribution from the new school board. They believed that the board would enact policies resulting in a loss of school funding, and/or the closure of the African American public schools. These fears worried the editors of the *Mobile Daily Register*, the organ for the Democratic and Conservative Parties who now dominated the school board. Shortly after the election, the editors of the *Mobile Daily Register* published an editorial as a means of calming their fears.

Titled "The Colored Public Schools," the editorial addressed the charges leveled at the new school board by several black Mobilians and their white allies. "The colored people have had their minds stuffed with many false and injurious ideas by Putnam and others, in regard to the treatment they would receive at the hands of the new Superintendent and School Commissioners," the editorial opened. In response to the "false and injurious ideas," the editorialist recommended that parents and community leaders meet and fully discuss their concerns with the new superintendent and school commissioners. The editorialist concluded that officers, as elected officials, considered "the proper care of colored children" to be "as much a duty imposed upon them, and one that they have as much at heart, as the education of white children." For the editorialist, proper care entailed the allocation of school funds, as white and black taxpayers equally contributed to the school fund. Black Mobilians' fears were misguided. The editorialist reasoned, "If the colored people suppose the Democratic and Conservative party, which now holds sway in Alabama, desires to keep the black people in ignorance, they are greatly mistaken." Hence black Mobilians had nothing to fear.[9]

Instead, the editorialist encouraged the community's use of the schools. This would allow black Mobilians to draw their own conclusions rather than listening to individuals like Putnam. If they did, they would not be "made the dupes and instruments of designing strangers, who come here for the express purpose of using them as pawns to play their game of plunder and office-seeking." The editorialist concluded by advising them "to look into the matter and judge for themselves. So far from finding obstacles and enmity, they will find that they have only kind, considerate and well-wishing friends for their improvement, not only in the school board, but in the community at large." As suggested by the editorialist, the new school board and the broader white community pledged to fill the roles held by George L. Putnam and the previous school board.[10]

Despite this editorial, black Mobilians quickly realized that the majority of white Mobilians endorsed African American public schools solely out of a sense of obligation. Unlike in Richmond, major newspaper editors limited their recognition of the African American public schools. In the *Mobile Daily Register*, "our schools" referred only to the white public schools, as evidenced by its coverage of the schools' closing exercises. Direct mention of the African American public schools occurred primarily during the announcement of teachers elected for employment. Obligation rather than a true commitment to African American education guided most white Mobilians' actions. In short, African American public schools never reached the level of "our schools" and remained on the periphery.[11]

The discourse surrounding the March 1871 school board election even embroiled students. Motivated by lingering doubts over the public schools, the youths ridiculed the Decoration Day rituals celebrating local Confederate veterans. According to Maria Waterbury, a white teacher at Emerson Institute, the children taunted the white women decorating the graves of Confederate soldiers in a nearby cemetery with a loud rendition of "John Brown's Body" from the safety of the schoolyard. After hearing the children sing, "John Brown's body lies moldering in the grave / But his soul is marching on," she immediately ended recess. "Over a hundred of them," she recounted, marched "reluctantly into the house, and to their seats." She then delivered a stern lecture regarding the importance of respecting "the feelings of people, when they go to the graves of friends; that this school is trying to work by the golden rule." She felt that the young scholars had sunk to a level of immaturity shown by the adults in dealing with racial politics. Afterward, she noted that a group of ten or twelve boys had put away the rocks they had planned to throw at the Decoration Day processional while growling the word "Rebs." With her rebuke, Waterbury successfully prevented a "small rebellion." Unlike in other racially motivated fights, these youths had the benefit of a levelheaded and caring schoolteacher. Her strong rebuke helped to diffuse the post–school board election climate within the school.[12]

This incident revealed the intersections between politics and education. Broader politics surrounding the school often spilled into the classroom. As a microcosm of the society, children attempted to resolve the sociopolitical tensions present in their environment. When words proved inadequate, the children used their fists and projectiles. The schools acted as important sites for negotiating broader questions pertaining to race and politics. Public schoolteachers, such as Waterbury, proved essential in securing better political and racial relations beyond the classroom.

Black Mobilians' political participation did not end with the failed March 1871 elections. They continued endorsing candidates, primarily Republican, at the national, state, and local levels. As extensively discussed by historian Michael

Fitzgerald, black Mobilians' electoral participation remained a major influence in the city's politics over the course of the decade. Political meetings occurred throughout the city's churches, including Emerson Institute's chapel. On Election Day, they showed that support en masse often protected voters from intimidation and bribery. The community's endorsement, protection, and votes ensured that black Mobilians had a voice in the affairs shaping their lives. From observing the community's political engagement, school-age children understood the importance of electoral politics as it affected their ability to obtain an education. Following the 1872 presidential election, Waterbury recalled, "The whole school rose and sang the doxology." From adults to children, black Mobilians remained steadfast in their use of electoral politics as a strategy for quality schools. While not always fruitful, electoral participation gave them a voice.[13]

Shortly after the March 1871 election campaign, the community suffered another major loss with the passing of John Carraway. Less than two months after Berry's suicide, Carraway's death dealt another blow. Carraway was Mobile's "most distinguished politician," according to historian Michael Fitzgerald, "having served in the constitutional convention, the legislature, and as a city councilman." The death of two senior African American politicians posed unexpected challenges to the community's efforts.[14]

As a result, black Mobilians actively sought their replacement from within. In 1872 they endorsed W. Irving Squire for the 1873 school board elections. Squire and his wife conducted a "large and flourishing" night school in the city. Squire also formerly served as a city engineer under the Harrington administration. They viewed his commitment toward education and political experience as a reason to endorse his nomination. Riding high from the 1872 presidential and local elections, Squire noted the community's optimism for potentially defeating the Democratic–Conservative coalition in the upcoming elections in a letter to E. M. Cravath. He wrote: "In the last election we beat the Democrats by nearly five thousand majority. We expect to [regain] our County Schools Superintendent." Squire then commented on the black Mobilians' endorsement of him and his reluctant acceptance of it. "I will accept the nomination," Squire wrote, but he preferred that they "find anyone else to take it, who is competent and our friend." Squire's hesitation showed the reluctance shared by other African American educators in entering the political arena. For Squire and others, competence in the classroom did not necessarily equate to competency in the administration of the public school system. Squire, though, still wanted to support the community who afforded him with a "comfortable position." This motivated his acceptance. However, he acknowledged his own weakness and preferred that someone else ran. Consequently, black Mobilians had many difficulties finding suitable school board contenders. However, this did not stop their efforts to secure a voice on the school board.[15]

Black Mobilians' electoral participation yielded few political gains. Democrats, in their coalition with conservatives, continued to achieve electoral success by capitalizing on the lessons of the March 1871 school board elections in 1873, 1875, and 1877. A Democrats coalition held the county superintendent position and the majority of school board positions. By 1877 the Democrat–Conservative coalition held firm control over not only the school board but city politics as well. Mobile had been redeemed. Recognizing the political shift, black Mobilians adapted their politics in order to maintain a political voice.[16]

Some black Mobilians even considered switching political parties as a strategy for securing a voice in shaping political affairs. In May 1877 Rev. E. D. Taylor, Jackson Clay, James Allen, George Miller, and Samuel Jones petitioned the mayor, board of alderman, and city council. These men had been staunch Republicans and were quite active in the black Mobilian community's political mobilization since 1867. Throughout the petition, these former Republicans unabashedly employed the racial rhetoric of the Democratic Party. "The undersigned citizens representing the colored element of the City of Mobile respectfully suggest your honors consideration," the petition opened, "that prior to all the elections held in the City of Mobile for the different offices, they have been led into wrongs by unprincipled and unscroupulous men whose guize have been spacious and showy, but their aim have proved to be plunder." With this opening, the men appealed directly to the white supremacist notions undergirding the Democrats' return to political power. They admitted to being duped by unprincipled and unscrupulous men, like Putnam. As a result, the petitioners concluded in the opening that "they have left us as enemies to the people that have ever been our friends immemorial, and have ever been the first to favor us in all troubles and it is intelligent for us to confess the same." Thus their political allegiance to the Republican Party and white northerners made them the political "enemies" of local elites. According to the opening, they should have been aligned with local southern elites and the Democratic Party. They now humbled themselves to the ruling elite.[17]

Petitioners discussed the negative outcomes of their political decisions in the next section. Therein, they specifically addressed the detrimental effects of their community's political "infidelity." They argued, "Notwithstanding our infidelity in all past elections and our actions in fighting politically against those who have ever been at service to our relief when in trouble," had placed the community "in a despairing attitude among those who can only favor us." The petitioners recognized that these wrong political choices resulted in poor conditions in the community and a dearth of political friends to alleviate their desperation. They requested relief from the mayor, board of alderman, and common council. Desired relief, according to the petitioners, entailed patronage appointments: "Your petitioners would ask or pray that you would give them a recognition in the giving out of the public spoils . . . [and] that you give our petition your most careful and serious consideration." The petitioners then presented the mayor, board of alderman, and city council with the names of seven individuals for corporation positions and ten individuals for positions in the police department. In adopting a submissive stance, black Mobilians, as represented by the petitioners, desired a real political voice in influencing the decisions affecting their community. In this instance, the mayor, board of alderman, and common council did not act on their suggestions. The political entities eventually tabled the petition. The petition also led to harsh criticism from the local newspapers. However, black Mobilians' acknowledgment of their "infidelity" showed the lengths in which they would go to achieve results.[18]

While petitioners only asked for noneducational positions, black Mobilians hoped that the petition's success would result in meaningful change in school board administration. This is evident in the fact that Rev. E. D. Taylor acted as the chairman of the petitioners. Taylor was not a stranger to the African American public schools. His church housed a public school. He regularly spoke at school functions such as picnics, graduations, and dedication ceremonies of new schools. Taylor's participation and the petition itself reflected the black Mobilians' political savvy. They firmly understood the shifting political currents within Mobile. They adopted any strategies that permitted them to have a voice in shaping political affairs. They also understood that it was necessary to embrace the new political regime. Positions of patronage and electoral success would only improve the schools and the overall community. Hence Taylor's participation reflected black Mobilians' reading of the political climate wrought by Redemption.[19]

Furthermore, black Mobilians embraced the advice given in the April 1871 *Mobile Daily Register* editorial by holding elected school officials accountable. They made their opinions known to the school board primarily through petitions. Since 1867, petitioning had been a tactic employed by the community in dealing with the school board. By 1871, black Mobilians had honed it into an art form. First, they held special mass meetings to discuss the problem at hand. From these meetings, they developed a course of action, which often entailed the creation of a petition committee. The designated committee would then create a petition for the community's approval. In the same meeting or another meeting, the community voiced any concerns regarding the proposed petition before voting on it. After the community approved the petition, it would be sent to the appropriate parties and signees would be listed as "undersigned representatives" of the black Mobilian community. Rev. E. D. Taylor regularly spearheaded petitions ranging from repairs to the construction of new schools to the hiring of teachers. Through petitioning, black Mobilians held elected officials accountable and challenged their hegemonic control. Their scrutiny, in the form of the petitions, made school board officials aware of their decisions pertaining to the African American public schools. If they made an unpopular decision, black Mobilians would definitely alert them of it. As a result, petitioning remained an important strategy in assuring that black Mobilians had a voice in school board affairs.[20]

Educational accessibility, such as school accommodations and night schools, represented another concern addressed by the quality campaigns. Demands for educational access centered on several realities. The system lacked a sufficient number of schools to accommodate the city's African American school-age population. The school census reported 10,099 African American school-age children during the 1870–1871 academic year. However, actual enrollment was much lower. During the 1870–1871 academic year, only 2,560 African Americans enrolled in the schools, with an average attendance of 1,930. As the numbers suggest, existing schools simply could not handle the population as reported by the school census. Administrators often turned away students due to the lack of suitable accommodations.[21]

Moreover, school facilities were either rented or in disrepair. During the 1870–1871 academic year, the county rented six buildings for the purpose of African American education. The number reduced to five during the following academic year. Putnam's removal resulted in the removal of Emerson Institute as a public school. The majority of the remaining schools were either "totally unfit for school purposes," or "not large enough" to accommodate the number of students desiring a public school education. Instead of constructing schools, the school board maintained a policy of renting African American churches. Dickson noted this practice in his report to the state superintendent of public instruction: "The colored people's Churches being generally the most suitable places for their schools, have been procured, so far as practicable, for the purposes of instruction. In some instances for repairs, in others free of rent." Though the schools resided primarily within the African American church system, the lack of permanent school structures bothered parents and community leaders. They found the poor school conditions "demoralizing." As a result, parents and community leaders, according to Waterbury, believed that the scholars were "losing what the A.M.A.

have taught them." On this concern, African Americans found support from the superintendent. Dickson acknowledged that the "colored schools have no school buildings as such, and considering the cost of erecting such buildings." While he recognized the need for permanent structures, Dickson understood that "it will require time to procure [them]." But it was uncertain how long the community would have to wait for better school accommodations.[22]

The system also lacked flexibility in terms of school offerings. The initial public school system did not include night schools or Sabbath schools. Under the Freedmen's School system, these alternative day school programs allowed for the attendance of nontraditional students. Mobile had state approval for offering night schools for "persons over the age of twenty-one" but chose not to create them. Furthermore, state law restricted any implemented programs to "persons over the age of twenty-one." Designed for adult education, this provision still excluded a large portion of school-age children unable to attend the public schools even were it adopted. The lack of flexible course offerings and restrictive state laws left little choice for individuals such as Spencer Snell.[23]

Work prevented Spencer Snell from attending the day schools. Instead, between 1869 and 1873 he attended private night schools operated by local black Mobilians. In a May 1889 *American Missionary* article the future minister recalled his plight to obtain an education: "My first lessons from books I received in night school. At this time I was employed as [a] dining room servant by a family in Mobile. I did my work during the day, taking a little time here and there for study as best I could, and went to school at night." His unconventional educational path led to better wages: "I suppose they considered my services more and more valuable as I became more enlightened, for, during the four years, my wages increased from $3.50 to $10 per month." Snell used the increase in his earnings for furthering his education. While the school's expense caused some personal economic hardship, Snell considered the payment a great investment in which he "would have paid five dollars had it been required." Whereas Snell overcame the financial burden posed by the lack of public night schools, others were not as fortunate.[24]

The public schools also proved less accommodating to irregular attendance than under the Freedmen's School system. Administrators enforced a culture that punished sporadic attendance and shifting between schools during an academic year. In his first report as superintendent of education, Dickson bitterly complained about the board's efforts at maintaining consistent school enrollment. He placed the blame solely on the integration of African American schoolhouses: "The trouble caused by changing schools is very much enhanced since the colored children have been a part of the public schools." In order to rectify this problem, he explained, "Steps were immediately taken to prevent pupils from changing schools without the written permission by the Superintendent. This for a while seemed to be quite sufficient, but means were soon discovered by which the order amounted to nothing." Students attempted to bypass the new measures by even assuming a new name in order to enter another school. However, "means have been found by which this trick is exposed," Dickson reported. "The teacher asks the school what that boy's name was before he came, and the newcomer generally finds some one ready to expose him." For Dickson, consistent attendance at one school, rather than several, permitted academic success. "We may by keeping the colored children at one school during a term, hope to give them proper instruction," Dickson concluded, "and make their time at school a source of profit and culture, which certainly was impossible under former regulations."[25]

Dickson's attendance difficulties revealed a shift in expectations and school culture between the Freedmen's Schools and the public schools. Under the former system, students transferred between schools for a variety of reasons. In this instance, it is unclear why the youth left the school and assumed a new identity for entry into another school. He may not have liked the school's instructor. The new school may have been more convenient to his home and/or employment. It is evident, though, that Dickson's desire for a strict school culture greatly differed from that of the students and parents. For Dickson, the "trouble of changing schools" was a new challenge for his administration of the city schools. For some students, the inability to change schools at will and the stricter attendance policies represented new challenges to their educational choice and access to education.[26]

Dickson's difficulties also resulted from the imposition of a new grade classification system and curriculum. Under the new classification in public schools, Dickson found African American students lacking. He noted in his 1871 report, "The schedule of studies has been changed in a great measure for colored pupils. I found pupils in the colored schools studying geography and grammar who could not write at all." By the end of the academic year Dickson saw success: "Now every pupil, as soon as he can read simple sentences, begins to learn writing." However, parents, as evidenced by Maria Waterbury's correspondence with E. M. Cravath, wanted their children instructed in courses not offered by the schools, such as higher mathematics, music, art, and Latin. These courses were only available in the private school system.[27]

Poor school conditions motivated black Mobilians' support of local private schools. Private schools offered better conditions than did the public schools, in terms of accommodations, curriculum, and instructors. M. H. Leatherman cited the poor quality of the public schools for her decision to send her daughter to private schools. In a letter to the American Missionary Association, she noted, "There are a great many free schools about the city but as they do not amount to much, the people do not care to send their children, so long as there is any alternative." Withdrawal from public schools gave parents, like Leatherman, more control over school conditions. Student enrollment at Emerson Institute and other private schools increased during the decade. Tuition costs, though, prevented many from utilizing this option.[28]

Emerson Institute served as a viable alternative to the public schools. Its overall conditions far surpassed those of the Mobile public schools. Enrolled students noted the difference in the quality of instruction. Maria Waterbury reported in a letter to E. M. Cravath, "One scholar the first who came to the inst. came from the best free school in the place said she had but one spelling lesson there in two weeks." The irregularity in which spelling lessons occurred suggests an overcrowded schoolroom and a high student-to-teacher ratio. Emerson Institute provided transfer students with an education not available in the public schools.[29]

Affordability also made Emerson Institute a suitable alternative to most private schools. Administrators purposely kept the tuition costs low in order to ensure a "large and prosperous" school. While some parents objected to the nominal tuition costs, school administrators found that parents preferred "a pay school." The school expanded its program to include additional day and night classes in order to accommodate the large number of students seeking admission. As a result, enrollment increased to 125 in November 1873, 167 in April 1874, and 210 in January 1876. Based on these numbers, parents found Emerson Institute as their best alternative to the poor public schools.[30]

Emerson Institute's night school program addressed the needs of black Mobilians who were unable to attend the day schools. W. Irving Squire and his wife initiated the school's program in the winter of 1872–73. They appealed directly to organizational aims regarding African American education by mentioning the targeted population of the night school—children unable to attend the public schools. He concluded, "By complying with my request you will secure school facilities for many who are now deprived of them." American Missionary Association executives approved the proposition. Squire's night school relocated to Emerson Institute. By 1877 the night school program was a major feature of course offerings. Educational accessibility and school prestige attracted the untraditional students to the school. As a result, African American parents and children continued supporting the program, as it was the best available option to them.[31]

Students, like Spencer Snell, flocked to Emerson Institute's night school. Snell recalled how he learned about Emerson Institute and its night program. "While I was a student in one of these night schools, I chanced one day to see a newspaper which a colored man who knew me had thrown into the yard for me," Snell remembered. Happanstance resulted in Snell's discovery of the program. He recalled, "In this paper I read an article telling about Emerson Institute, a school of the American Missionary Association, and the commencement exercises soon to occur there. The school had been in Mobile for several years, but I had heard not of it till now." Upon discovering the school's existence, Snell actively prepared for his entry into Emerson during the spring 1874 term. He proclaimed his thanks to the unknown deliveryman, because he was "quite a different man to-day from what I would have been but for reading that article." Indeed, the night school program changed his life. He wrote, "Precious to me is the memory of those days during which I took tuition in the night-school, where the key was put into my hand and the door of knowledge was opened to me." The night school system, whether at private schools operated by black Mobilians or Emerson Institute, benefited a population unaddressed by the existing public schools. Without the initiative of black Mobilians and their educational partners, Snell and other individuals may not have received an education.[32]

For the majority of parents with children in the public schools, the private school system was not an option. These parents strongly objected to paying tuition for their children's education, as their taxes funded the public schools. Some viewed private schools as "swindling humbugs." Parents could either improve the quality of schools and educational opportunities available, or not send their children to the public schools. Since the latter countered directly with black Mobilians' aim to become an educated people, they chose the former. Student withdrawal and the thriving private school system gave these parents ammunition in their struggle. Specifically, they pressured the school board to look for better accommodations and often cited withdrawal for the private schools as evidence. They understood that the growth of the private school system reflected poorly on officials' ability to provide them with public schools. Parents argued that students would not have left the public schools had school conditions been better. With quality school accommodations, parents reasoned that the public schools would thrive.[33]

School board officials agreed. Prior to the start of the 1872–1873 academic year, they sought to improve school accommodations for African American children. In August 1872 Dickson approached American Missionary Association executives in order to secure Emerson Institute as a public school and renew their previous relationship. Dickson and the school board first considered renting the property, as was done under Putnam's administration. Community pressure, though, made the school board reverse its original plan. In September 1872 Dickson offered to purchase Emerson Institute instead of renting the property. He offered "$15,000 in five annual installments without interest" for the property, but the American Missionary Association refused. While continuing their efforts to negotiate a sale, school commissioners rented school accommodations. They also expanded the number of schools whenever funding became available. Although newly established schools were consolidated with older schools under intense financial difficulties, the school board made real attempts to address black Mobilians' demands for school accommodations. Their efforts, though, neither staved off student withdrawal nor ended the complaints over the poor conditions. School officials remained under pressure to secure suitable school facilities.[34]

The school accommodation campaign produced modest gains. Black Mobilians achieved greater educational access with additional public schools and slightly improved school accommodations. Parents and community leaders effectively used petitions, student withdrawal, and community support of the private schools as strategies. However, a large percentage of the population reported in the school census remained uneducated. In 1879, 1,793 out of 9,836 school-age children enrolled in the African American public schools. Private school enrollment accounted for a small percentage of those not attending the public schools. Black Mobilians recognized the discrepancy between the school census population and actual enrollment. They realized that obtaining adequate school accommodations remained at the heart of the problem and hoped that continued activism would lessen this discrepancy.[35]

Black Mobilians made the employment of African American public school-teachers an early objective of the quality campaigns. They found the city's hiring practices appalling. Even though the Board of School Commissioners claimed in April 1871 that it considered white, Creole of color, and black applicants equally, it rarely hired black and Creole of color teachers. With the exception of Sara Stanley Woodward, black and Creole of color Mobilians found employment as assistant teachers, aides, or supernumeraries in the schools and not in the capacity of principal instructor. Often mistaken as white, Sara Stanley Woodward found employment as the principal of the St. Louis School from 1871 to 1874. This confusion permitted her from sharing the fate of other nonwhite educators.[36]

Instead of African American teachers, parents and children often endured un-sympathetic white public schoolteachers such as Maria Wilhelm. Wilhelm had served as the principal teacher in the Creole School for two years without complaint. When the board gave her an appointment as a "Negro School Teacher" in October 1874, she declined "that to which I have been appointed, knowing that I have neither the qualifications [nor] disposition to fit me for a Negro School Teacher." Although she did not have another job, Wilhelm wanted a position that was more suitable to her "qualifications and disposition." Dickson granted her a transfer from the "Negro School" to the Creole School during the 1874–1875 academic year and appointed Miss M. F. Dubroca, a Creole of color, as her assistant. Wilhelm found this arrangement acceptable as she completed the year at the Creole School. The following year, Wilhelm received a position outside the African American and Creole schools. As evidenced in her letter to Dickson, Wilhelm regarded her appointment as a "Negro School Teacher" as subpar. She could tolerate a position in the Creole School, but a position in the African American public school proved too much for her. Other white teachers shared Wilhelm's disdain. They regarded an appointment as a "Negro School Teacher" to be the worst possible position in the public school system.[37]

Students did poorly under Wilhelm and similar teachers. While students made some progress in their annual examinations, Dickson noted the difficulties of the white teachers in their instruction of African American students. "The colored children of primary grades, are most easily taught orally than by requiring them to study set lessons," Dickson reported. This difficulty perplexed Dickson as well as white educators in the African American schools. He wrote, "They take an interest in repeating what they learn, and will learn very readily in this way, when it is very difficult to induce the same pupils to study a set task." It is evident that Dickson and the white educators viewed the students' oral learning as contrary to common school pedagogy, which demanded a silent curriculum and monitorial system in shaping students into responsible adults. When the teachers forced another teaching method onto the children, such as inducing students to study a set task, they encountered problems. Instead of adapting their teaching methods, they remained inflexible. Consequently, students were not advancing scholastically as previously done under the Freedmen's Schools.[38]

Parents discerned the effects of the lack of African American teachers on their children's scholastic progress. Teachers like Wilhelm impeded academic achievement. Parents wanted control over the quality of teachers, as it affected their child's academic success. If they could not have African American teachers, they wanted teachers who were sympathetic to their students' development as citizens. In short, parents wanted teachers like Maria L. Waterbury.[39] She utilized a holistic approach in her teaching. She was not merely instructing students in reading, writing, and arithmetic but also developing them into useful citizens. She often used classroom and schoolyard incidents as teaching moments. In diffusing community problems that spilled into the classroom, Waterbury and other teachers remade their charges into productive citizens. In this environment, students thrived.[40]

In 1871, black Mobilians launched their campaign for African American teachers for the African American public schools. One strategy involved having educated members of their community apply directly to the Board of School Commissioners. The community encouraged Alice and Mattie Summerville, daughters of James A. Summerville, to apply. These women had been regularly featured in the *Nationalist* for their scholastic achievement under the Freedmen's School system. Their father's reputation as a successful businessman also made them appealing candidates. On paper, the Summerville sisters, along with Mary E. Weeman, Leanna Saxon, Laura A. Branch, and Miss E. J. Robertson, met the stringent state teaching requirements and were suitable candidates. Coupled with submitting qualified candidates, parents and community leaders sent petitions to the Board of School Commissioners.[41]

These strategies had limited success. Alice Summerville received a teacher appointment at the Lawrence and Augusta Streets School. Other candidates were not as fortunate. School commissioners either rejected the qualified candidates or hired them as assistant teachers, aides, or supernumeraries. For instance, Saxon, Branch, and Mattie Summerville received assistant appointments while Weeman and Robertson received supernumerary appointments. According to the meeting minutes, the Board of School Commissioners stated that it considered all applicants equally and based its decision on the applicants' meeting the stringent Alabama qualifications, prior teaching experience, and letters of recommendation. In response to complaints received, the school commissioners argued that they found that the white candidates often proved more qualified than the nonwhite applicants. Despite its failure, Rev. E. D. Taylor and other community leaders continued this course of action.[42]

The teacher campaign raised alarm among school officials. Dickson regularly defended the schools' predominantly white teaching staffs. He often centered his argument on the low rate of absenteeism. In 1875 Dickson reported that in "the higher grades absentees are few. I have noticed that, even on stormy, rain and cold days, in a room of over 200 girls, there were not five absent." He attributed this low rate directly to the quality of the predominantly white teaching staff.

Dickson reasoned, "Such regularity and attention shows a very high appreciation of these schools by parents and faithful work on the part of teachers." Dickson's use of low absenteeism was a plausible argument. If the teachers lacked the trust of students and parents, absenteeism would have been higher.[43]

However, the focus on low absenteeism addressed neither black Mobilians' complaints nor those of the parents who withdrew their children from the public schools due to the inferior quality of teachers. This focus also ignored complaints received from Maria J. Wilhelm and other teachers about teaching in the African American public schools. Black Mobilians' efforts placed the Board of School Commissioners on the defensive. Thus the teacher campaign forced school officials to continually assess and reconsider their decisions pertaining to the African American public schools. Their hegemony never went unchallenged.

Black Mobilians' reform efforts also prompted responses from several white Mobilians. Using the local press, they defended school commissioners and the white teachers placed in the African American public schools. In 1873 the *Mobile Daily Tribune* addressed the teachers' campaign. By focusing on public school attendance by African Americans, the editorialist argued, "A fact which speaks volumes for the progressive spirit of the black man and his determination to prepare himself for the higher duties of citizenship, is that the percentage of school attendance among the colored children is relatively larger than among the whites." For evidence, the editorialist used the schools' enrollment statistics: "The reports for November show an enrollment of nearly 1100 colored and about 1900 white pupils, the total white population by recent estimate being double that of the colored." This evidence undercut the activists' objectives. If the teachers were so bad, then why did the parents of the nearly 1,100 students send their children to the Mobile public schools? The editorialist concluded that the quality teachers hired under Dickson's administration contributed to this high percentage of school attendance. The editorialist reasoned that these parents recognized the quality of the "carefully selected" teachers and the application of the same standards for "scholastic attainments" and "experimental knowledge of teaching being applied to them as to teachers for white schools"—the benefits of which resulted in their continued patronage of the schools. Thus Redemption ensured quality public schools by employing "competent and efficient teachers."[44]

Indeed, the editorialist presented a persuasive argument. Parents still sent their children to the public schools. The predominant white teaching staff never resulted in high absenteeism among the enrolled students. This superficial assessment, though, never considered why parents would continue sending their children to the public schools. It purposely ignores the existence of the thriving private school system. It also ignores the fact that parents supported the schools in order to fulfill a communal desire to become an educated people. Abstaining from the public schools may not have been a choice. Hence continued patronage more reflected the lack of choice in educational options available than the quality of teachers.[45]

Unconvinced, parents, ministers, and other black Mobilians persevered by adopting another strategy. As noted in an earlier chapter, they appealed to and convinced the American Missionary Association executives to implement a formal normal program that met Alabama teaching standards. Emerson Normal emerged from this partnership. The school graduated its first students in 1876. Upon the graduation of William A. Caldwell, Artemesia Europe, and Mary Europe, parents and community leaders encouraged their application for teaching positions. Rev. E. D. Taylor and others felt confident that the Board of School Commissioners would not reject these candidates. Their efforts failed. None of the Emerson Normal graduates received teaching positions during the 1876–1877 academic year.[46]

Frustrated, Rev. Taylor, Rev. Albert F. Owen, and several parents with children in the public schools demanded a change in the school board's hiring practices. In September 1878 the board thoroughly discussed another petition received. On behalf of parents and the entire community, Rev. Taylor and petition committee members demanded that the board appoint African American teachers in existing African American public schools and whenever new schools were established. Swayed by their petition and the existence of Emerson Normal, the school board amended its policy. School commissioners promised that "the Claims of Colored applicants . . . will receive consideration and when equally competent in Scholarship and ability to govern will have the preference in selection." During the 1878–1879 academic year the school board granted William A. Caldwell an appointment as the principal of the Good Hope School.[47]

Though Caldwell's hiring represented a victory, black Mobilians and their allies remained dissatisfied. African Americans and Creoles composed a small percentage of the teachers employed in the public schools. They desired an end of the board's hiring of white teachers in the African American public schools. Emerson Normal and other regional normal programs had created a corps of African American teachers, which made such hiring practices unnecessary. Therefore, they would continue to fight for African American public schoolteachers until all positions were filled either by an African American or by a Creole of color educator into the next decade.

Funding represented a final aspect of the quality campaigns. As in Richmond, funding was essential to the success of public schools. Without it, school buildings could not be built, repaired, or outfitted with proper school apparatus. Funding also underpinned the teacher's campaign, as employment secured the economic livelihoods for some community members. Black Mobilians recognized the importance of adequately funding the schools. However, they also understood that they had little control over this issue. The Board of School Commissioners and the broader community concurred. Public schools were expensive. Yet, all agreed that public schools were necessary for Mobile's citizens, regardless of race, class, gender, and/or former servitude.

Events during the 1870–1871 academic year impeded Mobile's ability to adequately fund the public schools. At the start of the decade, Mobile suffered from a lack of school funds but was able to sustain the public schools with the assistance of the Peabody Education Fund and the American Missionary Association. However, the dual school board debate, Putnam's ousting, and the March 1871 school election caused the Peabody Education Fund to withdraw its financial support. Without reapplication and evidence of a stable city administrative structure, the organization refused "to renew engagement." Putnam's removal also resulted in the withdrawal of American Missionary Association's financial support. The events leading up to Putnam's removal convinced the organization of the futility in working local and state school officials. The withdrawal of these crucial financial sources resulted in the city's heavy reliance on taxation, the state's school fund, and deficit spending.[48]

The lack of school funds made it impossible for the Board of School Commissioners to adequately support the schools. Paltry in comparison to Richmond, the state education fund allocated approximately $13,400 for the African American public schools and approximately $18,000 for white public schools. The board supplemented these funds through taxation and creative financing. Still, the supplemental funding never eradicated the board's financial difficulties. School finances forced Dickson to eliminate inefficiency wherever possible, especially in salaries. In 1871 he noted that "many . . . have been employed without due regard to the service to be rendered." As evidence, he revealed that "in one school a teacher with a small school of boys received two hundred and twenty five dollars per month, while a principal of a girls school numbering one hundred and eighty pupils, receives only one hundred and twenty-five dollars per month." As a solution, he proposed equalizing salaries based on grade and position. His plan alleviated one financial burden by netting a savings of $267 per month. While streamlining the system's budget, Dickson's efforts were hindered by the city's financial situation. In the end, he could only provide for the schools to the best of his abilities.[49]

Like Richmond administrators, Dickson attempted to maintain a consistent policy by distributing school funds in proportion to the number of students documented in the annual school census at the same rate per student. This policy ensured that African American taxes supported the African American public schools without the negative effects of non-enrollment. Fluctuations of the school census, not absenteeism, determined allocations. State financial difficulties had the greatest effect. Apportionment of state funds declined for all public schools, regardless of race. Parents and community leaders strove for as much money as possible and could not easily complain about the overt use of race.[50]

Effects of the Panic of 1873 and the resulting depression reverberated throughout Mobile. As in other urban centers, the national financial crisis profoundly affected black Mobilians. It also coincided with a major yellow fever epidemic in Mobile. Both proved devastating to the city's African American population. Edward P. Lord described the dual impact in a letter to E. M. Cravath: "The fever panic however with the money panic has made it impossible." He explained, "The people here cannot raise any money even those who have money in the bank as that requires sixty days notice. Those who have been at work or teaching can collect nothing." Owing to severe financial hardships, public school enrollment and average attendance increased among black and Creole of color Mobilians. Enrollment decreased to pre-panic levels only during brief periods of recovery. These enrollment fluctuations demonstrated the economic impact on some parents who simply could not afford private school tuition, even the affordable Emerson Institute. Despite poor economic conditions, Emerson Institute and other private schools remained open. Lord hoped that the financial difficulties would not last long. He concluded his letter: "I trust the clouds are to be blown away soon." The financial woes, though, were not "blown away soon." The financial panic started a long recession in which the majority of black Mobilians suffered much of the brunt. Moreover, the overall African American population increased in response to a rural flight for jobs, schools, and city services. This influx strained the social services designed for residents. Indeed, the 1873 financial panic affected all black Mobilians.[51]

Starting at the state level, the financial crisis affected the public school system. The crisis took a toll of the state education fund. The state superintendent of public instruction reported, "The financial depression experienced by all branches of the State Government for the last year has been specially embarrassing for the public school system." Prior to the financial panic, the state legislature approved an act on April 19, 1873, in which the state retained a certain portion of school money collected by counties for the state fund. This relief effort failed, as the financial panic made the collection of these monies impossible. Alabama's educational finances, according to Superintendent Joseph H. Speed in his 1874 report, had "been neither removed nor lessened. On the contrary, some new complications have, unfortunately, arisen out of measures adopted for relief of the school system." As a result, state fund distributions to county and city school districts decreased. Allocations from the "Colored fund" fluctuated from a high of $12,106 to a low of $6,147 between the 1873–1874 academic year and the 1879–1880 academic year. While these allocations never amounted to the money allotted during the pre-panic years, the fund survived. Hence state fiscal policies sustained the public school system amid the crisis.[52]

The decrease in state funds caused Alabama school districts to make difficult decisions. Some shortened their school year. Others consolidated the number of schools. Mobile chose another option. City officials implemented a special tax solely for the support of their schools. They also relied on deficit spending to cope with any shortfalls. Overall, the Board of School Commissioners economized as much as possible. On average, Mobile still contributed $10,000 to $20,000 per year in excess of the state fund allocations between 1873 and 1879. The board still maintained its distribution policy for the funds. In comparison with other major southern cities, however, Mobile spent less money on its public schools. Dickson noted this fact with pride at the school board's fiscal efficiency and reduced spending in his 1875 report. The city spent slightly less than $13.00 per student whereas Richmond, Virginia, allocated $15.88 per student. But the school board's economy did not help. The city went increasingly into debt as its citizens endured a heavy tax burden for its public schools.[53]

By 1875 the city's indebtedness raised questions over the need to sustain the public schools, regardless of race. State officials questioned Mobile's appropriation of the dwindling school fund. As a result, fewer state funds flowed into Mobile. African American appropriations from the state declined from $12,106 to $8,175 in the year following reorganization. With dwindling state appropriations, city officials resorted to taxation and deficit spending. These measures were neither sufficient nor popular among white, black, and Creole citizens. Their communities had suffered from the crisis. Deteriorating city services, high taxation, and repayment of city debts added to their financial burden. Some objected to these measures and began openly questioning the necessity of free public schools. Their objections placed the Board of School Commissioners and advocates of the public schools on the defensive.[54]

In 1875 a *Mobile Daily Tribune* article defended the importance of sustaining the public schools. In discussing the role of government and public education, the author explained, "The theory is this. In a government like ours, it is supposed that the permanency of it depends on the education of the people." He reasoned, "Without this there can be no permanency; therefore it is the duty of the State to cram the people with reading, etc." This rationale harked back to the arguments made after the American Revolution and the during the national common school movement during the 1840s and 1850s. Without an educated citizenry, the national republic would fail. Public common schools ensured the perpetuation of a republican government. These philosophical debates, though, placed the defense of public schools in more abstract terms. Average citizens remained unconvinced by such arguments, including the *Mobile Daily Tribune* author. However, the author still believed in the public school system.[55]

The *Mobile Daily Tribune* article then addressed the benefits of the public school system as a means of convincing naysayers. The author employed another popular argument in defense of public schools. Public schools, he argued, remained cheaper than jails: "To our impoverished people of Mobile the public schools are a great blessing. Hundreds of citizens have children who, without these schools, would grow in idleness, ignorance, and probably vice." In preventing "idleness, ignorance, and vice," the public schools contributed to the city's overall public welfare. He reasoned, "It is much cheaper to pay for schoolhouses than it is for penitentiaries and jails, without reference to the general public security from theft, arson, and other crimes." Instead of using abstract terms, this argument illuminated the debate in terms most understood by average citizens. In its conclusion, the author hoped that white, black, and Creole Mobilians would not become bogged down by the philosophical rationale for the necessity of the public school system. He concluded, "And thus, although the right is not entirely demonstrable of the schools, it is certainly true of their benefits, we suppose, is conclusive of the argument in their favor." The use of this concrete example allowed the argument to secure more support for the public schools. Most individuals may not have understood the intellectual arguments espoused in the defense of public schools as a right of citizenship. However, they understood the need for public welfare and public security. These arguments helped to lessen the opposition to the continuation of public schools amid the national financial crisis.[56]

School funding still posed a challenge by the end of the decade. Nearly bank-rupt by the public schools, Mobile faced another crisis on the Board of School Commissioners in 1878. School officials disagreed over the financing of the school system and the powers of the school superintendent. As in previous crises, state officials acted as mediators. Leroy Box, the state superintendent of public in-struction, reorganized the Mobile school system by ordering new elections and redefining the powers of the board according to mandates established under the 1875 Alabama Constitution. Compliance with the new constitution and a subse-quent 1877 state law brought significant changes to city appropriations. New state mandates established a loophole in which funding would no longer be equitable between African American and white schools. County superintendents now had the discretion of not using the state school census when making appropriations to the public schools. Instead, they could make appropriations based on "the number of children of his district . . . who will probably attend each school, and apportion the district fund to the several schools of his district as nearly per capita as practicable." Prior state laws had not given any school official the au-thority to "discriminate racially for or against either racial group." This act made race and actual usage the determinants in school funding. As a result, school officials changed the system of allocations to public schools in accordance with state mandates.[57]

Changes to school fund allocations had unintended consequences. Originally designed as a relief measure, the change would prove detrimental to African American public schools. Private school attendance and non-enrollment now affected school funding. Since, proportionally, more black Mobilians attended the schools than did white students, the schools had even fewer funds for materi-als and suitable accommodations. Second, school superintendents now had the power to discriminate on the basis of race in the distribution of school funds. Using their discretion, superintendents could divert more money to the white public schools than to the African American public schools. Equitable distribu-tion was no longer guaranteed and race became a significant factor. These conse-quences became increasingly apparent during the next decade.[58]

African American public schools survived the immense financial hardships. Students, parents, and community leaders understood that the fate of their schools hinged on city and state finances as the national financial crisis thwarted their ability to sustain them. Throughout the decade, they found unexpected al-lies. Mobile's Board of School Commissioners and state officials remained com-mitted to public schools for all citizens regardless of race. While the issue of school funding went unresolved, black Mobilians felt reassured by the Mobile's financial commitment to African American education as the public schools entered its second decade.

African American public schools faced many obstacles at the beginning of the 1870s. New challenges entailed new educational partners, the loss of outside financial support from previous educational partners, an inadequate number of school buildings, and lack of educational offerings. Some challenges remained unresolved from the Freedmen's School era and the transition to public schools. The effects of bipartisan politics within the school board and the political return of the Democrat–Conservative coalition remained unresolved challenges. Despite these new and old challenges, black Mobilians and their allies remained committed to education as a right of citizenship. They embarked on the quality campaign as a means of addressing the educational challenges.

Over the course of the decade, parents, students, and leaders slowly made gains in the improvement of the public schools. They had the most success in securing African American teachers in the public schools. However, their quest for quality schools was far from complete. Adequate school accommodations, flexibility in course offerings, representation on the school board, and funding still needed improvement. While success was limited, black Mobilians had developed the strategies for continuing their struggle into the second decade of African American public schools. As a result, they began the 1880s prepared to build on the gains and lessons of the previous decade in their quality campaigns. For them, their struggle for quality schools continued.

IV

PERFECTING THE AFRICAN
AMERICAN SCHOOLHOUSE

7   Walking Slowly but Surely

*The Readjusters and the Quality
School Campaigns in Richmond*

On December 29, 1883, *New York Globe* readers were presented with a surprising New Year's request from Petersburg, Virginia. Signed "Femme," the unknown African American woman's letter requested prayers for education and the accumulation of wealth for all urban black southerners for the upcoming year. Probably considering the likely removal of two African American school board members in nearby Richmond, she felt that education and wealth were the only weapons against the region's poor material and racial conditions. Thus she penned to the newspaper's predominantly African American readership, "At the close of the war we were left to crawl, we crawled as well as we could, and when the time came for us to walk we had no one to stretch out their hands to encourage us to walk, but we did walk; true it was slowly, but surely." During the 1870s, she argued, they lacked the "support from the whites, and our own people in the North were not able to help us." Instead of merely casting blame, she concluded that education "helps to make a man brave and money makes him braver." For these reasons, she implored readers, "Now again I entreat you to pray that we may continue to get education and wealth, and then we will be able to go along by the side of our white brother[s] unmolested." The prayers demanded by Femme echoed the pleas of black Richmonders. For Femme in neighboring Petersburg and black Richmonders, education remained essential in their quest for citizenship, equality, and protection from molestation.[1]

In the 1880s, black Richmonders continued to walk "slowly, but surely" in their struggle for quality public schools. Unlike in other urban centers, black Richmonders' efforts greatly benefited from a statewide political revolution. The emergence of the Readjuster Party accelerated the gains achieved by the quality campaigns by producing a more conducive environment. Capitalizing on the momentous period of change, activists overcame many of the previous decade's obstacles and made significant progress in their overall campaign objectives by 1885. Yet black Richmonders and their allies strove for additional success. They remained firmly committed to Educational Reconstruction, quality public schools, and educational access for all Virginians, black and white. No longer crawling, black Richmonders and their allies wanted to sustain the gains made while striving for additional success in the latter part of the decade.[2]

Since the departure of the Freedmen's Bureau from education, black Richmonders sought direct representation on the Richmond school board. Like other African Americans across the state, region, and nation, they felt that direct political representation would resolve existing problems with the African American public schools and ensure success in terms of future educational opportunities for their children. However, racial attitudes toward African American representatives thwarted success until the Readjuster regime appointed R. A. Paul and Richard Forrester to the Richmond school board in early 1883. Their appointment represented not merely a victory within city and state politics but also a national victory for African American education. In achieving a milestone coveted by African Americans across the state, region, and nation, Paul's and Forrester's appointment signified to black Richmonders that African American public education was a legitimate right of citizenship and freedom in the postwar South and that their efforts since 1865 had not been in vain.

African Americans in Richmond, unlike those in other urban centers, made real progress in terms of civil and political rights during the Readjuster movement. The Readjuster Party was a political coalition of urban African American and white immigrant workers, black tenant farmers and landowners in heavily African American eastern counties, and white Western landowners. The party catapulted into power by tapping into widespread resentment over the existing government's inefficiency amid poor economic conditions. Readjusters offered a new vision for Virginia. They promised social mobility, racial justice, an industrialized economic order, and a sustainable public school system for all Virginians, regardless of race. The Readjuster movement, as argued by historians James T. Moore and Jane Dailey, represented a revolt from below.[3] With African American electoral support, Readjusters achieved a significant victory by becoming the political majority in the state after the 1881 elections. Indeed, interracial and interclass cooperation prevailed over white supremacy.[4]

The new Readjuster legislature quickly enacted reform measures that benefited its African American constituents. The legislature abolished the whipping post. It doubled the number of public schools and established a state normal school for African Americans in Petersburg. It also placed African American physicians in charge of asylums for African Americans and appointed more African Americans to civil servant positions in Virginia. But the Readjuster regime's greatest show of power occurred when it brought major reform to the Richmond

school board, transforming the nature of black Richmonders' activism, specifically their struggle for board representation.[5]

Through happenstance and political maneuverings, the Readjusters' reform
yielded success in activists' campaigns. In January 1883 E. M. Garnett, superintendent of the city schools, realized that none of the Richmond school board members took the required oath of office. Garnett notified the state attorney general
of the situation. By not taking the oath of office, they violated state law. Attorney
General F. S. Blair ordered them to take the required oath within thirty days or
vacate the office. The city council then would have another thirty days to replace
any vacancies or have the state board of education fill the vacancies. However,
the affected individuals did not. The historical record is silent on their reasons for
not taking the oath or why the city council did not simply fill the vacancies. Their
actions had major consequences. On February 17 the state board of education
appointed a new Richmond school board, comprising Republicans, Readjusters,
and two African Americans. With the appointments of Richard Forrester and
Capt. Robert A. Paul, black Richmonders finally had direct representation in the
operations of city's public schools. Without these unexpected developments and
patronage, this victory would not have been possible.[6]

With their appointment, black Richmonders, though, expected the men's assistance in achieving "colored teachers in the colored schools" and quickly made
their demands known. According to the petition developed at the May 22, 1883,
meeting at the First African Church, petitioners asked "that while we would not
presume to dictate as to the management of the Richmond public schools, we
respectfully petition the Richmond School Board, as an act of justice to ourselves
and as an advantage to our children, that they appoint colored principals and
teachers to all our colored schools." Paul and Forrester paid heed. After the men
convinced their colleagues to listen to the petitioners' demands, African American applicants received teaching positions in all of the African American public
schools except Richmond Colored Normal. Persuaded by a passionate argument
made by Paul, the school board also promoted Albert V. Norrell, James H. Hayes,
and James Hugo Johnston to become the principals of the Navy Hill, Valley, and
Baker schools, respectively. Without direct school board representation and continued community pressure, the struggle for African American teachers and
principals would have remained at a stalemate.[7]

African Americans in Richmond and across the nation celebrated. Not only
had black Richmonders achieved direct representation on the Richmond school
board, they were able to secure black teachers and administrators in the public

schools. Parents, community leaders, and activists had every reason to feel victorious. The Virginia correspondent for the *New York Globe* professed their feelings of vindication after laboring for over a decade: "At last we can assuredly say the battle has been fought and the victory is won." Indeed, they had achieved a major victory in terms of education, politics, and racial progress. Thus Paul's and Forrester's political and leisure activities were widely reported on in Richmond but also as far away as New York City.[8]

On the other hand, white Democrats immediately voiced their opposition. They strongly objected to Paul's and Forrester's presence on the Richmond school board. Moreover, the creation of African American teaching staffs and the appointment of the three African American principals fueled their rage. As a result of the actions of the "mongrel board," according to the displaced Navy Hill principal, a "revolution began." State Democratic Party organizers seized on the displacement of the white principals and teachers as justification for removing the Readjusters from power. They argued that the Readjuster experiment on the Richmond school board resulted in job loss for white principals and teachers in order to place African Americans on "an equal footing." Through such arguments, the party successfully convinced white Virginians that similar experiments would occur in their cities, towns, and counties if the Readjusters remained in power. And just as political maneuverings allowed for the appointment of Paul and Forrester, state and city politics permitted the men's removal.[9]

After a coordinated statewide campaign, Democrats regained power in the 1883 elections. Almost immediately, they began the process of removing Paul and Forrester. Since the Virginia Court of Appeals had upheld the legality of Paul's and Forrester's appointments, the new state legislature devised and adopted legislation that required all school boards to vacate office within thirty days of the bill's passage. This legislation also required new elections to fill the mandatory vacancies. African Americans in Richmond and across the nation recognized the legislation's true intent—the removal of Paul and Forrester. Although black Richmonders petitioned the state legislature demanding "colored trustees for colored schools," Paul, Forrester, and others vacated the Richmond school board. Voters elected a new, all-white school board. Within a short period, Democrats successfully overturned activists' gains.[10]

Black Richmonders quickly returned to previous strategies in dealing with the school board, but not their previous submissiveness. They became increasingly critical of the new board. After the required elections, African American parents, community leaders, and activists remained skeptical of the claims that "politics should have nothing to do with the management of the schools." They hoped that the new school board would "practice what they preach." When their initial interactions were unfavorable, they criticized the newly elected members as being "dumb as oysters." For activists, their harsh critiques and subsequent relationships with the Richmond school board resulted from a sense of duty not only to African American students but also to the legacy of Paul and Forrester. In speaking of Paul, the Virginia correspondent for the *New York Globe* asserted, "The Captain has ably defended the rights of his people and proved that he was a man of courage in the higher sense of the word. The colored people have much to thank him for as their representative and when the proper time comes they will not be backward in showing their appreciation." Hence black Richmonders continued petitioning. Now, they openly questioned the board's decisions while hoping for another political revolution.[11]

Black Richmonders also relied on their remaining political allies. Since the state legislature never forced new elections for councilmen and aldermen, Edwin Archer Randolph remained on the Richmond city council. Randolph was born in Richmond on January 19, 1850, to free parents, James and Rebecca Archer Randolph. After serving as a driver for a white Richmond physician, he left the city to pursue postsecondary education. He attended Wayland Seminary in Washington, D.C., before entering Yale Law School in 1878.[12] After becoming the first African American graduate of Yale Law School, Randolph returned to Richmond, where he opened a law office, served as the first editor of the *Richmond Planet*, and actively participated in the Acme Literary Association. In 1881 he was elected to a two-year term on the Richmond city council and then served on the board of aldermen.[13] In this capacity he regularly advocated for allocating necessary appropriations for new school accommodations, the appointment of African American principals and teachers, and other educational matters. Furthermore, Superintendent E. M. Garnett was not included in the mandatory elections. Given his prior sympathies with African American education, activists were not concerned that he would stop advocating on their behalf. While they lost direct representation, parents, community leaders, and activists were not completely powerless. Through electoral politics, petitioning, and securing important government allies, black Richmonders retained a voice in the administration of the public schools.[14]

By navigating a favorable political environment, black Richmonders temporarily secured direct representation on the Richmond school board. With this victory, the Richmond public schools benefitted. The system expanded with new schools, African Americans found employment as teachers and briefly as principals, and the schools benefited from the infusion of state and city funding.

Therefore, the brief tenure of Paul and Forrester suggests that this period was not a "nadir" in terms of African American education or politics. Rather, it demonstrates the importance of critically reassessing prior understandings of Reconstruction, politics, and African American education. By extending the chronology of Reconstruction, it is possible to appreciate the ways black Richmonders employed newer and older protest strategies in order to make African American public schools enduring institutions.

During the 1880s, the school accommodation campaign's central objective entailed providing accommodations for all school-age children desiring a public school education. Despite their previous efforts, parents and activists became increasingly frustrated that the city school system lacked an adequate number of school facilities. As a result, enrollments represented a fraction of the city's school census. In their activism, African American parents, community leaders, and activists sought to redress this discrepancy.[15]

The Readjuster movement greatly assisted the school accommodation campaigns. Starting in 1879, Readjusters funneled more state monies to cities, towns, and counties to be used in the public schools. Using state funds, the Richmond school board responded to prior demands for school accommodations. The board opened the East End School and also renovated and enlarged existing city schools for African American students. The capacities of Valley, Baker, and Navy Hill schools expanded as a result of the renovations. These improvements, though, never resolved the problem. To be sure, the number of enrolled students increased from 2,591 at the start of the decade to 3,140 two years later. But enrolled students only represented approximately 35.7 percent of the school census population. Since the enrolled students reflected the schools' capacity, it is evident that the city simply lacked a sufficient number of schools to serve the school census population. Thus the city schools remained inaccessible to the majority of children.[16]

During the 1883–1884 academic year, parents and activists became frustrated with the Readjuster regime. The employment of African American principals and teachers prompted a surge in community interest. A large number of African American parents actively sought admittance in order to have their children receive the benefits of African American faculties. On the first day of classes, the state's *New York Globe* correspondent reported that "parents could be seen marching their children to the schools, only to be refused admittance. The school accommodations here are totally inadequate. About one thousand pupils were turned away." With those nearly one thousand students denied entry, activists demanded additional school accommodations from the city council and school board. Furthermore, they expected Paul, Forrester, and Randolph to assist them. By October 1883 Randolph secured city appropriations, which allowed for the opening of two schools on "the grounds formerly occupied by the Moore Street Industrial School." Paul also pushed through a resolution requesting additional city appropriations for the creation of another school in the West End neighborhood. While Paul's and the city council's efforts were applauded, parents and other community members remained unsatisfied. In an October 1883 article, the *New York Globe* commented, "It is a crying shame that there should be one thousand children thrown upon the streets from the fact that there is no room for them in the public schools." As a result, parents and activists maintained their agitation with the support of their political allies on the Richmond school board and city council. Even with the adoption of these measures, school accommodations remained a source of frustration for activists.[17]

Democrats' political return never stopped activists' agitation. Residents, especially in areas woefully without adequate accommodations, resumed a strategy of petitioning. Unable to ignore activists' demands, the Richmond school board responded with five major additions between 1884 and 1890. Three specifically addressed the needs of the residents living in the West End section of Richmond. Overcrowded conditions precipitated the restoration of half-day sessions. Superintendent Garnett felt that the half-day sessions were an "injustice" to the students, teachers, and parents. On their behalf, Garnett recommended the immediate construction of a schoolhouse. In 1887 the Moore School opened with Garnett as its principal. School officials re-rented the Moore Street Baptist Church property in order to accommodate student and resident demand the following year. The newly created Brook School provided some relief, but it quickly became overcrowded. Activists then forced school officials to purchase and renovate an armory that was used by African American soldiers. As the armory was located adjacent to the Brook School, school officials opened and renamed the school complex as the Monroe School. Similar agitation by residents in the eastern and southeastern sections of Richmond resulted in the last two additions. The Fulton School opened during the 1889–1890 academic year. The East End School received a major renovation that expanded its overall capacity. These additions came directly as a result of activists' initiative. While black Richmonders lacked direct school board representation, their perfection and application of older protest strategies allowed them to make inroads on the issue of school accommodations.[18]

Overall, these additions increased the number of children who could access the city's public schools. Enrollments increased from 3,110 students during the 1885–1886 academic year to 4,968 students during the 1889–1890 academic year. Student enrollments nearly doubled since the beginning of the decade. The newer facilities also allowed for an increase in the percentage of school-age children attending the public schools. In relation to the school census, enrolled students steadily increased from 34.7 percent during 1885–1886 to 48.8 percent by the end of the decade. While this increase can be seen as a testament to black Richmonders' activism, a large number of African American children could not attend. Demand for the African American public schools still exceeded the number of available seats.[19]

These gains also never resolved the realities encountered by enrolled students and those denied admittance. Enrolled students faced overcrowded conditions in order to obtain an education. Some endured half-day sessions, an unpopular measure designed to increase educational access. For students not enrolled in the public schools and their taxpaying parents, they coped with the humiliation and frustration of being denied entry to a school system sustained by African American taxes. The lack of school accommodations forced them to rely on private schools or other, informal means of obtaining an education. Consequently, parents and community leaders celebrated the increased number and percentage of enrolled African American public school students. However, they never stopped agitating for additional and better school accommodations. For black Richmonders, they continued to walk slowly but surely in their struggle for school facilities.[20]

Activists maintained the employment of African American teachers as a third and crucial objective of their quality campaigns. At the start of the decade, hiring practices remained the primary obstacle. Despite the combined efforts of parents, community leaders, and Richmond Colored Normal graduates, success was limited. The Navy Hill School represented the only school with African American teachers and a white principal at the start of the decade. Richmond Colored Normal graduates filled all the available positions. Through petitioning, black Richmonders retained African American teachers at the newly created East End School in 1881. Likewise, these teachers received their training from Richmond Colored Normal and had a white principal supervising them. While success was limited, these schools evoked a sense of hope in black Richmonders that school officials would "see that it is best for all concerned to appoint colored teachers for all of our colored schools."[21]

Moreover, scholastic results of Navy Hill and East End schools justified the continued activism. Students excelled academically as their teachers instilled pride in academic achievement. Teachers, such as Daniel B. Williams, James Hugo Johnston, and James Hayes, conveyed to their students that academic success permitted racial progress. As the "hope of the race," these teachers promoted to their young charges the necessity of regular attendance, studying, and performing to the best of their abilities. "You, a part of the rising youth of our race, hold within your grasp the possibility of adding rich and lasting benefits to your race and country," Williams informed students at a Moore Street Church Sunday school picnic. "I desire to state in a plain, practical manner how you can do this. You must set before your minds a lofty standard of physical, intellectual and moral excellence." Seeking not to disappoint their teachers, students regularly outperformed their peers on the semi-annual examinations. They also were promoted at a greater rate because the teachers, according to a former student, "guided our childish feet, trained our restless hands, and created within our youthful souls an unquenchable search for knowledge, an undying ambition to be something, and to do something." These rewards made parents, students, and community leaders continue their teachers' campaign.[22]

Despite these rewards, Navy Hill and East End teachers and students still experienced discrimination. African American teachers faced severe repercussions if they dared to question any discriminatory practice. In 1883 Daniel B. Williams advocated for better treatment from Hubbard G. Carlton. In questioning the Navy Hill school principal, Williams faced "insubordination and mutinous conduct" charges, putting his position in jeopardy. According to Carlton, Williams charged him with "unjust and unfair discrimination in the promotion of pupils." By not promoting the students deemed competent by the teachers, Williams felt that Carlton undermined the teachers' abilities for making such decisions. Although the school board agreed to promote all students who passed their examinations, Williams received a suspension without pay. After rejecting Williams's petition for reinstatement, the board agreed that he could reapply for his position during the next academic year. Despite this guarantee, he never regained his employment in the Richmond public schools. Instead, Williams taught in the Henrico County schools and at a private school operating from his residence while pursuing a degree from Brown University during the summer months. Ultimately, he found employment as a professor at Virginia Normal and Collegiate Institute in nearby Petersburg. For activists, this incident reinforced the need for teachers as well as principals. Navy Hill students lost a valuable teacher and mentor when William's questioned Carlton's authority. Neither the students nor the community activists could afford to lose more teachers from these highly valued institutions.[23]

Excluding Navy Hill and East End, the reality of white teaching staffs made activists continue their "colored teachers for colored schools" campaign. Local newspapers, such as the *Virginia Star*, vocalized black Richmonders' demands for African American public schoolteachers. A November 1882 article demanded recognition of African American civil and political rights as conferred by the state constitution and the Reconstruction amendments. In the appeal, the *Virginia Star* article extended the definition of civil and political rights to include their demands for African American public schoolteachers. The article's author remarked, "No candid white person in the South will deny that the colored people have been denied their civil and political rights. For, are they not as a class excluded from our juries, from holding office, aye, from teaching their own children in the capacity of public free schoolteachers?" In demanding the recognition of African American civil and political rights, the *Virginia Star* article concluded with a plea for fairness, equality, and dignity. "Give us our rights which belong to us. Give us fair and living wages for a fair day's work. Treat our women with the respect due to their sex. Open the doors of lucrative business to our young men and women. Assist and encourage us to educate our children and bring them up in refinement whenever our means will admit of it." Without fair and equitable wages, dignity, and education, as articulated by the *Virginia Star*, black Richmonders realized that full citizenship was not possible. Hence African American public schoolteachers were integral to their quest for full citizenship by ensuring that current and future school-age children had access to better wages and respectability through education.[24]

By December 1882, local newspapers became more aggressive in their demands for African American public schoolteachers. This militancy resulted from a growing frustration with the Readjusters' inability to satisfy their demands. A front-page *Virginia Star* editorial implored the Richmond school board to follow the model set by other major cities in Virginia. "Lynchburg, Petersburg, Norfolk, Hampton, Danville, Charlottesville, and Manchester have put colored teachers in their colored schools," the editorial opened. "Only Richmond and a few other localities in this State persist in refusing to give the colored people teachers of their own race." After recognizing the success of the Navy Hill and East End schools, the editorial concluded that the School Board's refusal stemmed from "motives of sordidness, spite and Bourbon blindness." The editorial applauded Superintendent Garnett for his continued efforts to assist them against a determined foe. But they recognized his inability to overcome the primary obstacle to their goal—obstinate school board members. The editorialist hoped that "a sound sense of justice will, before a great length of time, induce our School Board to do unto as they would that they should do unto them." Through comparison with other major urban centers, activists hoped that public shame would bring change.[25]

Activists also turned to the state's Readjuster regime for assistance. They used the *Virginia Star* as a sounding board for their demands. One December 1882 letter to the editor made a case for state intervention. "The white people have white teachers to instruct their children. We want colored teachers to instruct our young; when we can find them competent," the letter's author argued. "We have asked for colored teachers, but the School Board says; 'No' you must have the white ones." The author demanded state intervention. He called on the Readjuster regime to enact "a good honest government that does not make a difference on account of the color of the skin." Activists expected the Readjuster regime to make the Richmond school board more amenable. In requesting state intervention, African Americans elevated their teachers' campaign from a city to a state demand.[26] After laboring for over a decade, parents, community leaders, and activists had every reason to feel victorious over Readjuster intervention and the actions of Richmond school board in 1883. Without it, the struggle for African American teachers and principals would have remained at an impasse.[27]

Therefore, parents clamored to have their children take part in the historic moment. Administrators reported high enrollment and low absenteeism for the year. Community leaders also praised the programs developed by the principals. The former Navy Hill teachers devised a weekly lecture series in order to aid first-time Richmond schoolteachers. Each month, three experienced teachers gave lectures on teaching pedagogy and issues, such as the initial meeting topic of "Corporal Punishment." Local and regional newspapers regularly reported on this continuous education series as evidence of the principals' ingenuity and competency for the positions held. From enrollments to teacher training, black Richmonders had every reason to celebrate the fruits of their activism. The academic year demonstrated that their efforts had not been in vain.[28]

They also reveled in the praise received from school administrators and curious visitors. Superintendent Garnett and other officials regularly visited the schools. At a December 1883 visit to the Valley School, Superintendent Garnett said that "he was pleased with what he saw. He thought, at first, that the colored schools, under the new management, would cause him much trouble; but he found them doing as well as they had ever done" since the creation of the public school system. Comments such as this only vindicated the activists' previous struggle. In response to his remarks, the state's *New York Globe* correspondent commented, "Many persons prophesied a dark day for the schools when the change was made. The above speaks for itself." Similarly, published tourist accounts also galvanized activists. In early 1884 William R. Granger toured the schools. The future Bucknell graduate and physician found Hayes, Norrell, and Johnston to be competent and intelligent men who were ably assisted by the teachers. Granger was greatly impressed by the students' scholastic progress and their respect for the teachers. He wrote, "In conduct and decorum, the pupils reflect the care of the teachers. Strongly refractory spirits are seldom met; and then such receive prompt attention. Respect for teachers is a characteristic feature in each of the schools. No loud rebukes are necessary, nor frequent calls for order." In his visit to Richmond Colored Normal, Granger noticed a sharp difference in the students' interactions with their white teachers. The "lack of that deep regard for the teacher shown in the primary grades" at the normal school reinforced the success of African American faculties and principals. Students thrived under African American public schoolteachers and principals. Indeed, official reports and published tourist accounts demonstrated success rather than failure. However, it proved short-lived. After regaining power, the new Democratic-majority Richmond school board removed the African American principals at the end of the academic year.[29]

Black Richmonders immediately expressed their anger and disappointment through the African American press. In a *New York Globe* article, the Virginia correspondent voiced these sentiments. "Again have the Bourbons shown their greed for office by the ousting of Messrs J. Highland Hayes, J. H. Johnston and A. V. Norrell, the colored principals of this city, from the colored schools, and putting white men in their places," the article opened. "There was no charge against them, in fact the record made by the respective schools under their control is unparalleled in their history." Owing to the qualitative and quantitative progress made under the three men, the correspondent astutely recognized that race and political partisanship motivated their removal. Despite being the recipients of diplomas from "an institution that a Democratic board sanctioned," the correspondent argued that the "partisan Board went to work and scraped up persons from far and near to supply their places." As a result, the correspondent as well as most African Americans considered the school board's actions to be "the first time in the school life of Virginia that a School Board has been the reflection of a revolutionary legislature." For parents and activists, the principals' removal reinforced that competency no longer mattered in the selection of school principals—race and political affiliation did.[30]

Simultaneously, parents, children, and community leaders coped with the removal of eleven male African American teachers for their political activities.

These men had received their appointments as a result of patronage. Whereas Hayes, Johnston, and Norrell returned to their former teaching positions, the Richmond school board replaced eleven men with African American female educators. Although viewed as less threatening than their male counterparts, these women actively participated in local politics. However, they could not physically cast a ballot that would oust elected school officials. It was for this reason that the school board fired the eleven male teachers. Their removal epitomized that race, political affiliation, and gender mattered more than competency in the selection of teachers.[31]

Although African Americans served as principals for one year, African American teachers remained. White teachers lost their monopoly on employment in the African American public schools. During the 1884–1885 academic year the school board rejected a petition of displaced white teachers and white community leaders for their reemployment. After the Readjuster revolution, white educators only served in African Americans schools either as principals or as faculty members at Richmond Colored Normal. As a result of the changed hiring practices, by 1885 black Richmonders turned their attention to other objectives in the quality campaigns. With African American public schoolteachers, they felt reassured that the children would be treated with respect and dignity. They were no longer concerned over the quality of education received under the educators' tutelage. Thus they felt that the campaign for African American public schoolteachers could end, as they had achieved the desired result.[32]

As in the previous decade, the quality campaigns' success was contingent on funding. At the end of the 1870s, the city's financial situation remained as such —all public schools, regardless of race, were underfunded. The emergence of Readjuster Party, though, transformed city and state officials' attitudes toward school funding and broke a major barrier. While black Richmonders continued seeking as much money as possible for the schools and equity in the distribution of said school funds, the Readjuster movement made their crusade easier.

Readjusters ended much of the funding challenges from the previous decade. William Mahone and other Readjusters made school funding a priority for the nascent party. Indeed, the 1879 party platform endorsed sustaining a system of adequately funded public schools. The party pledged to reform how the state distributed school fund monies to cities, towns, and counties and increase the amount of state monies appropriated. Their 1879 platform promised funding reform in which "no child shall be deprived of the blessings of education." The party's pledged educational reform accounted for its success in the 1879 elections. Upon achieving political success, the party immediately fulfilled its educational platform by increasing state aid to Richmond during the 1879–1880 academic year. As state contributions increased from $5,188.50 to a staggering $24,904.80, the crisis ceased.[33]

The infusion of money set the tone for state and city appropriations for the entire decade. While state appropriations slightly decreased for the next two years, state educational contributions never dwindled to pre-Readjuster amounts. Even with the decline of the Readjuster Party, annual state funds provided between $23,000 and $30,000 to the Richmond public schools. Moreover, increased state funds correlated with an increase in city allocations. By reaffirming the state's commitment to public schools, specifically African American public schools, the city council contributed even more money. Through taxation and fiscal management, the city allocations increased from approximately $50,000 to over $100,000 by the end of the decade. Indeed, state and city allocations to the public schools greatly surpassed the amounts allocated to the city public schools during the previous decade. Hence the city's ability to fund its African American schools greatly improved.[34]

Richmond school officials now could fulfill parents, children, and community members' demands for quality public schools. To be sure, increased state and city appropriations never completely eradicated the funding shortfall. City officials also could not completely address all of the problems associated with the public schools. But they now had more capital in order to acquire additional accommodations and to staff the new school facilities. As a result, the quality campaigns greatly benefited from the infusion of state educational funds. Black Richmonders and their allies no longer dealt with debates over the fiscal feasibility of public schools or the legitimacy of African American education. Liberal state and city expenditures cemented African American public school education as a right of citizenship.[35]

Black Richmonders and their allies now sought to maximize the amount of educational funds given to the public schools. Parents, community leaders, and other allies fought against any measures that diverted school monies away from black Richmonders. For instance, activists refused to support school choice legislation. In 1886 Richmonders and other urban Virginians advocated against the Berry bill, a proposed state legislative measure which would "allow the children in county or city to attend the public schools in any other city or county." Weary of rural Virginians seeking consistent and regular schooling for their children, black Richmonders recognized that the proposed state legislation would have worsened the issue of school accommodations. Such a bill, as articulated by the *Dispatch*, would allow for the exclusion of more Richmonders, particularly black

Richmonders, in order "to make room for the children from other parts of the State, whose parents pay nothing into the city treasury." Hence many found the bill to be "very injurious to the Richmond public schools" and advocated that their state representatives vote against it. Richmonders' objection also revealed the continued dilemma associated with school funding. Despite the seemingly ample local financial support managed by a bureaucratic school administration, Richmond still experienced real financial difficulties in sustaining its public schools. Other than by raising taxes, city officials remained unable to overcome this obstacle and resorted to maximizing the money spent for its citizens.[36]

Activists also engaged in national educational funding debates. Black Richmonders strongly endorsed the Blair education bill. In supporting the bill, designed to provide federal funding to the nation's schools, black Richmonders and their allies recognized that federal intervention could overcome the remaining obstacles to school funding. "Much interest is manifested here in the bill for National Aid to Education," the Virginia correspondent for the *New York Globe* reported. "It is a bill that should certainly be the means of lifting the colored man to the foreground." In addition, activists believed that federal intervention would also provide the necessary surveillance of southern states in distributing the funds equitably. In the same *New York Globe* article, the correspondent wrote, "When the accommodations for the whites are the accommodations for the colored, then, and not until then, will we believe in the possibility of the whites doing justice to Negroes in this respect." The correspondent concluded, "To consign such a bulk of money to the keeping of these Southern Bourbons would be worse than folly, and fatal to the interests of the Negro." As evidenced by this article, black Richmonders' support of the Blair education bill reflected a belief that the school funding issue was a national rather than a city, state, or regional struggle. By the 1880s, black Richmonders firmly believed in the transformative nature of education in relation to citizenship and progress. Based on their experience, activists felt obligated to support the passage of this federal legislation. The legislation would aid not only their efforts but those of all African Americans across the South and the nation.[37]

In supporting the national funding bill, black Richmonders also desired a restoration of their earlier relationship with white northerners and the federal government. Their public discourse surrounding the federal educational legislation included discussions of the nation's previous commitment to African American education. The Virginia correspondent reminded *New York Globe* readers that the majority of "all the fine institutions of the South for the colored youth were reared by Northern contributions." As articulated by the *New York Globe* correspondent, activists played up this relationship as a reason for supporting the bill's passage. This discourse also called into attention the perceived abandonment of northern and federal support after the departure of the Freedmen's Bureau. The correspondent remarked, "The South passed laws before the war to crush the educational abilities of the black man, and it [has taken] more than twenty years to wipe out that spirit." In highlighting the length of time, the correspondent chastised New Yorkers, northerners, and the federal government alike. For fifteen years, the efforts of black Richmonders and other Virginians eradicated most of the local sentiment "to crush the educational abilities of the black man." Their efforts sustained the foundation established by northern and federal contributions. Yet the correspondent and Richmond activists hoped their rebuke would convince *New York Globe* readers of the legislation's necessity. They and other black southerners would willingly overlook previous abandonment if they secured enough northern support for the bill's passage and implementation. If the bill failed, activists feared for the future of their quality public school campaigns but also of campaigns across the rural and urban South. On this issue Richmond activists did not want to walk alone in the struggle.[38]

Changes in attitudes at the city and state level allowed for black Richmonders and their allies to make substantial gains in their struggle for school funding. Unlike in other southern cities, black Richmonders experienced the benefits of liberal school expenditures, which allowed them to secure funding for the construction and staffing of additional school accommodations. Yet these liberal expenditures never stopped their agitation in securing more state and city monies for their schools, especially after Readjusters' demise. They also demanded that the region use Richmond as a model in the funding of African American education. Hence black Richmonders engaged in national debates addressing the funding of not only their schools but also the schools of their southern brethren who were not as fortunate. Although black Richmonders' experience can be classified as atypical, they still engaged in a struggle for equitable and sufficient school funding that was common across the region. It may have been easier for them to achieve results, but they still had to fight for this campaign objective.

Over the 1880s, black Richmonders and their allies made significant progress in their quest for quality public schools. Maneuvering in a favorable political environment, activists temporarily secured direct representation on the Richmond school board. The school system expanded with new schools. The new facilities allowed more African American children to access a public school education. Black Richmonders also found employment as teachers and briefly as principals. With the infusion of state and city funding, activists ensured that the schools received sufficient financial support. Through protest strategies old and new, activists greatly improved the Richmond public schools. Indeed, black Richmonders and their allies could claim success by the end of the decade.

Activists still strove for more progress, as the schools remained far from perfect. African American children were still being denied access to a public school education because of a want of adequate accommodations. After brief success, black Richmonders lacked direct representation on the Richmond school board. The removal of Paul and Forrester reestablished a dependency on their white allies for the education of African American children. Activists also proved unable to fully overcome the remaining funding shortfall affecting their schools. Yet parents, community leaders, and activists remained undeterred by the remaining school problems. Congressional debates over a federal educational funding bill offered hope. Their activism kept the schools open and made them better institutions. Without the activists' perfection of the previous decade's protest strategies and adaptations, these setbacks may have been greater in Richmond.

8

Still Crawling

Black Mobilians' Struggle for Quality Schools Continues

Femme's bold New Year's request must have elicited mixed emotions when *New York Globe* readers saw her remarks. While some may have been confused or shocked by her prayer request for education and wealth, it would have deeply resonated among black Mobilians. Her synopsis characterized their experience. Like Femme, they "crawled as well as we could, and when the time came for us to walk we had no one to stretch out their hands to encourage us to walk, but we did walk; true it was slowly, but surely." Moreover, black Mobilians would have received Femme's words differently than black Richmonders. With the exception of two northern missionary associations, a few local white allies, and briefly the Peabody Education Fund, they, too, lacked "support from the whites, and our own people in the North were not able to help us." Yet the promise of education guided their hard and slow struggle and permitted several gains after the Freedmen's Bureau departure. As they entered the second decade of the quality school campaigns, black Mobilians, like Femme in Petersburg, Virginia, required spiritual assurances in their quest for education, freedom, and citizenship.[1]

In the 1880s, black Mobilians continued a "slowly, but surely" crawl in their struggle for quality public schools. Unlike the case with their Richmond counterparts, a more conducive political environment never manifested itself for Mobilians. Perseverance and continued activism allowed them to make modest yet steady progress in their quality campaigns. Their unwavering insistence on quality public schools and a firm commitment to becoming a literate people ensured that African American children would continue to access a public school education.[2] Through continued pressure on their allies and resilience in the face of adversity, activists achieved steady progress in their quest.

Unlike their Richmond counterparts, black Mobilians proved less successful in securing direct representation on the Mobile County Board of School Commissioners. Throughout the 1880s, a Democrat–Conservative coalition firmly controlled the city's political system. While black Mobilians maneuvered the terrain and secured various patronage positions, they proved unable overcome the party's white supremacist views of having African American school commissioners. They, like Richmonders after the fall of the Readjusters, could not persuade elected officials or voters that African Americans were capable of managing the schools.[3]

Despite the lack of direct representation, parents, religious leaders, and activists relied on strategies honed during the previous decade. They continued the practice of petitioning, which afforded them a political voice over the schools by forcing the school board to address their concerns at official meetings. While not always successful, petitioning allowed them some control over the schools. Moreover, black Mobilians employed the ballot as a strategy. Using their electoral power, the African American and Creole communities forced candidates to address their community's needs in their campaigns in exchange for votes. Afterward, they held the officials accountable for action with threats of removing their support in the next election. These strategies reflected their ability to effect change in school operations even without African American and Creole commissioners. While hamstrung, black Mobilians and their allies were never silenced by this lack of representation.[4]

Black Mobilians' fought for school accommodations on three fronts during the 1880s. First, black and Creole Mobilians sought to maintain existing accommodations accessible to anyone desiring a public school education. Second, they sought to expand the school system in order to increase the number of students enrolled. Third, they fiercely protected the private school system. During the previous decade, activists found the existence of private schools beneficial in their quality school campaigns. Private schools ensured choice while providing a model for what the public schools could become. Over the course of the decade, black Mobilians and their allies experienced both success and setbacks as they crawled their way to quality public schools.

Black Mobilians and their allies sought to keep existing schools open. At the start of the decade, the city offered five public schools for African American children and one school for Creole children. Student enrollment reflected approximately 30 percent of the city's school census population. Though meager in number, activists fought to ensure that the number of schools never decreased, as it would have prevented educational access to more African American children. In maintaining six schools, activists could still claim a victory, as the available physical buildings remained the same. Thus activists desired to keep the number of schools at this minimum of six, which would ensure continued access to students already enrolled in the public schools while establishing a minimum enrollment standard.[5]

In struggling to maintain the existing schools, black and Creole of color activists often reinforced social differences between the groups as they protected the educational interests of the other. Since the end of the Civil War, a separate school existed for Creole of color children without much debate. At the February 16, 1881, meeting, school commissioners contemplated a petition received from Ben Johnson requesting his child's admittance into the Creole Free School. In discussing the petition, the board debated the necessity of the separate school for Creole of color children and felt that consolidating the Creole Free School into Augusta Street School would prove adequate. However, public outcry from Creole and black Mobilians enabled the school's survival. Activists realized that closing the Creole Free School would have decreased the number of public schools to five. It did not matter that the school had a small enrollment or that it reinforced division between the Creole and black Mobilian communities. Removal threatened all nonwhite schools. Activists equated threats to one group's educational interests as threats to the other. Although internal division remained, unity prevailed in the protection of the public schools. In this instance, activists convinced the Board of School Commissioners of the necessity of maintaining the Creole Free School until 1887, when the school permanently closed.[6]

For the existing schools, activists also sought necessary school repairs, which made the schools into functional facilities, helping activists to sustain a positive public image of the schools. Poor conditions often deterred parents from sending their children to the public schools. Indeed, they opted for the city's private school system or non-attendance, as evidenced by the student enrollment figures. Student enrollment decreased from 2,225 students during the 1880–1881 academic year to a decade-low of 1,818 students during the 1882–1883 academic year. Owing to their activism, public school enrollment steadily increased to 2,356 students by the end of the decade. Officials used the improved facilities as evidence of their response to citizens' demands and a measure of educational progress in official state reports. Improvements to facilities, though often cosmetic, attracted parent, student, and communal support.[7]

The construction of new schools was a second objective of the school accommodations campaign. Bleak city finances thwarted activists from securing new accommodations for African American children. While school officials attributed low enrollment to racial differences, activists understood that the heart of the problem was the lack of school accommodations provided between 1880 and 1886. Their failure resulted in a majority of African American children and their parents continuing to be denied access to a public school education. Hence activists continued their school accommodation campaign.[8]

Limited success occurred only when activists requested new facilities in order to replace school facilities closed by the Board of School Commissioners. Citing inefficiency, the board closed the Creole Free School in 1887. Activists successfully persuaded the board to open the Monroe Street School for the displaced Creole student population and the neighborhood's growing school-age African American population. Although many displaced Creole students enrolled at the Augusta School or at a private school, black Mobilians received a new facility and maintained the school offerings at six schools. In 1888 another reduction occurred. Activists acquired the Broad Street Academy, but they lost the St. Louis Street, Good Hope, and Monroe Street schools. Enrollment figures show that displaced students flocked to the newly built Broad Street Academy and other schools. However, activists suffered a major setback. The city's public school system decreased its offerings to African American and Creole children from six schools to four by the end of the decade. The number of physical structures mattered in terms of assessing success. The clear reduction represented the marginalization of the African American schoolhouse and the possible return to antebellum conditions. Thus black Mobilians and their partners viewed even enlarged facilities amid the loss of two schools as failure in their quest for educational access.[9]

A third component of the school accommodations campaign consisted of sustaining the private school system as an alternative to the public school system. In their long struggle for education, black Mobilians and Creoles supported private schools as a means of providing parents and children with choice. But they also supported private schools as a means of improving public schools. During the 1880s, black Mobilians continued to depend on the existence of Emerson Institute in order to press school commissioners for better accommodations and expanded programs. Without Emerson Institute, they would have lost an important bargaining chip with school officials. As a result, they fiercely protected the school.[10]

During the winter of 1881–1882, arsonists again attempted to permanently close Emerson Institute. Their efforts were thwarted when Rev. Albert F. Owens and other African American religious leaders immediately found temporary locations for the school until it could be rebuilt. This solution often placed the private school within the same buildings rented as public schools. For instance, Rev. Owens, pastor of the Third Baptist Church, made his church's basement available as a temporary site while other sections of the church operated as a public school. These leaders' initiative enabled classes to resume within days of the fire. In an *American Missionary* article, Emma Caughey, school principal, reported that the school reopened "on Monday, Jan. 30, with three departments, at the Third Baptist Church, about one mile from the 'Home' and two departments in the basement of the Little Zion Church, about three blocks distant from the Home." Like the 1876 arson of Emerson Institute, black Mobilians' outpouring of support demonstrated their refusal to give into opposition to the school and, more broadly, African American education. Similar to the public schools, Emerson Institute allowed black Mobilians to make progress in becoming an educated people. As it fulfilled an important function, parents, religious leaders, and activists felt the institution warranted their support and protection. Arson only reinforced their commitment to educational access for all. Hence black Mobilians and their allies contributed their money, space, and time to the school's rebuilding. As a result, Emerson Institute and Normal School reopened in a larger facility in October 1882.[11]

In their struggle for school accommodations, black Mobilians achieved limited success. Activists could not prevent the closure of some public schools. However, they secured improved facilities at the remaining schools as well as newer facilities. They also sustained a vibrant private school system as an alternative to the public schools. While their activism never achieved a substantial increase in overall enrollments, their activism permitted the continuation of the African American public schools in improved facilities.

During the 1880s, black Mobilians and their allies had two objectives in their teachers' campaign. First, they sought the employment of African American teachers and principals. Second, they demanded the creation of a public normal school option within the city's school system. African Americans achieved their greatest success in this struggle for quality public schools and fulfilled both objectives.

Activists viewed the employment of African American teachers as a high priority. Parents and other activists used the board's promise of employing African American teachers and the emergence of African American teaching corps in the city as the basis for their activism. In September 1878 the African American community, through a petition, secured the board's commitment in hiring of "Colored Teachers for [the] Colored schools." While the board affirmed its commitment with the hiring of William A. Caldwell in 1879, parents, religious leaders, and other activists continued to demand the hiring of African American teachers and principals in all of the schools. At the start of the decade, African Americans still composed a small percentage of the teachers and principals employed in the city's African American public schools. They demanded that school commissioners uphold their promise, which would be "in the best interest" of the schools, as an 1884 *Mobile Item* resolution argued. In pressuring the board, black Mobilians made some gains. More African American public school teachers received positions but they never reached the majority of the teachers employed. Often, they held subordinate positions to their white counterparts. These gains, though, did not stop parents from demanding African American teachers in all of the city's schools.[12]

By 1885, activists reevaluated their protest strategies. They demanded that the Board of the School Commissioners hire L. W. Cummings and F. A. Stewart. Although better qualified than the white teachers employed at the Davis Avenue School, the recent Fisk University graduates received subordinate teaching positions. In their appeal, the men turned to the community for support. Agreeing with Cummings and Stewart, approximately thirteen hundred black Mobilians signed petitions "contending that black teachers would do a better job and that those who pursued higher education deserved encouragement." Several white political elites also signed the petitions, as they felt that the African American and Creole schools should have African American and Creole teachers as a matter of fairness. However, the school board remained firm in its hiring decision. When petitioning failed, Cummings, Stewart, and the residents surrounding the Davis Avenue School considered more aggressive tactics.[13]

Activists proposed a boycott. Cummings, Stewart, and residents held a mass meeting in order to discuss "colored people for colored schools, and demand that the colored people have their rights." Stewart called for a boycott in order to "compel them to give us colored teachers." Four-fifths of the meeting attendees agreed. The 1885–1886 academic year opened with a boycott at the Davis Avenue School. Though attendance remained "quite small," the monthlong boycott quickly lost momentum and ultimately failed. School commissioners held firm in their decision. Support from white political elites dematerialized as a result of the new militancy. Yet the Davis Avenue community's very public discontent forced the board to again reconsider its hiring practices. The following year, the board hired several "colored teachers for the colored schools" while professing that race did not factor into the selection of teachers. This concession would not have been possible without the boycott or the activism of black Mobilians and their allies.[14]

Activists' greatest achievement occurred with the creation of the Broad Street Academy, a public normal school. In their struggle for African American public school teachers, activists worked with the American Missionary Association in the development of a normal school. Emerson Normal trained a corps of teachers that received teaching positions in the city and county schools throughout the decade. Owing to the success of Emerson Normal and black Mobilians' partnership with the American Missionary Association, the Board of School Commissioners created a new school that would serve as both a primary school as well as normal school for city residents. In 1887 the Broad Street Academy opened. The two-story clapboard school also fulfilled another community demand. Unlike Richmond Colored Normal, it featured an all–African American faculty that drew on the city's educated African American ministry, Emerson Normal graduates, and Emerson Institute graduates. In the normal program, faculty assisted with the training of future teachers. The primary school faculty, especially William A Caldwell, instilled racial pride and the rhetoric of racial progress to their students through education. Through its normal school and faculty, Broad Street Academy symbolized progress and success. Thus they achieved two victories with the creation of one institution.[15]

These victories produced an unintended consequence. The more militant protest style caused white political elites to seek alternative black leadership outside of Mobile. They took notice of a young man who was developing a school in rural Alabama. The effects this decision had on Educational Reconstruction manifested itself in the next decade with the meteoric rise of Booker T. Washington.

Born in Franklin County, Virginia, Booker T. Washington came of age during the early years of Educational Reconstruction in the rural South. Seasonal labor demands, availability of teachers, and family domestic economies in Malden, West Virginia, meant that Washington, like many rural black southerners, remained largely self-taught. As described in his autobiography, Washington cobbled an education from formal classroom learning, books supplied from his mother, private night school instruction, and lessons learned under the tutelage of Viola Ruffner. Indeed, Washington's "struggle for an education" revealed the limits of Educational Reconstruction and its slow outreach toward the rural South.[16] His more positive experience with Educational Reconstruction came with his enrollment in Hampton University. While at Hampton, he learned some of the key tenets of Educational Reconstruction—the importance of interracial cooperation and the necessity of refashioning one's education inside and outside the classroom to include racial uplift. Washington differed greatly from black Mobilians and other urban black southerners in that he focused on the rural South as the driver of change rather than as the trickle-down recipient. This shift in focus enabled him to develop the industrial education model as a countermovement to the more urban-centered Educational Reconstruction.[17]

Selected to lead Tuskegee Institute in 1881, Washington undertook the process of ensuring its financial stability and longevity. Like black Mobilians, Washington understood the importance of local white support, state recognition, and funding in the struggle for African American education. He fund-raised extensively and created a network of partners, often with the assistance of his mentor Samuel Chapman Armstrong, early founder and administrator of the Hampton Institute. He and his partners lobbied local and state officials for increased funding and recognition in a manner that appealed rather than threatened their racial sensibilities. But more important, Washington built Tuskegee from a few buildings to a leading institution officially recognized by the state of Alabama with annual appropriations. His style of leadership allowed for increased educational access, development of Tuskegee, and legitimacy of an institution aligned with the needs and lives of African Americans in Tuskegee and rural Alabama.[18]

Over the 1880s, both rural and urban Alabamian solutions coexisted. They served the needs of distinct populations without competition over state appropriations and support. As previously discussed, educational access, rather than the type of educational model, mattered to black Mobilians. This permitted cooperation between the competing urban and rural black Alabamian interests. Approximately a year after opening his church as a temporary location of Emerson Institute, Rev. Albert Owens delivered a closing address at the 1883 Tuskegee Day celebration, which received favorable reviews by students, faculty, and administrators.[19] Washington even solicited Rev. Owens's support in the 1887 relocation of Alabama State University from Marion to Montgomery. He feared that the "Col'd Baptist State Convention will make some effort to influence the Governor," and asked Warren Logan, Tuskegee educator and confidant, to "get Pettiford, Rev. A. F. Owen [sic], and Hawthorne to oppose the State Convention's meddling with the matter."[20] As evidenced by these two examples, meaningful cooperation occurred as the differing interests complemented the other. Ultimately, differences in approaches and educational models would change African American public education. Coexistence ended after the defeat of the Blair education bill of 1890.

Hindsight, though, must not overshadow the achievements of black Mobilians' most successful campaign. They gradually eroded the city's discriminatory hiring practices over a two-decade-long fight. In demanding that school commissioners uphold their 1879 promise, black Mobilians and Creoles of color steadily received teaching positions in the city's schools. They also secured all-black faculties at several city schools. While black Mobilians and Creoles still competed with white candidates, the overall number of those employed was greatly improved from the start of the decade. Moreover, they secured a public normal school option within the city. Broad Street Academy expanded the curriculum offered but also created a pool of candidates from which the city could draw for

employment. Perseverance and continued activism resulted in the gradual transformation of the city's schools for African American children. By 1890, enrolled
students were most likely taught by an African American or Creole teacher than
by a white teacher.[21]

In terms of school funding, black Mobilians' experience greatly differed from
that of black Richmonders. Indeed, it typified the experiences of most African
American struggles in cities, towns, and counties across the South. Neither Mobile nor areas outside of Virginia experienced a political revolution similar to the
Readjuster movement. For activists, the situation in Mobile remained bleak as
city and county officials could not adequately fund the public schools, whether
white or black. New state laws also proved to be an obstacle for the activists.
Despite these major challenges, black Mobilians and their allies recognized that
the success of the quality campaigns hinged on funding. As a result, they sought
as much money as possible for the school system, but they recognized that they
faced an uphill battle.

As in the previous decade, state and city financial difficulties posed the greatest obstacle to their efforts. During the 1880s, changes to the state distributions
from the "Colored fund" had major ramifications for black and Creole of color
Mobilians. Monies from the fund subsidized not only primary education but also
secondary education. Although state officials provided generous appropriations
to Tuskegee and other secondary schools, the public schools suffered. Overall,
this equated to less state funding. While Mobile received nearly two-thirds of the
state funds received by the county, state appropriations ranged between $4,000
and $5,000 for the entire decade. City officials never sufficiently overcame this
shortfall, as the 1875 constitution specifically prohibited local taxation for school
purposes. Thus school funding still posed a challenge during the 1880s.[22]

Unlike their Richmond counterparts, the Board of School Commissioners in
Mobile abandoned its policy of equitable school fund distributions. At the start
of the decade, Mobile city and county schools complied with the 1875 state constitutional mandates for school funding. The constitution and the resulting state
legislation gave school superintendents the authority to discriminate on the basis
of race in the distribution of school funds. Using their discretion, superintendents could divert more money to the white public schools than to the African
American public schools. As the city's ability to finance the public schools worsened, superintendents chose to apply monies from the "Colored fund" in order
to ensure that the white public schools completed a full academic year.[23]

This decision had major consequences. African American and Creole of color
students typically experienced shorter academic years than their white counter-

parts. They went to school fewer days than white students for seven academic years from 1878 to 1890. Students only once experienced a near equitable term, and twice did students experience a longer academic year than white students. This decision also affected teachers' salaries. The average monthly salaries for African American teachers were less than for white teachers. Moreover, the salaries received were much less than in the previous decade, when white teachers filled the majority of the teaching positions in the African American public schools. While this decision resulted in less classroom instruction and inequitable teacher pay, the city never closed the schools and officials attempted to respond to some of the activists' demands. Though the schools remained underfunded, activists maneuvered the poor economic terrain and achieved some success in the overall campaign for quality schools.[24]

In light of the ongoing school funding difficulties, black Mobilians and their allies looked to Washington, D.C., for assistance. The proposed Blair education bill, according to parents, community leaders, and activists, would greatly assist their efforts to create quality public schools. Activists found common ground with some white Mobilians on this issue. In 1880 the *Mobile Register* favored federal aid as a means of furthering the progress made by African Americans across the city and state. The newspaper asked its readers, "Do we not today see a great improvement in the race compared with that they were ten years ago?" In his 1887 annual report, State Superintendent Solomon Palmer also expressed his support for federal intervention: "Without assistance from the general government, I fear the State will never be able to give thousands of her children, now verging into manhood and womanhood, that education so necessary to qualify them for useful lives, to make them ornaments in society, a blessing to the State and benefactors or mankind; and without which they will have to grope their way in the darkness of ignorance, eking out a miserable existence through life." However, black Mobilians desired not only the infusion of federal monies but also the necessary oversight in the equitable distribution of said funds. State and city school fiscal policies demonstrated the need for federal oversight. Like black Richmonders, they recognized the promise of the bill in correcting southern fiscal mismanagement and elevating all southern African Americans. Hence they strongly endorsed the restoration of a partnership with the federal government. But as these national debates continued throughout the decade, black Mobilians and their allies pressed forward in their efforts to secure adequate funding for the city's schools.[25]

Black Mobilians and their allies experienced their greatest setback in the campaign for school funding, proving unable to overcome state and local forces to secure additional school funds. Despite these challenges, activists could claim a minor victory as the city's African American public schools never ceased. Though the schools were woefully underfunded, the parents of enrolled children continued to have access to a system supported by city and state taxes. As the decade progressed, it became increasingly clear that only federal intervention would overcome the school funding obstacles. Hence they hoped for the passage of the Blair education bill while "crawling" in their struggle for quality public schools.

In the 1880s, black Mobilians and their allies continued their slow advance toward quality public schools. They effectively read the political climate in Mobile and the state in general. They recognized that success would not occur as a result of political revolution. Instead of giving up hope, they persevered amid a bleak political landscape with petitioning, electoral politics, and even boycotting. Through their various campaigns, they made some progress by building on the previous decade's gains and lessons. They sustained student enrollments and won renovations to existing schools and the construction of new facilities. They protected Emerson Institute and other private schools. In so doing, they maintained academic choice for the city's black and Creole of color citizenry. They successfully agitated for African American public school teachers. Thus activists' reading of the political landscape dictated not only the overall quality campaign's progress but also how they operated within it.

However, black Mobilians and their allies proved unable to overcome several obstacles. Political realities prevented them from securing direct representation on the Board of School Commissioners. But their greatest failure lay in securing adequate city and state funding. The schools remained underfunded. While black Mobilians pressed on, they understood that overcoming the school funding issue remained their greatest challenge. It was a challenge that required more than their activism. It required national intervention.

Like black Richmonders, they increasingly realized that federal funding and oversight would permit additional public school facilities for every school-age child desiring an education while decreasing the discrepancy between enrolled and non-attending children. It would also ensure that enrolled students had access to quality conditions and quality teachers. Hence black Mobilians hoped for the passage of Blair education bill, strove for additional success in their respective quality campaigns, and persevered for future generations of children.

Epilogue

*The Blair Education Bill and
the Death of Educational
Reconstruction, 1890*

After twenty-five years of steady progress, the events of 1890 provoked unexpected commentary from two individuals invested in African American education. In December 1890 Maria L. Waterbury surveyed the
contemporary African American educational efforts in the city of Mobile, state
of Alabama, and across the South. The former Mobile Freedmen's School educator found the lack of adequate local school funding and northern philanthropy
disturbing. To city and state officials, Waterbury demanded, "In view of this state
of things in one of the Gulf states, will the South please the North, a chance to
keep still, by giving free schools to all its people." But for her northern audience
she offered a stronger rebuke. Their perceived abandonment of the eight million
southern African Americans prompted Waterbury to conclude her autobiography with a pointed question: "Reader, have you done you duty by them?"[1]

Thirteen years later, W. E. B. Du Bois offered similar commentary on the re-
treat from Educational Reconstruction. Like Waterbury, he questioned why conditions had deteriorated since 1890. In his essay, titled "Of the Training of Black
Men," Du Bois argued that the "years of constructive definite effort toward the
building of complete school systems" crumbled as a result of "new obstacles." He
reasoned, "In the midst, then, of the larger problems of Negro education sprang
up the more practical question of work, the inevitable economic quandary that
faces a people in the transition from slavery to freedom, and especially those who
make that change amid hate and prejudice, lawlessness and ruthless competition." Hence Du Bois concluded that these new obstacles, specifically the rise of
industrial education, attacks on the liberal arts tradition instituted in the postwar
African American public schools, and worsening race relations, permitted the
deteriorating conditions.[2]

After the gains of Educational Reconstruction, what had transpired that
would allow Waterbury and Du Bois to make such remarks? The answer lies in
the events surrounding the Blair education bill in 1890 and the shared realization
of the two divergent port cities that the future of African American education

rested on this legislation. By extending the traditional Reconstruction chronology, as I have argued throughout, these events signaled the real closure of the post-emancipation moment and the opening of another phase of African American education, which would last for the next sixty-four years. More significantly, the new phase symbolized the triumph of rural southerners in shaping African American education over their urban brethren.[3]

Educational Reconstruction ended in 1890 when Congress failed to pass the Blair education bill. Like the Compromise of 1877, their failure represented another compromise, but in terms of education rather than politics. Motivated by concern for the plight of the former slaves and inadequately financed public schools for white and black children in the South, Senator Henry W. Blair initially proposed the bill in 1880, which allotted $77 million in federal funds for public schools to be distributed to the states, proportionate to their illiteracy rates, over eight years. As illiteracy was much higher in the southern states, black Mobilians, black Richmonders, and the superintendents of public instruction in Virginia and Alabama supported the bill, which would have ensured the stability of the public schools for white and African American children. Together, they convinced several congressmen to support its passage in an almost-decade-long fight. This support allowed for the bill to almost pass three times during the 1880s.[4]

It is not possible to highlight the effects of the bill, campaign, and defeat of Educational Reconstruction without understanding the man who championed it. Born in Campton, New Hampshire, Henry William Blair was the third child of William Henry and Lois Baker Blair. As his most recent biographer has shown, hardship and loss marked his early years. His father was severely hurt in an accident while demolishing a building and died within a month, in December 1836. His father's death forced Blair's mother to place his two older siblings into family homes while she, Henry, and her young infant moved between family members until she permanently placed him with the Richard Bartlett household in May 1843. Within this house Blair found stability as well as a strong educational foundation, and he eventually became a lawyer.[5] These formative childhood experiences convinced him of the transformative nature of education and profoundly influenced his later fight for the Blair education bill. During the Civil War, he enlisted as a major in the 15th Regiment of the New Hampshire Infantry and rose to the rank of lieutenant colonel. Following the war, Blair entered politics and worked his way through several state representative positions in the New Hampshire legislature before being elected as a midterm replacement to the U.S. Senate in 1879.[6]

A fateful alliance with William Mahone, the Readjuster senator of Virginia, led to Blair's appointment to the Senate Education and Labor Committee and the subsequent birth of the Blair education bill in 1880. As the chairman, Blair developed and pushed this legislation through committee. The bill, like the man, was influenced by the first phase of Educational Reconstruction under the Freedmen's Bureau and congressional reformers who had proposed federal aid for public education during the 1870s. Differing from previous education bills, the Blair legislation "called for the creation of a permanent, uniform, national, public school system in America supported with federal funds."[7] The bill not only required shifting public school operations from the states to the federal government, but also attempted to fulfill "the promises made to educate blacks during Reconstruction." Since the majority of the funds, roughly 75 percent, would assist southern schools, the bill would have infused southern African American public schools, more than any others, with essential monies. This would have rectified the major challenges endured by black Richmonders and Mobilians in their quest for quality public schools and the extension of educational gains beyond the urban South into the rural South. Their respective state and local government partners would have been able to fully fund the educational systems created in the Reconstruction-era constitutions without difficulty and satisfy their obligation to citizens, white and black. Most important, federal oversight would have prevented any distribution irregularities and ensure a degree of protection similar to the Freedmen's Bureau school phase of Educational Reconstruction.[8]

While it was not the only educational bill under consideration at the time, the Blair bill received the most serious attention as a feasible solution. Unlike the other piece of legislation, Blair crafted his around strong qualitative and statistical data collected by J. L. M. Curry of the Peabody Education Fund, John Eaton of the National Educational Assembly, local and state government reports, and the 1880 U.S. census.[9] He devised a plan that allowed for success, centered on this research project as well as a public relations campaign and state superintendents' appearances at formal hearings conducted by a joint meeting of House of Representatives and Senate education committees. He not only personally answered any questions received but also defended the bill and its constitutionality in such a manner that his critics could not easily dismiss the legislation outright as had been done with the other bills. As a result, his seemingly sensible plan easily passed in the Senate in 1884 and 1886 but passed only narrowly a third time in 1888 by a vote of thirty-nine to twenty-nine. Unfortunately, it stalled in the House of Representatives each time. Democrat Speaker John G. Carlisle of Kentucky stated that he "refused to squander the House's precious time on it."[10] It often never left the House Committee on Education and Labor, and it never reached a full vote, despite the efforts of Thomas H. Browne, Republican representative and Confederate veteran of Accomack County, Virginia, John M. Brower, Republican representative of Mount Airy, North Carolina, and other proponents. Factionalism within the Republican Party prevented any meaningful defense against Speaker Carlisle and other critics in the House.[11]

Beyond Congress, the northern media voiced opposition. Publications like *The Nation* made racial as well as economic arguments to oppose the bill. Edwin L. Godkin and his staff laid the intellectual foundation that would later form the basis of the opposition mounted by the *Mobile Register* and other southern newspapers by the end of the decade. Citing the 1880 census data, a *Nation* editorialist argued, "It is absurd to say that the South in 1888 needs federal aid to educate their children because in 1880 there were three million grown-up illiterates, born either slaves or 'poor whites' of the slavery era."[12] In a way, *The Nation* editorialist employed language concerning the status of African Americans and the Gilded Age nation akin to that used in Justice Joseph P. Bradley's majority opinion in the *Civil Rights Cases* of 1883. In this regard, the Supreme Court and editorialist concurred. The obligation of the nation toward former slaves had ended. Self-reliance and hard work, not federal subsidies and special protections, served as the most effective remedies to this regional problem.[13]

The Nation then highlighted the flaws in Blair's data. Blair relied heavily on information gathered from southern superintendents of education. These superintendents cited continuous but slow progress without any federal aid within their respective state; therefore, *The Nation* concluded that "outside help is not needed," especially in Virginia and Alabama. The rhetoric of progress proved especially salient for Democrats and Republicans tied to Gilded Age corporations. New South industrialism successfully brought the region "impoverished by the war" into economic recovery through the ingenuity and innovative efforts of southern industrialists rather than the federal government. Thus, *The Nation* concluded, "The South has shown herself able to overcome the difficulties of the situation, and her success is another tribute to American self-reliance."[14] Blair and his proponents combated such critiques with the support of letters to the editor and the African American press. Letters, such as those by George Groff in *Science*, and regular commentary in the *Christian Recorder*, extolled the benefits for southern education, white and black, but also highlighted the importance in continuing the successes of Educational Reconstruction. A January 1887 *Christian Recorder* article pragmatically noted the fruits of the national activism: "It is a nice thing for the white people of this country to clamor for the Blair bill on account of our poor people. It matters little to us on what ground the clamor is made, but let it continue. We want the national educational law." By 1890, arguments for and against the Blair bill were quite developed and entrenched.[15]

As national support waned, Blair, black urban southerners, and other proponents of the Educational Reconstruction felt that the 51st Congress, better known as the Billion-Dollar Congress, was its last best chance. The political demographics of Washington, D.C., changed as a consequence of the 1888 elections. Republicans now controlled the House of Representatives, Senate, and White House. Most significant, the 1890 congressional agenda centered on questions of race, the status of southern African Americans, and race relations with debates on the Butler emigration bill and federal elections bill. Unlike with previous attempts, Blair and his proponents had every reason to believe that Congress would ensure the bill's passage.[16]

The formal debate showcased Blair's confidence in the political moment. While the Senate raised the issue on February 6, 1890, Blair launched a "one-man filibuster on many afternoons over the next six weeks." Speaking continuously for two weeks in mid-February, his nuanced argument rested on the core tenets of Educational Reconstruction: "An educated South, white and black, would be good for the party, national economy and race relations in the America." He depicted his southern critics as members of the antebellum slave regime who, in the fight to maintain power, refused to recognize the new postwar America. He provided examples from outside the region to show the benefits of a national rather than regional solution. In illustrating that Charleston spent more money per capita on education than did Boston and other non-southern areas, he appealed to some northern critics. He also addressed the economic arguments made by *The Nation* and industrial capitalists by linking the Blair bill to the expectant ascendancy of the United States as a global power. After the filibuster, Blair and his allies deftly responded to those opposing the legislation from Texas, West Virginia, Wisconsin, and Kansas on the grounds of constitutionality and preferential treatment of African American education. Ignoring the negative national media attention, including the coverage in the *Mobile Daily Register*, and the silence of President Benjamin Harrison, on the eve of the March 20 vote Blair felt he had secured enough support for a "one-vote victory."[17]

The nature of the Blair education bill debate, national support, and political reality convinced black Richmonders and Mobilians of a forthcoming successful outcome. Whereas black Mobilians had the *Huntsville Gazette*, black Richmonders employed the *Richmond Planet* in articulating their confidence.[18] As in the previous decade, the newspaper pursued a more aggressive campaign in coalescing white and black support. John Mitchell, Jr., Richmond Colored Normal graduate and editor, and his staff reminded readers of Senator Blair's support during the concluding years of the Readjuster moment in the city and state whose "intelligent opinion" could be trusted to secure a unified voice behind the Blair bill. As a friend of the editor and the city, the *Richmond Planet* openly endorsed the legislation and the man.[19]

More important, the seemingly imminent Blair bill emboldened Mitchell and his staff in counteracting local white opposition. Less than three weeks before the final vote, a *Richmond Planet* article targeted Frank G. Ruffin, a Confederate veteran and the second auditor of Virginia. Using the successful Richmond public schools as evidence, the unknown author, presumably Mitchell, charged that the underlying purpose of Ruffin and his colleagues in using state appropriations for African American education was "not to make a better citizen of him, but to make him a willing tool—a Democrat. And in a failure to bring about this result, he would declare the money expended wasted."[20] He immediately followed this assertion by attacking Ruffin's loyalty to the state: "We veil our eyes in shame and beg the world not to look upon the denegation of a Virginia citizen. The shades of WASHINGTON and JEFFERSON stand aghast."[21] The author's brazen questioning showed Mitchell's and black Richmonders' firm belief that the Blair bill would pass. This strong faith in the political moment and Senator Blair's abilities empowered Mitchell and his staff, as the Readjusters had done a few years earlier with the appointment of two African American school board members. As discussed in an earlier chapter, they felt that the political landscape was in their favor.

The March 20 vote revealed otherwise. Although Republicans controlled Congress and the presidency, the issue of national school funding and African American public school education failed to unite all Republicans. As historian Michael Perman has demonstrated, "Sectional post–Civil War problems were no longer sources of cohesion in the party but instead to served to divide it." While older Republicans like Henry W. Blair, President Harrison (albeit not publicly), and John Sherman still championed a federal education bill, younger Republicans assisted with its defeat. In a forty-three to thirty-nine vote, twenty-seven Republicans and twelve southern Democrats voted for the bill while eighteen Republicans, sixteen northern, midwestern, and western Democrats, and nine southern Democrats voted against the bill. Despite almost succeeding, supporters lost their best chance in securing the bill's passage, and the legislation never reappeared. Blair's continued revival attempts failed. Interestingly, Congress briefly debated and successfully passed the second Morrill bill of 1890, which contributed to the formation of seventeen historically black colleges. African American public school education and Educational Reconstruction simply failed to unite Congress and the nation as it had both in 1865 and after the departure of the Freedmen's Bureau. Thus bitter feelings and a profound sense of mourning reigned across the urban South, the African American press, and even Maria L. Waterbury's memoir. The 51st Congress and the party of Lincoln had betrayed them.[22]

In Richmond and Mobile, the Blair education bill defeat stunned residents. The *Daily Dispatch* of Richmond announced its defeat with the simple headline "Blair Bill Dead," while the *Mobile Daily Register* informed readers with the front-page article titled "The Bill Was Lost."[23] The African American press reflected the shock as well. The *Huntsville Gazette* offered gratitude to Senator Blair for "his able and manly fight in behalf of Education" but offered no real recourse other than hope for the revival attempts and perseverance in general.[24] After a brief hiatus, the *Richmond Planet* pressed readers into preventing the Republican majority from failing them again with the national election bill while simultaneously urging readers to remain hopeful for the bill's revival in July 1890. They did not accept the finality of its defeat until November.[25] Recognizing the blow to Educational Reconstruction, this defeat called for more introspection regarding the its reasons and effects in their respective communities and states.

In some respects, the defeat of the Blair education bill highlighted the failures of the national Republican Party to shape the postwar South. Reconstruction policy required a quick restoration of government in order to change the southern society and provide southern African Americans with basic protections.[26] President Andrew Johnson and southern white terrorism stymied this policy, in which political parties served as temporary agents of reform. The Reconstruction reforms required a military occupation, a strong federal government, and southern Republican governments supported by an African American electorate. These essential elements, however, invited attacks of corruption, patronage, and bad government by individuals from both within and without the Republican Party.[27] Although doomed from the start of Educational Reconstruction, Republicans managed to provide some educational access by partnering with black southerners, especially black Richmonders and Mobilians. Indeed, they ensured some basic protections in the Reconstruction-era state constitutions, which legitimated the African American schoolhouse. By 1890 the Republican Party's vision proved inadequate. Finding common ground in the language of good government, the national Republican Party abandoned its southern black allies.

The success of Educational Reconstruction also facilitated the defeat of the Blair education bill by making it easier for some white northerners to abandon southern African American education. As with the Reconstruction constitutional amendments, the former Confederate states' extension of education to include all citizens, white and black, demonstrated that the national project worked. African American public schools and even some normal schools received state funding as well as basic protections. African American school-age children had access to an education just as white children did, albeit not always convenient in terms of location or the nature of accommodations. With state-funded normal schools, such as Richmond Colored Normal and Broad Street Academy, African American teachers found employment in the classroom. Hence the common school system produced under Educational Reconstruction succeeded by contributing to the rise of productive citizens, white and black. In understanding Reconstruction as an "era of citizenship," some white northerners felt that the nation had fulfilled its duty to southern African Americans in their transition from slavery to freedom.[28]

For other white northerners, changing attitudes toward southern African Americans stemmed from their fears about labor and an activist government. Educational Reconstruction required an expanded activist government on a state and national level. Such government intervention exacerbated northern white fears that a labor underclass "would use government to redistribute wealth," undermine their power, and ultimately destroy American society. Therefore, these white northerners championed the defeat of the Blair education bill in order to limit further government activism for southern African Americans and other "disadvantaged groups" in the nation.[29] In short, the Blair education bill represented "the use of government to provide extraordinary benefits for African Americans." These white northerners felt that it was the responsibility of local government, not the federal government, to handle such matters. Opponents successfully argued that the passage of the bill would be catastrophic for the nation's future by linking the Blair bill to white northern labor concerns. The national upheaval over the Blair legislation further contributed to northern acceptance of disfranchisement in order to prevent the "creation of a paternalistic government catering to those unwilling to work."[30]

Most significantly, the failure of the Blair education bill demonstrated that black Richmonders and Mobilians never shared the goals and objectives of even well-intentioned white northerners. Their unwavering desire to become an educated people outweighed any consideration of federal policy or changing white northern opinions. This fundamental tenet of Educational Reconstruction guided their actions after the Blair defeat. Now, black Richmonders, black Mobilians, and their remaining allies realized that they could no longer rely on the federal government to intervene on behalf of African American education.

In addition to these setbacks, new obstacles emerged with the meteoric rise of Booker T. Washington. Unlike the challenges that arose with end of the Freedmen's Bureau, southern urban African American proponents of Educational Reconstruction could not readily overcome this challenge from within the African American community. Indeed, Du Bois correctly identified the triumph of industrial education as a major consequence of the Blair defeat on African American education. Washington's charisma, philosophy, and network of partners signaled the real closure of Educational Reconstruction, more so than the March 20 vote, the failure of the national Republican Party, and the sharp decline in national white support which they had enjoyed since 1865.

Born under slavery, Booker T. Washington haphazardly experienced Educational Reconstruction in rural West Virginia. Work and the seasonal academic school year caused the young man to be largely self-taught. As professed in his autobiography *Up from Slavery*, he acquired his education from Ms. Viola Ruffner and others prior to attending Hampton Institute. Although Hampton might not have existed without Educational Reconstruction or the efforts of black Richmonders, Washington found the experience transformative in ways that made him turn against the urban-centered philosophy that helped him. His experiences and mentorship as a student and faculty member profoundly influenced his educational philosophy, attitude toward Educational Reconstruction, and, ultimately, the Blair education bill.[31]

Washington's views on the Blair bill resembled those of his mentor Samuel Chapman Armstrong, a former Freedmen's Bureau agent instrumental in the establishment and early administration of Hampton Institute. As an early opponent, Armstrong regarded it as the antithesis of the Hampton Model and encouraged the *Southern Workman* readership, students, faculty, and alumni to oppose it. "As for federal aid to education in the Blair Bill," Armstrong firmly believed that its "fatal error" was being "opposed to doctrine of self help."[32] At this point in his career, Washington actively sought Armstrong's counsel as he developed Tuskegee Institute, so would not have come out against him. It becomes evident that Washington embodied his mentor's reasoning on the Blair bill when one examines his correspondence, public speeches, and editorials over the decade.

Washington made explicit reference to the legislation in a letter to John E. McConnell. In this December 17, 1885, letter, Washington gave a passionate argument to the white Republican lawyer from Wisconsin on the necessity of educational pre-qualifications in order to bring about peaceful elections and race relations in the region. He saw that the adoption of new voting qualifications would "create an ambition in the minds of the ignorant Negroes that would soon lead them to seek education."[33] In calling for the creation of essentially literacy tests, Washington wrote, "The passage of the Blair Educational Bill will bring about the most speedy remedy for illiteracy. In my mind, the political condition will be most speedily remedied by a division of the present political parties. At present, the Democratic party is composed almost entirely of whites and the Republican party is composed almost entirely of blacks—it is one race against the other. When both races are largely represented in both parties, there will be fair and peaceable elections."[34] In responding most likely to a question posed by McConnell's original letter, he acknowledged the bill as a possible solution to the issues surrounding voting, but he did not come out for or against it. Rather, Washington immediately followed the sentence with his solution of amiable local southern race relations in lieu of a forced congressional one. The Blair bill, therefore, represented a possible but mostly likely ineffective solution. Ultimately, Washington's seemingly evasive remark serves as a critical assessment more of the effectiveness of congressional legislation in remediating race relations than of the bill itself.

Beyond this sole explicit reference, Washington's indirect Blair education bill references remained consistent with his developing philosophy of self-help, education, and race relations later articulated in his 1895 Atlanta Exposition address. Washington argued at the 1882 meeting of the Alabama State Teachers' Association in Selma, "It is true that we need lawyers and doctors, and at the same time we need inventors, machinists, builders of steamboats and successful planters and merchants. Such persons will do more to banish prejudice than all the laws Congress can pass."[35] Without specifically mentioning the bill, he concluded that individuals trained in the industrial education system would have better success than Congress would in ending prejudice. He expressed similar sentiments in an April 1885 letter to the editor of the Montgomery *Advertiser* protesting his discriminatory treatment experienced in a railroad incident: "My faith is that the influences which are going to permanently right such wrongs are going to come from within the South and from the Southern people. National legislation and other outside attempts fail."[36] As in the 1882 speech and 1885 McConnell letter, Washington disparaged national legislation in favor of localism and African American self-help. Agitation against the Blair education bill, whether directly or indirectly, remained consistent with his remarks on congressional legislation as remedies to race or educational issues as well as those of his mentor.

Washington's views differed greatly from black Richmonders and Mobilians who fully supported the legislation. These activists relied on the national support of African Americans who feared the bill's defeat as a blow to Educational Reconstruction. The black press, such as the *Christian Recorder*, organ of the African Methodist Episcopal Church, regularly implored readers to demand that Congress "pass the Blair educational bill" and, if necessary, "pray [for] the passage of the Blair Educational Bill now before the Congress of the United States."[37] This commentary would have reassured members of the Emanuel African Methodist Episcopal Church of Mobile and Ebenezer African Methodist Episcopal Church in Richmond in their struggle to pass the educational funding legislation. Therefore, black Richmonders and Mobilians could and did ignore the young man at Tuskegee. Unlike with other issues, as discussed previously, divergent urban and rural educational interests prevented cooperation on the Blair education bill.

After Washington's Atlanta Exposition address, black Richmonders, black Mobilians, and their white partners took notice. His open support of the changing race relations and the industrial education model represented the future, and Educational Reconstruction became regulated to the past. Coupled with the 1890 Blair bill defeat, the consequences of this shift ultimately closed the door on the revolutionary moment in African American education.

Long-standing white partners of Educational Reconstruction abandoned their black urban proponents for Washington's advice and support. His industrial education model provided them with a convenient exit. As discussed in previous chapters, the Peabody Education Fund had been an essential source of funding for primary African American public education since its creation in 1867. Black Richmonders and black Mobilians had previously relied on this partnership to establish security for the state-funded public schools. The organization's reoriented funding model, from primary liberal arts education to secondary education with a strong emphasis on industrial education, now excluded them. Trustees actively sought Washington's counsel on the distribution of funds, from amounts to recipients. Whereas Tuskegee and other schools that adopted industrial education greatly benefited, black Richmonders and Mobilians found themselves shutout from not only the Peabody Fund but also the Slater and Rosenwald Funds. By switching focus, furthermore, these philanthropists maintained their commitment to African American education without any guilt, as the "public schools had to be kept open, and at the same time, the private schools which were furnishing teachers and leaders were depending not on state aid but on Northern philanthropy." The substitution absolved them, in their minds, from the negative consequences encountered in Mobile and Richmond.[38]

Most significantly, black Richmonders and Mobilians lost the support of Senator Henry William Blair. After the 1890 defeat, Blair shifted the focus of the bill to include industrial education in order to secure its passage. Blair openly courted the support of Washington instead of his previous African American allies across the urban South and nation. Blair explained in his February 1896 letter, "Your wonderful address at the Atlanta Exposition together with the embodiment of your great life-work in the Industrial Institute point you out as the one man whose endorsement of this movement will make it successful, and the opportunity for its conspicuous inauguration at the Conference seem to be Providential."[39] With this shift and personal plea, Washington supported the revamped bill. By 1906, in a letter to Samuel L. Williams, Washington acknowledged Blair as "one white friend on guard at Washington."[40] While the modified legislation never materialized, black Richmonders and Mobilians found themselves excluded from the national educational debate, in which the tenets of Washingtonian industrial education instead of Educational Reconstruction dominated.

Building on a rich legacy, black Richmonders and Mobilians responded to these new setbacks as they had previously done. They shifted strategies to deal with the new political and racial climate. Since Confederate defeat, they had used education as a means to position themselves as leaders who could uplift both the race and the post–Civil War nation. As race relations worsened, educator–activists and other middle-class reformers were essential in preparing a new generation for future challenges and social mobility, advocating on behalf of the less-educated African Americans, and promoting a vision of freedom, citizenship, and equality still centered on education. They firmly felt that education remained the best vehicle.

Black Richmonders and Mobilians found encouragement in the achievements of a recent past rather than their slave past. Through Educational Reconstruction, they overcame the concerted efforts to limit the growth of African American education in their respective cities, states, and regions. They moved African American education from being a nonentity to a legitimate institution, established a professional class of African American public schoolteachers, developed educational resources essential to daily school operations, and ensured its continuation for future generations. As partners and circumstances changed over the twenty-five-year period, Educational Reconstruction had profoundly assisted their transition from slavery to freedom and inclusion in the body politic. For black Richmonders and Mobilians, the Blair education bill defeat, failed

federal intervention, white northerners' abandonment of Educational Reconstruction, and the emergence of Booker T. Washington could not overshadow
the triumph of the Freedmen's Schools or state-funded public schools yielded by
their educational networks.

Educational Reconstruction reinforced in the minds of black Richmonders
and Mobilians that realizing its promise required continual negotiations, vigi-
lance, perseverance, compromise, and, above all, patience. Indeed, the twenty-
five-year period cemented the necessity of flexibility and adaptability in resolving
challenges and obstacles through creative solutions without sacrificing the larger
mission embarked on in 1865. Nonetheless, the promise of its benefits continued
to motivate individuals who came of age during Educational Reconstruction at
the turn of the twentieth century.

Thus Daniel Webster Davis continued to find hope in the tenets of Educational
Reconstruction as W. E. B. Du Bois and Maria Waterbury mourned its end with
the failure of the Blair bill. Employing language similar to Washington's Atlanta
Exposition address, Davis informed 1900 Richmond Colored Normal graduates
that their destiny remained in the South, and that white southerners were integral to future racial progress. He informed the graduates, "Another blunder you
are likely to make, my young friends, is to think that every white man is your
enemy." He firmly believed "with all my heart, with all the past before me, with
all the gloomy outlook that nowhere under God's sun will the negro find truer,
kinder, more considerate friends than right here in the southland, among these
white people, where we were born, where we have lived, and where we expect to
die." Saddened that the races "seem to be growing further apart," he offered the
graduates a remedy through their postgraduation mission of "politeness, honesty
of purpose and soberly to bring about a better relation."[41]

On the surface, Davis's embrace of Washingtonian philosophy seems to pan-
der to the prominent white audience members, who found its conciliatory nature appealing. An article in *The Times* heralded his remarks as "excellent advice
given to young colored people" in which white elites "approve of the sentiments
expressed."[42] Davis, though, epitomized the sentiments of individuals like himself who came of age in the immediate postwar period and were its chief beneficiaries. Schooled in the tenets of Educational Reconstruction, they refused to
abandon it. Interracial cooperation and establishing strategic alliances enabled
Davis's own success as well as the success of countless of other urban African
Americans. Thus it was not contradictory for him to request that the graduates
not distrust all whites and to align themselves with individuals who shared a

common belief in racial uplift in the city, state, or region. After all, Davis saw himself "by nature and training a Virginian" who fought for the racial uplift of all Virginians through liberal arts as well as industrial education.

Recognizing that not all could "be preachers, teachers, lawyers, doctors, scientists and philosophers," Davis instructed the Richmond Colored Normal graduates to "remember it is as honorable to saw planks in a carpenter shop as to saw bones in the dissecting-room; as noble to dig the roots out of the soil as to extract the square root in the class-room." Regardless of their future professions, these graduates as well as other school-age children had a larger duty. Davis reminded them in the concluding paragraphs, "Go forth, young men and women, find places for yourselves, whether in school, shop or farm, and preach the eternal gospel of the elevation of your people. Tell the young negro that he must behave himself, that he must have more respect for himself, his race, and those by whom he is surrounded."[43] They were expected, as his generation trained under Educational Reconstruction, to refashion their education to work on behalf of racial uplift at their place of employment, their homes, and, more important, their community.

Unlike in 1865, the 1900 Richmond Colored Normal graduating class, black Richmonders, and black Mobilians were better equipped for such an undertaking. They continued to build on a legacy of interracial networks that had yielded them success since emancipation. Assessing the new landscape, black Richmonders and black Mobilians continued to push through an educational agenda for their respective cities and states without sacrificing their commitment to a larger struggle for legitimacy, educational access, and citizenship. As partners and conditions changed, they never lost sight of these aims.

Though Educational Reconstruction ended, African American public school education did not. It merely entered a new phase as the Jim Crow era posed new challenges. Using the lessons learned over a twenty-five-year period, black Richmonders, black Mobilians, and other urban African Americans refined older strategies, adopted new tactics, and sought new partners. They maintained an unwavering support of interracial cooperation, the transformative nature of education, and their non-slave status in the post–Civil War urban South. Although never neatly fitting within the Washington and Du Bois paradigm, they remained true to the goals of Educational Reconstruction.

Hence Daniel Webster Davis and Giles Jackson articulated these fundamental tenets of Educational Reconstruction in their preface to the 1908 edition of *Industrial History of the Negro Race of the United States*. "Every race has its history written by its own members. This, to our minds," proclaimed Davis and

Jackson, "is a special reason why the Negro should have a history of himself, written by members of his own race, and that history should be taught in the schools of the youth of the race."[44] The authors as well as others who came of age in Educational Reconstruction understood that their work remained unfinished. Using the knowledge acquired since escaping "the clutches of those who held [them] in slavery," they made Wallace Turnage's earlier words palatable to a new generation.[45] Thus they hoped by "showing the strides made by the race" that it "would prove beneficial, not only to the adult, but especially the youth."[46] No longer crawling, Educational Reconstruction and its legacy enabled black Rich-monders and Mobilians to continue their "walk . . . slowly, but surely" into the twentieth century.[47]

Acknowledgments

Educational Reconstruction could not have been completed without the assistance and support of many people. The late Gerald R. Gill provided guidance when I began my initial foray into the subject in 2002. Dr. Heather A. Williams's encouragement and editorial suggestions enhanced the overall project; however, her calming voice of reason motivated me as I revised the initial manuscript while teaching at Elizabeth City State University. In revising subsequent drafts of the manuscript, Andy L. Slap's editorial eye was invaluable. His patience and confidence in the project greatly assisted in producing the final product. Thank you.

I would like to also express my gratitude to family, friends, and colleagues for their support during the entire process. My parents, Millicent and Nathaniel Green; brothers, Joshua and Zachary; and relatives have always encouraged me in this endeavor with their unconditional love, support, and sympathetic ears. They have endured all of my anxieties and ramblings without complaint. Stretching the boundaries of a typical friendship, Marja Humphrey, Catherine Connor, Elizabeth Gritter, and Dwana Waugh have read, commented on, and offered advice on several sections of the final project. Critical feedback and insights received at the following conferences helped with honing key sub-arguments: the New Perspectives of Black History and Culture conference, the Annual Meeting of the North Carolina Association of Historians, the Hawaii International Conference on Arts and Humanities, the Urban Historical Association conference, the Society of Civil War Historians conference, and the Association of the Study of African American Life and History conference. Lastly, my colleagues at Elizabeth City State University and the University of Alabama have been instrumental in revising several manuscript drafts. I want to thank especially Rebecca Seaman, Charles Reed, Ted Mitchell, Utz McKnight, Jennifer D. Jones, Jennifer Purvis, Jennifer Schoaf, and Cassander Smith. Thank you for providing critical feedback and commentary during every phase of this project.

The manuscript would not have been possible without several fellowships and archives. Travel funds and fellowships received from the Center for the Study of the American South, the Massachusetts Historical Society, the Virginia Historical Society, the History Department at the University of North Carolina, the Doris G. Quinn Fellowship, Elizabeth City State University, the NEH Summer

Programs for College and University Teachers, and the University of Alabama allowed me to conduct necessary research. I would like to give many thanks to the archivists and staff at the following facilities: the Massachusetts Historical Society, the Virginia Historical Society, the Library of Virginia, the Richmond Public Library, the Maggie Lena Walker National Historical Site, Virginia State University, Vanderbilt University, the University of Virginia, Duke University, the University of South Alabama, the Mobile Municipal Archives, the Mobile Public Library, the Historic Mobile Preservation Society, Davis Library at the University of North Carolina, the North Carolina Collection at Wilson Library, Mercer University, the Alabama Department of Archives and History, and the University of Alabama.

Finally, I dedicate this study to my mother, whose poignant question inspired the project. I never forgot it as I journeyed to completion.

Notes

Introduction

1. David W. Blight, ed., *A Slave No More: Two Men Who Escaped to Freedom, Including Their Own Narratives* (Orlando, Fla.: Harcourt, 2007), 214–15.

2. Ibid.

3. Daniel B. Williams, *Freedom and Progress, and Other Choice Addresses on Practical, Scientific, Educational, Philosophic, Historic, and Religious Subjects* (Petersburg, Va.: Daniel B. Williams, 1890), 7–8, 82, 86–87.

4. Ibid., 86–87; Henry Wadsworth Longfellow Dana, "'Sail on O Ship of State!': How Longfellow Came to Write These Lines 100 Years Ago," *Colby Quarterly* 2 (February 1950): 209–14.

5. Christian G. Samito, *Becoming American under Fire: Irish Americans, African Americans, and the Politics of Citizenship during the Civil War Era* (Ithaca, N.Y.: Cornell University Press, 2009), 4.

6. Ibid., 5–12.

7. Midori Takagi, *Rearing Wolves to Our Destruction: Slavery in Richmond, Virginia, 1782–1865* (Charlottesville: University Press of Virginia, 1999), 21–23; Gregg D. Kimball, *American City, Southern Place: A Cultural History of Antebellum Richmond* (Athens: University of Georgia Press, 2000), 3–36.

8. Harriett Amos, *Cotton City: Urban Development in Antebellum Mobile* (Birmingham: University of Alabama Press, 1985), 7, 22–24, 26–47, 196.

9. Census records, 1800–60; "Richmond Population, 1742–1860," African American Lecture Series, September 25, 2001, Vertical File-Richmond Slavery, VHS; Amos, *Cotton City*, 85.

10. Howard N. Rabinowitz, *Race Relations in the Urban South, 1865–1890* (1978; repr., Athens: University of Georgia Press, 1996), 3, 31; John Hope Franklin and Alfred A. Moss, Jr., *From Slavery to Freedom: A History of African Americans* (New York: Alfred A. Knopf, 2000), 141; Steven Hahn, *A Nation under Our Feet: Black Political Struggles in the Rural South from Slavery to the Great Migration* (Cambridge, Mass.: Belknap Press, 2003), 22; Amos, *Cotton City*, 85, 88–89.

11. Henrico County (Va.): Register of Free Negroes and Mulattoes, 1852–63, LVA; Society for the Prevention of the Absconding and Abduction of Slaves, Richmond, Va., Minutes of Directors' Meetings, 1833–49, VHS; Nancy C. Frantel, *Richmond Virginia Uncovered: The Records of Slaves and Free Blacks Listed in the City Sergeant Jail Register, 1841–1846* (Westminster, Md.: Heritage Books, 2010), 5–7, 95–98; Amos, *Cotton City*, 146–48; Michael W. Fitzgerald, *Urban Emancipation: Popular Politics in Reconstruction Mobile, 1860–1890* (Baton Rouge: Louisiana State University Press, 2002), 12; Petitions to Become Slaves, 1860–62, Mobile County Probate Court, Archives and Records Depart-

ment, Mobile, Alabama; Christopher Nordmann, "Free Negroes in Mobile County, Alabama" (Ph.D. diss., University of Alabama, 1990).

12. Rabinowitz, *Race Relations in the Urban South*, 152; Peter H. Wood, "Nat Turner: The Unknown Slave as Visionary Leader," in *Black Leaders of the Nineteenth Century*, ed. Leon Litwack and August Meier (Urbana: University of Illinois Press, 1991), 23–24; Heather A. Williams, *Self-Taught: African American Education in Slavery and Freedom* (Chapel Hill: University of North Carolina Press, 2005), 203, 208–10.

13. John T. Gillard, *The Catholic Church and the American Negro; Being an Investigation of the Past and Present Activities of the Catholic Church in Behalf of the 12,000,000 Negroes in the United States, with an Examination of the Difficulties Which Affect the Work of the Colored Missions* (1929; repr., New York: Johnson Reprint Corporation, 1968), 12–14; United States Census Bureau, *Statistics of the United States (Including Mortality, Property, &c.) in 1860: Compiled from the Original Returns and Being Final Exhibit of the Eighth Census, under the Direction of the Secretary of the Interior* (Washington, D.C.: Government Printing Office, 1866), 507.

14. Karl Kaestle, *Pillars of the Republic: Common Schools and American Society 1780–1860* (New York: Hill and Wang, 1983), 64, 68–71, 76, 82, 91–92, 105, 113, 192.

15. Margaret Meagher, *History of Richmond* (Richmond: Virginia Division of the Works Progress Administration, 1939), 97–99, 107–9; J. L. Blair Buck, *The Development of Public Schools in Virginia, 1607–1952* (Richmond: Commonwealth of Virginia State Board of Education, 1952), 53–62. For additional information on the common school movement in Virginia, see William Arthur Maddox, *The Free School Idea in Virginia before the Civil War: A Phase of Political and Social Evolution* (New York: Teachers College, Columbia University, 1918); Amos, *Cotton City*, 189–90; Nordmann, "Free Negroes in Mobile County, Alabama," 204–5, 210–12; Peter Kolchin, *First Freedom: The Responses of Alabama's Blacks to Emancipation and Reconstruction* (Westport, Conn.: Greenwood Press, 1972), 79; United States Census Bureau, *Statistics of the United States . . . in 1860*, 507.

16. Franklin and Moss, *From Slavery to Freedom*, 155, 179–80; Heather Andrea Williams, "'Clothing Themselves in Intelligence': The Freedpeople, Schooling, and Northern Teachers, 1861–1871," *Journal of African American History* 87 (Fall 2002): 372–73; Carter G. Woodson, ed., *The Mind of the Negro as Reflected in Letters Written during the Crisis, 1800–1860* (Washington, D.C.: Association for the Study of Negro Life and History, 1926), 15–47, 54.

17. Willie Lee Rose, *Rehearsal for Reconstruction: The Port Royal Experiment* (New York: Bobbs-Merrill, 1964).

18. Williams, *Self-Taught*; Ronald E. Butchart, *Schooling the Freed People: Teaching, Learning, and the Struggle for Black Freedom, 1861–1876* (Chapel Hill: University of North Carolina, 2010).

19. James D. Anderson, *The Education of Blacks in the South, 1865–1935* (Chapel Hill: University of North Carolina Press, 1988), 2–3; Butchart, *Schooling the Freed People*.

20. Heather Cox Richardson, *The Death of Reconstruction: Race, Labor, and Politics in the Post–Civil War North, 1865–1901* (Cambridge, Mass.: Harvard University Press, 2001);

Andrew L. Slap, *The Doom of Reconstruction: The Liberal Republicans in the Civil War Era* (New York: Fordham University Press, 2006).

21. David R. Goldfield, *Cotton Fields and Skyscrapers: Southern City and Region, 1607–1980* (Baton Rouge: Louisiana State University Press, 1982), 3–6.

22. Ibid., 6, 80–88, 103–5.

23. Don H. Doyle, *New Men, New Cities, New South: Atlanta, Nashville, Charleston, Mobile, 1860–1910* (Chapel Hill: University of North Carolina Press, 1990).

24. Thomas W. Hanchett, *Sorting Out the New South City: Race, Class, and Urban Development, 1875–1975* (Chapel Hill: University of North Carolina Press, 1998).

25. Rabinowitz, *Race Relations in the Urban South*; Peter Rachleff, *Black Labor in Richmond, 1865–1890* (Philadelphia: Temple University Press, 1984); Fitzgerald, *Urban Emancipation*; Jacqueline Jones, *Saving Savannah: The City and the Civil War* (New York: Alfred A. Knopf, 2008).

26. Richardson, *Death of Reconstruction*, 207.

27. Williams, *Freedom and Progress*, 86.

28. Blight, *Slave No More*, 215.

1. Remaking the Former Confederate Capital: Black Richmonders and the Transition to Public Schools, 1865–1870

1. Ann Field Alexander, *Race Man: The Rise and Fall of the "Fighting Editor," John Mitchell, Jr.* (Charlottesville: University of Virginia Press, 2002), 13; Daniel Webster Davis, "Old Normal," in *Idle Moment: Containing Emancipation and Other Poems by D. Webster Davis; with an Introduction by Hon. John H. Smythe* (Baltimore: The Educator of Morgan College, 1895), 37.

2. Arthur R. Henry Report, 1865, 1–9, VHS; Rabinowitz, *Race Relations in the Urban South*, 18–22; Nicole Johnson, "Rosa Dixon Bowser," *Richmond Times-Dispatch*, February 9, 2009; A. A. Taylor, "Religious Efforts among the Negro," *Journal of Negro History* 11 (July 1926): 442; Rev. George Stinson to Rev. M. E. Strieby, April 13, 1865, reel 4, AMA Archives, Virginia, ARC; "Peter Woolfolk," *Freedmen's Record* 1 (July 1865): 119.

3. "Cheering News from Richmond: Glorious Surprise!" *Anglo-African*, May 6, 1865, 2.

4. Hannah E. Stevenson, April 9, 1865 letter, folder 15, box 5, Curtis–Stevenson Family Papers, 1775–1920, MHS; "New England Report of the Teacher's Committee," *The American Freedmen* 1 (May 1866): 29, MHS; Joe M. Richardson, *Christian Reconstruction: The American Missionary Association and Southern Blacks, 1861–1890* (Athens: University of Georgia Press, 1986), 19–20; "State Superintendent's Monthly Reports, July 1865 to June 1867," reel 11, VA-BRFAL-ED.

5. "New England Report of the Teacher's Committee," *The American Freedmen* 1 (May 1866): 29, MHS; quoted in Rachleff, *Black Labor in Richmond*, 11; Williams, *Self-Taught*, 7–29.

6. Stinson to Strieby, April 13, 1865.

7. Ibid.

8. Henry A. Bullock, *A History of Negro Education in the South: From 1619 to the Present* (Cambridge, Mass.: Harvard University Press, 1967), 43; Regular Weekly Meet-

ing, Minutes, May 12, 1865, folder Teacher's Committee, 1864–66, box 2, NEFAS Records, MHS.

9. "Peter Woolfolk," 119; W. L. Coan to M. E. Strieby, April 20, 1865, reel 5, AMA Archives, Virginia, ARC; "R. H. J. in Richmond City," *Anglo-African*, August 5, 1865, 2.

10. Eric Foner, *Reconstruction: America's Unfinished Revolution, 1863–1877* (New York: Harper and Row, 1988), 69; Randall M. Miller, "Introduction. The Freedmen's Bureau and Reconstruction: An Overview," in *The Freedmen's Bureau and Reconstruction: Reconsiderations*, ed. Paul A. Cimbala and Randall M. Miller (New York: Fordham University Press, 1999), xvii–xviii.

11. John A. Carpenter, *Sword and Olive Branch: Oliver Otis Howard* (New York: Fordham University Press, 1999), 1–87; John Cox and LaWanda Cox, "General O. O. Howard and the 'Misrepresented Bureau,'" *Journal of Southern History* 19 (November 1953): 432; Foner, *Reconstruction*, 142–44.

12. Cox and Cox, "General O. O. Howard and the 'Misrepresented Bureau,'" 452.

13. Miller, "Introduction," xxvii; Luther Tracy Townsend, *History of the Sixteenth Regiment, New Hampshire Volunteers* (Washington, D.C.: Norman T. Elliott, 1897), 348; Leo Weldon Wertheimer, ed., *The Twelfth General Catalogue of the Psi Upsilon Fraternity* (New York: Executive Council of Psi Upsilon Fraternity, 1917), 432.

14. "Roster of Sixteenth New Hampshire Volunteers," in New Hampshire, *Journal of the Honorable Senate of the State of New Hampshire*, June Session, 1864 (Concord: Amos Hadley, State Printer, 1864).

15. Townsend, *History of the Sixteenth Regiment*, 348–49; "Muster-Out Roll of R. M. Manly, Chaplain, 1st U.S. Col'd Cavalry," Ralza M. Manly Collection, Richmond Public Library, Richmond, Virginia; Betty Mansfield, "That Fateful Class: Black Teachers of Virginia's Freedmen, 1861–1882" (Ph.D. diss., Catholic University of America, 1980), 150–51; Alexander, *Race Man*, 12.

16. Quoted in Mansfield, "That Fateful Class," 150–51.

17. Brooks Smith and Wayne Dementi, *Facts and Legends of the Hills of Richmond* (Manakin-Sabot, Va.: Dementi, 2008), 18–19; September 3 Meeting, Minutes, September 3, 1866, folder Teachers Committee, 1866–70, box 2, NEFAS Records, MHS.

18. For statistics, see "State Superintendent Monthly Statistical Reports, July 1865 to June 1870," reel 11, VA-BRFAL-ED; Michael Chesson, *Richmond after the War, 1865–1890* (Richmond: Virginia State Library, 1981), 133–34.

19. Helen Corwin Fischer, "Monthly Report, October 1865," reel 15, VA-BRFAL-ED.

20. R.M. Manly to Hannah E. Stevenson, December 22, 1866, printed pages 138–39, reel 1, VA-BRFAL-ED.

21. R. M. Manly to J. M. McKim, July 23 1866, reel 1, VA-BRFAL-ED; R. M. Manly to Rev. Woolsey, August 24, 1866, reel 8, AMA Archives, Virginia, ARC.

22. Jacqueline M. Jones, *Soldiers of Light and Love: Northern Teachers and Georgia Blacks, 1865–1873* (Chapel Hill: University of North Carolina Press, 1980), 14–15; Richardson, *Christian Reconstruction*, 19–22.

23. For monthly racial breakdowns of teachers from 1865 to 1867, see "State Superintendent Monthly Statistical Reports, July 1865 to June 1870."

24. Earle H. West, "The Harris Brothers: Black Northern Teachers in the Reconstruction South," *Journal of Negro History* 48 (Spring 1979): 127–28; William D. Harris to George Whipple, December 1, 1865, reel 6; Harris to Whipple, April 9, 1866, reel 7; Harris to Whipple, February 17, 1866, reel 6, all in AMA Archives, Virginia, ARC.

25. Chesson, *Richmond after the War*, 100–101; "State Superintendent Monthly Statistical Reports, November 1865 to May 1867," reel 11, VA-BRFAL-ED.

26. December 30, 1868, entry, letter from Peter Woolfolk, Daily Record, 1868–69, box 1; February 21, 1866, entry, letter from Andrew Washburn, Daily Record, 1865–66, box 1; March 21, 1866, entry, letter from Sarah F. Foster, Daily Record, 1865–66, box 1, all in NEFAS Records, MHS.

27. Figures comes from manual computation of correspondence referencing the Bakery incident in AMA Archives, Virginia, ARC, April to July 1866; and NEFAS Records, MHS, April to July 1865. For promises made to Washburn, see A. Merrill, *Circular*, June 2, 1866; and O. Brown, *Circular*, June 2, 1866, both in AMA Archives, Virginia, ARC. For promises made to Chase, see R. M. Manly to William G. Hawkins, June 9, 1866, reel 1, VA-BRFAL-ED.

28. O. Brown to Rev. J. H. Chapin, July 4, 1866, reel 1, VA-BRFAL-ED; C. Thurston Chase to George Whipple, July 2, 1866, reel 7, AMA Archives, Virginia, ARC; letter from Andrew Washburn, June 4, 1866, entry, Daily Record, 1865–66, box 1, NEFAS Records, MHS; R. M. Manly to Hannah Stevenson, July 20, 1869, target 2, reel 1, VA-BRFAL-ED; "Soldier's Memorial Society, Register," clipping, circa 1869, scrapbook 4, folder 2, Caroline Dall Papers, MHS; Adams Ayer, "List of Teachers Commissioned and Employed in Virginia by the Soldiers Memorial Society, December 1, 1869," reel 1, VA-BRFAL-ED.

29. American Baptist Home Mission Society, *Thirty-Fourth Annual Report of the American Baptist Home Mission Society, Convened at Boston, Mass., May 17 and 18, 1866* (New York: American Baptist Home Mission Rooms, 1866), 17–18; Charles H. Corey, *A History of the Richmond Theological Seminary, with Reminiscences of Thirty Year's Work among the Colored People of the South* (Richmond: J. W. Randolph, 1895); Adolph H. Grundman, "Northern Baptists and the Founding of Virginia Union University: The Perils of Paternalism," *Journal of Negro History* 63 (January 1978): 26–41.

30. R. M. Manly to John Walter, October 10, 1866, printed pages 90–91; R. M. Manly to Robert L. Murray, August 25, 1866, printed pages 75–76, both in reel 1, VA-BRFAL-ED; American Baptist Home Mission Society, *Thirty-Fifth Annual Report of the American Baptist Home Mission Society, Convened at Chicago, Ill., May 23 and 24, 1867* (New York: American Baptist Home Missions Rooms, 1867), 17–18; Elizabeth Cartland, "Chimborazo School," *Virginia History Society: An Occasional Bulletin* 43 (December 1981): 10, VHS.

31. Julia Porter Read to Harriett Sublett (Read) Berry, circa April–May 1865, section 4, Read Family Papers, 1828–1914, VHS; Foster Gaines, *Ghosts of the Confederacy: Defeat, the Lost Cause, and the Emergence of the New South, 1865–1913* (New York: Oxford University Press, 1987), 21.

32. Read to Berry, circa April–May 1865; Gaines, *Ghosts of the Confederacy*, 31–33, 35.

33. Read to Berry, circa April–May 1865; Chesson, *Richmond after the War*, 101; Thomas Holt, *Black over White: Negro Political Leadership in South Carolina during Reconstruction* (Urbana: University of Illinois Press, 1977), 23, 25.

34. Karin L. Zipf, "'The Whites Shall Rule the Land or Die': Gender, Race, and Class in North Carolina Reconstruction Politics," *Journal of Southern History* 65 (August 1999): 499–500, 506; Martha Hodes, *White Women, Black Men: Illicit Sex in the Nineteenth-Century South* (New Haven, Conn.: Yale University Press, 1997), 146.

35. Zipf, "Whites Shall Rule the Land or Die," 509; Albert J. Raboteau, *Slave Religion: The Invisible Institution in the Antebellum South* (New York: Oxford University Press, 1978); quoted in Rabinowitz, *Race Relations in the Urban South*, 152–53; Gaines, *Ghosts of the Confederacy*, 17–18.

36. "Untitled," 2; and "Commencement at the University of Virginia," 2, both in *Richmond Daily Examiner*, June 30, 1866. For more examples, please see "Untitled," May 26, 1866, 2; "Untitled," July 30 1866, 2; and "The Freedmen's Bureau in Richmond," July 30, 1866, 3, all in *Richmond Daily Examiner*.

37. William D. Harris to George Whipple, December 11, 1866, reel 8, AMA Archives, Virginia, ARC; "Free Schools in Richmond," *Christian Recorder*, May 19, 1866; Hodes, *White Women, Black Men*, 159–65.

38. A Member of the Church, "The Rev. W. D. Harris Honorably Acquitted," December 13, 1866, clipping; "The Negro Abduction Case: The Negro Preacher Harris Discharged," clipping, both enclosed in Harris to Whipple, December 11, 1866.

39. West, "Harris Brothers," 128.

40. Gen. O. Brown to George Whipple, March 1, 1867, reel 8, AMA Archives, Virginia, ARC.

41. John Hope Franklin, *Reconstruction after the Civil War* (Chicago: University of Chicago Press, 1961), 102; Foner, *Reconstruction*, 316–21; Richard L. Hume, "Carpetbaggers in the Reconstruction South: A Group Portrait of Outside Whites in the 'Black and Tan' Constitutional Conventions," *Journal of American History* 64 (September 1977): 315.

42. J. N. Brenaman, *A History of Virginia Conventions* (Richmond: J. L. Hill, 1902), 76; "The State Convention," *Richmond Whig*, December 14, 1867, 1; Monroe N. Work et al., "Some Negro Members of Reconstruction Conventions and Legislatures and of Congress," *Journal of Negro History* 5 (January 1920): 64.

43. A. A. Taylor, "Giving Virginia a Democratic Constitution," *Journal of Negro History* 11 (July 1926): 478; "The Conservative Convention," *Richmond Whig*, December 12, 1867, 1.

44. Foner, *Reconstruction*, 319–33; Jane Elizabeth Dailey, *Before Jim Crow: The Politics of Race in Postemancipation Virginia* (Chapel Hill: University of North Carolina Press, 2000), 21; John C. Underwood, "Virginia: Disqualifications under the New Constitution," *New York Times*, January 10, 1869, 5.

45. Dailey, *Before Jim Crow*, 23; Edgar W. Knight, *Reconstruction and Education in Virginia* (Syracuse, N.Y.: Gaylord Brothers, 1916), 5–6, 8.

46. Knight, *Reconstruction and Education in Virginia*, 10; Foner, *Reconstruction*, 322; Rabinowitz, *Race Relations in the Urban South*, 165; William L. Barney, *Battleground for*

the Union: *The Era of the Civil War and Reconstruction, 1848–1877* (Englewood Cliffs, N.J.: Prentice Hall, 1990), 277; Brenaman, *History of Virginia Conventions*, 78–79, 117–18. For a discussion of the state legislative debates in Richmond, see Knight, *Reconstruction and Education in Virginia*, 15; A. A. Taylor, "Solving the Problem of Education," *Journal of Negro History* 11 (April 1926): 388; William Preston Vaughn, *Schools for All: The Blacks and Public Education in the South, 1865–1877* (Lexington: University of Kentucky Press, 1974), 73; and Charles William Dabney, *Universal Education in the South*. vol. 1 (Chapel Hill: University of North Carolina Press, 1936), 173–74, 318, 417.

47. Knight, *Reconstruction and Education in Virginia*, 4; Vaughn, *Schools for All*, 53; Dailey, *Before Jim Crow*, 21; "The Conservative Convention," December 12, 1867, 1; and "The State Convention," December 21, 1867, 1, both in *Richmond Whig*; John A McDonnell, "Sub-assistant Commissioner's (or Agent's) Monthly Report, December, 1869," reel 13, VA-BRFAL-ED; Rabinowitz, *Race Relations in the Urban South*, 152.

48. R. M. Manly to George Whipple, July 15, 1868, reel 10; and Gen. O. Brown to Whipple, August 7 1868, reel 10, both in AMA Archives, Virginia, ARC; Rabinowitz, *Race Relations*, 166; Table XI: Comparative Statistics, in Richmond School Board, *Twenty-Fourth Annual Report of the Superintendent of Public Schools of the City of Richmond, VA., for the Scholastic Year Ending July 31st, 1893* (Richmond, Va.: C. N. Williams, City Printers, 1894), 40–41, LVA.

49. "State Superintendent Monthly Statistical Reports, October 1865 to July 1870," reel 11, VA-BRFAL-ED.

50. Rabinowitz, *Race Relations*, 134–35, 143–44; George Whipple to R. M. Manly, May 19, 1870, Unregistered Letters Received, December 1869–August 1870, reel 10, VA-BRFAL-ED; Rev. Charles E. Hodge to Rev. S. J. Jocelyn, May 21, 1870, reel 12, AMA Archives, Virginia, ARC.

51. R. M. Manly to Rev. E. P. Smith, May 21,1870; R. M. Manly to George Whipple, May 26, 1870; Virginia Legislature, Acts of Assembly, 1872, 454–56; 460–61, all in reel 12, AMA Archives, Virginia, ARC.

52. "From Manly, Richmond," *American Freedman* 3 (May 1868): 414–15, in NEFAS Records, MHS; Cox and Cox, "General O. O. Howard and the 'Misrepresented Bureau,'" 452–54; Taylor, "Solving the Problem of Education," 385–86; "State Superintendent Monthly Statistical Reports, September 1869 to July 1870," reel 11, VA-BRFAL-ED.

53. Richardson, *Christian Reconstruction*, 109.

54. R. M. Manly to New England Freedmen Aid Society, July 22, 1869; Ednah Cheney to the New England Freedmen Aid Society, August 2, 1869, both in file Daily Record, 1868–69, box 1, NEFAS Records, MHS.

55. American Freedman's Union Commission, *The Results of Emancipation in the United States of America by a Committee of the American Freedman's Union Commission* (New York: American Freedman's Union Commission, 1867); Richardson, *Christian Reconstruction*, 111; "State Superintendent Monthly Statistical Reports, September 1869 to July 1870."

56. Lizzie Parsons to Rev. Edwin P. Smith, May 31, 1869, reel 11, AMA Archives, Virginia, ARC; Peter Woolfolk to the New England Freedmen's Aid Society, December 30, 1868, file Daily Record, 1868–69, box 1, NEFAS Records, MHS.

57. Lizzie Parsons to Rev. Edwin P. Smith, May 31, 1869, reel 11, AMA Archives, Virginia, ARC.

58. Peter Woolfolk to the New England Freedmen's Aid Society, December 30, 1868; Amy G. Browne to the New England Freedmen's Aid Society, December 23, 1868, both in file Daily Record, 1868–69, box 1, NEFAS Records, MHS.

59. Knight, *Reconstruction and Education in Virginia*, 15; Taylor, "Solving the Problem of Education," 388; Vaughn, *Schools for All*, 73.

2. No Longer Slaves: Black Mobilians and the Hard Struggle for Schools, 1865–1870

1. "The Song of the Black Republicans," *Black Republican*, April 29, 1865, 1.

2. T. W. C., "Joy among the Poor Colored People of Mobile," *Black Republican* (New Orleans), April 29, 1865, 1.

3. Arthur W. Bergeron, Jr., *Confederate Mobile* (Jackson: University Press of Mississippi, 1991), xi.

4. Kaestle, *Pillars of the Republic*, 64, 68–71, 76, 82, 91–92, 105, 113, 192.

5. E. C. Branch, "Report of Our Schools," *Nationalist* (Mobile, Ala.), January 18, 1866, 2; John B. Myers, "The Education of the Alabama Freedmen during Presidential Reconstruction, 1865–1867," *Journal of Negro History* 40, no. 2 (1971): 165.

6. Amos, *Cotton City*, 189–90; Nordmann, "Free Negroes in Mobile County, Alabama," 204–5, 210–12; United States Census Bureau, *Statistics of the United States . . . in 1860*, 507.

7. Kenneth B. White, "The Alabama Freedmen's Bureau and Black Education: The Myth of Opportunity," *Alabama Review* 34 (April 1981): 109; Kenneth White, "Wager Swayne: Racist of Realist?" *Alabama Review* 31 (April 1978): 93–95; "Mr. E. C. Branch," *Nationalist* (Mobile, Ala.), April 5, 1866, 3.

8. "Mr. E. C. Branch," 3.

9. White, "Alabama Freedmen's Bureau and Black Education," 109; Horace Mann Bond, *Negro Education in Alabama: A Study in Cotton and Steel* (1939; repr., Tuscaloosa: University of Alabama Press, 1994), 81–83.

10. Branch, "Report of Our Schools," 2.; "Monthly Reports of District Superintendents, September 1865–June 1870," reel 5, AL-BRFAL-ED.

11. Branch, "Report of Our Schools," 2.

12. Ibid.

13. John Silsby, "The Nationalist," broadside, October 16, 1865, reel 1, AMA Archives, Alabama, ARC; Fitzgerald, *Urban Emancipation*, 55, 62–64; "Children's Department," *Nationalist* (Mobile, Ala.), January 25, 1866, 3. For a history of the newspaper, see Kimberly Bess Cantrell, "A Voice for the Freedmen: The Mobile *Nationalist*, 1865–1869" (M.A. diss., Auburn University, 1989).

14. C. W. Buckley, "Draft Report Made to Major General Swayne Relative to Colored Schools, March 30, 1866," reel 1, AL-BRFAL-ED.

15. "Mr. E. C. Branch," 2.

16. "School Exhibition," April 19, 1866, 2; "Untitled," December 27, 1866, 2; "Private School," advertisement, December 27, 1866, 3, all in the *Nationalist* (Mobile, Ala.).

17. "Nott, Josiah Clark," in *A Cyclopedia of American Medical Biography*, ed. Howard A. Kelly and Walter L. Burrage (Baltimore: Norman Remington, 1920), 856.

18. Reginald Horsman, *Josiah Nott of Mobile: Southerner, Physician, and Racial Theorist* (Baton Rouge: Louisiana State University Press, 1987), 170–221.

19. Quoted in Wager Swayne, "Report to Major General O. O. Howard concerning the Continued Occupancy of the Medical College in Mobile and the Reasons Therefore, January 24, 1866," reel 3, AL-BRFAL-ED.

20. "The Recent Fires," *Nationalist* (Mobile, Ala.), March 18, 1866, 2.

21. Ibid.; quoted in Swayne, "Report to Major General O. O. Howard"; White, "Alabama Freedmen's Bureau and Black Education," 118, 123–24.

22. Horsman, *Josiah Nott of Mobile*, 296–301; Josiah Nott, "The Negro Race," *Popular Magazine of Anthropology* 1 (July 1866): 102–6, 116–18.

23. "Letter of J. C. Nott, M.D.," *Nationalist* (Mobile, Ala.), March 1, 1866, 2.

24. Ibid.

25. Ibid.

26. Ibid.

27. Ibid.

28. Swayne, "Report to Major General O. O. Howard"; "Proclamation," *Nationalist* (Mobile, Ala.), March 8, 1866, 2.

29. C. W. Buckley, "Draft Report Made to Major General Swayne, April 20, 1866," 3, reel 1, AL-BRFAL-ED.

30. "Education of the Freedmen," *Nationalist* (Mobile, Ala.), March 29, 1866, 2.

31. Ibid.

32. Branch, "Report of Our Schools," 2; Swayne, "Report to Major General O. O. Howard."

33. "First of January," January 11, 1866, 2; "E. C. Branch, "Notice," January 18, 1866, 2; "School at the College," June 28, 1866, 2, all in the *Nationalist* (Mobile, Ala.).

34. Jones, *Saving Savannah*, 257; "Glorious News," advertisement, *Nationalist* (Mobile, Ala.), April 18, 1867, 2; E. C. Branch to E. P. Smith, April 19, 1867, reel 1, AMA Archives, Alabama, ARC; "Union Meeting," *Nationalist* (Mobile, Ala.), March 7, 1867, 2.

35. G. W. Horton to W. E. Whiting, November 4, 1866, reel 1, AMA Archives, Alabama, ARC.

36. Swayne, "Report to Major General O. O. Howard."

37. George Tracey to C. W. Buckley, January 11, 1867; George Tracey to C. W. Buckley, January 24, 1867; William A. Talcott to C. W. Buckley, February 5, 1867, all in reel 3, AL-BRFAL-ED; Charles A. Church, *History of Rockford and Winnebago County Illinois: From Settlement in 1834 to the Civil War* (Rockford: New England Society of Rockford, Illinois, 1900), 334.

38. Amos, *Cotton City*, 185, 189–90; Fitzgerald, *Urban Emancipation*, 10–11; Ira Berlin, *Slaves without Masters: The Free Negro in the Antebellum South* (New York: Vintage, 1976), 131.

39. Fitzgerald, *Urban Emancipation*, 11–13; Virginia Meacham Gould, "Free Creoles of Color in Mobile and Pensacola," in *Creoles of Color in the Gulf South*, ed. James H. Dorman (Knoxville: University of Tennessee Press, 1996), 43–44.

40. Amos, *Cotton City*, 185; quoted in Nordmann, "Free Negroes in Mobile County, Alabama," 201–2; Peter Kolchin, *First Freedom: The Responses of Alabama's Blacks to Emancipation and Reconstruction* (Westport, Conn.: Greenwood Press, 1972), 79–80; United States Census Bureau, *Statistics of the United States . . . in 1860*, 507; Williams, *Self-Taught*, 208.

41. Mobile City Directories, 1865–66, Mobile Municipal Archives, Mobile, Alabama; A Subscriber, "Letter to the Editor," *Nationalist* (Mobile, Ala.), January 25, 1866, 2.

42. "Forty-Seventh Anniversary of Creole Fire Company No. 1," *Mobile Daily Advertiser and Register*, April 28, 1866, 3; Fitzgerald, *Urban Emancipation*, 12–13.

43. "Forty-Seventh Anniversary of Creole Fire Company No. 1," 3; "The Symposium of the Creole Fire Company," *Mobile Daily Advertiser and Register*, April 29, 1866, 3.

44. "A Talk with the Creoles," *Nationalist* (Mobile, Ala.), May 1, 1866, 2.

45. Fitzgerald, *Urban Emancipation*, 73.

46. "Time Makes No Changes," *Nationalist* (Mobile, Ala.), May 10, 1866, 2.

47. "Ball of the Creole Fire Co.," January 31, 1867, 2; "Creole Fire Co. No. 1," May 2, 1867, 2; "Colored State Convention," April 4, 1867, 3, all in the *Nationalist* (Mobile, Ala.); "Colored Mass Convention of the State of Alabama," *Mobile Daily Advertiser and Register*, May 4, 1867, 2.

48. "The Colored Men," *Nationalist* (Mobile, Ala.), July 11, 1867, 2.

49. Ibid.

50. Ibid.

51. "Letter from Montgomery," *Mobile Daily Register*, November 10, 1867, 2; Alabama Constitution of 1867, Civil War and Reconstruction Subject Files, SG011154, Article 11, Section 6, Alabama Department of Archives and History, Montgomery, Alabama; Foner, *Reconstruction*, 276.

52. "The Crisis," November 13, 1867, 2; "The Proposed Constitution," December 17, 1867, 2, both in *Mobile Daily Advertiser and Register*; and "Do Not Vote," February 4, 1868, 2; "The Constitutional Executive Committee," January 30, 1868, 1, both in *Mobile Daily Register*.

53. "The Election," February 4, 1868, 2; "List of White Voters," February 12, 1868, 2; "A Card," February 14, 1868, 2, all in *Mobile Daily Register*.

54. Statistics quoted in "Alabama Constitution of 1868-Ratification," *Alabama Constitution of 1868*, n.d., http://www.legislature.state.al.us/aliswww/History/constitutions/1868/1868rat.html.

55. Cantrell, "Voice for the Freedmen," 57, 67–68.

56. Bond, *Negro Education in Alabama*, 84; C. A. Bradford to C. W. Buckley, August 7, 1867, reel 3, AL-BRFAL-ED.

57. Bradford to Buckley, August 7, 1867.

58. "What Next?" *Mobile Daily Register*, May 3, 1849, clipping, Black Schools, Clippings File, Historic Mobile Preservation Society, Mobile, Alabama; Fitzgerald, *Urban Emancipation*, 10–11.

59. C. W. Buckley, "Entry of Letter to C. A. Bradford, Secretary Mobile County School Board, August 9, 1867," Register of Letters Sent, stamped page 102, Letters Sent, vol. 1, November 30, 1866–January 27, 1868, reel 1, AL-BRFAL-ED.

60. C.W. Buckley, "Second Annual Report of the Superintendent of Education, October 1867," 2–3 (handwritten pages), Reports Sent Annual, 1866–68, reel 1, AL-BRFAL-ED.

61. White, "Alabama Freedmen's Bureau and Black Education," 111; R. D. Harper, "Annual Report of the Superintendent of Education to Edwin Beecher, October 1868," 1–2 (handwritten pages), Reports Sent Annual, 1866–68, reel 1, AL-BRFAL-ED.

62. R. D. Harper to Major General O. O. Howard, October 9, 1868, Letters Sent Ledger, stamped page 98; R. D. Harper to Edwin Beecher, October 19, 1868, Press Copies of Letters Sent, September 1868–July 1870, both in reel 1, AL-BRFAL-ED.

63. R. D. Harper to the American Missionary Association, circular letter, September 1, 1868, reel 1, AMA Archives, Alabama, ARC.

64. "Sub-Assistant Commissioner's (or Agent's) Monthly Report, January 1869," Monthly and Other Reports, Alabama, September 1865–June 1870, reel 15, AL-BRFAL-ED; Mobile City Directory, 1869, 21; Mobile City Directory, 1870, 284, both in Mobile Municipal Archives, Mobile, Alabama.

65. Willis G. Clark, *History of Education in Alabama, 1702–1889* (Washington, D.C.: Government Printing Office, 1889), 271; Peabody Education Fund, *Proceedings of the Trustees Meeting, Held at Washington, 15 February 1870* (Cambridge, Mass.: Press of John Wilson and Son, 1870), 45, in file 1, box 11, Peabody Education Fund Collection, Jean and Alexander Heard Library, Vanderbilt University, Nashville.

66. Albert Griffin, "The School Question," *Nationalist* (Mobile, Ala.), October 3, 1867, 2; Cantrell, "Voice of Freedom," 58–60.

67. Cantrell, "Voice of Freedom," 6–7; Albert Griffin, "Address to the White People of Alabama," *Nationalist* (Mobile, Ala.), January 28, 1868, 3.

68. Alpha, "What's Next," *Nationalist* (Mobile, Ala.), February 27, 1868, 2; Cantrell, "Voice of Freedom," 64–68.

69. L. S. Berry et al., "Protest of the Colored People," *Nationalist* (Mobile, Ala.), September 5, 1868, 2–3; Fitzgerald, *Urban Emancipation*, 128–31.

70. "Monthly Superintendent of Education Reports, July 1867–July 1868," reel 15, BRFAL-ED.

71. "Colored Orphan School," *Nationalist* (Mobile, Ala.), October 25, 1868, 2, column 5, Transcriptions of the *Nationalist* (WPA Project), Mobile Municipal Archives, Mobile, Alabama.

72. W. M. Bush, "Monthly Report for the State of Alabama for February 1868"; R. D. Harper, "Monthly Report for the State of Alabama for April 1868 to Major General O. O. Howard, May 1, 1868," both in Monthly and Other Reports, Alabama, September 1865–June 1870, reel 15, AL-BRFAL-ED.

73. George L. Putnam to Jacob R. Shipherd, copy, October 28, 1868; Jacob R. Shipherd to Mother Whiting, January 7, 1868; George L. Putnam to Edwin P. Smith, January 8, 1868, all in reel 1, AMA Archives, Alabama, ARC. For general reflections of Emerson Institute, see Sara G. Stanley, "Colored Schools of Mobile," March 26, 1868, 2; and "Mo-

bile College," April 30, 1868, 2, both in the *Nationalist* (Mobile, Ala.); Fitzgerald, *Urban Emancipation*, 127.

74. Fitzgerald, *Urban Emancipation*, 144–45.

75. N. B. Cloud, "Official Report of the Superintendent of Public Instruction on the Troubles in the Mobile Free Public Schools," in Alabama State Board of Education, *Report of the Superintendent of Public Instruction of the State of Alabama to the Governor for the Year 1868–9 Ending 30 September 1869* (Montgomery: John G. Stokes and Company, State Printers, 1869), 35–36; Fitzgerald, *Urban Emancipation*, 145.

76. Cloud, "Official Report," 37, 39–47; and "Public School Notice," *Nationalist* (Mobile, Ala.), May 21, 1869, 3, column 4, Transcriptions of the *Nationalist* (WPA Project), Mobile Municipal Archives, Mobile, Alabama.

77. Gustavus W. Horton to E. P. Smith, July 31, 1867; Gustavus W. Horton to the Editors of *The Congregationalist*, September 10, 1870; James Gillette to E. P. Smith, March 16, 1869, all in reel 1, AMA Archives, Alabama, ARC. For Putnam's responses to attacks, see George L. Putnam to E. P. Smith, May 29, 1869; September 14, 1869; and July 14, 1870, all in reel 1, AMA Archives, Alabama, ARC.

78. A Republican, "The School Question and the Legislature," *Nationalist* (Mobile, Ala.), October 11, 1869, 1, columns 1 and 3, Transcriptions of the *Nationalist* (WPA Project), Mobile Municipal Archives, Mobile, Alabama; *Mobile Daily Republican*, October 31, 1870, 2, column 3, Transcriptions of the *Mobile Daily Republican* (WPA Project).

79. W. Irving Squire to E. P. Smith, February 21, 1869, reel 1, AMA Archives, Alabama, ARC.

80. "The School Muddle: The Big Gun Fire," *Nationalist* (Mobile, Ala.), October 1, 1869, 2, column 2, Transcriptions of the *Nationalist* (WPA Project), Mobile Municipal Archives, Mobile, Alabama.

81. George Tracey to C. W. Buckley, January 24, 1867; and George Tracey to C. W. Buckley, March 22, 1867, both in Unregistered Letters, December 1865–July 1870, reel 3, AL-BRFAL-ED; Cloud, "Official Report," 39–47; George L. Putnam to E. P. Smith, September 14, 1869; October 4, 1869; and July 14, 1870, all in reel 1, AMA Archives, Alabama, ARC.

82. Peabody Education Fund, *Proceedings of the Trustees Meeting, Held at Philadelphia, 15 February 1871* (Cambridge, Mass.: Press of John Wilson and Son, 1870), 34, file 2, box 11, Peabody Education Fund Collection, Jean and Alexander Heard Library, Vanderbilt University, Nashville.

3. To "Do That Which Is Best": Richmond Colored Normal and the Development of Public Schoolteachers

1. The quotation in the title of this chapter comes from Daniel Barclay Williams, *A Sketch of the Life and Times of Capt. R. A. Paul: An Authentic and Abbreviated History of His Career from Boyhood to the Present Time; Containing a Reliable Account of the Politics of Virginia from 1874 to the Present Time* (Richmond, Va.: Johns and Goolsby, 1885), 68. The quotation in the first paragraph comes from J. A. C. Chandler to the Principals of

the Colored Schools, memorandum, October 27, 1913, Section 6, Daniel Webster Davis Papers, VHS.

2. "Daniel Webster Davis," Section 8, Daniel Webster Davis Papers, VHS; Virginia Department of Education, *Virginia School Report, 1889: Nineteenth Annual Report of the Superintendent of Public Instruction of the Commonwealth of Virginia with Accompanying Documents, School Year Ending July 31, 1889* (Richmond, Va.: J. H. O'Bannon, Superintendent Public Printing, 1889), 51–73; Virginia Department of Education, *Virginia School Report, 1890: Twentieth Annual Report of the Superintendent of Public Instruction of Public Instruction of the Commonwealth of Virginia with Accompanying Documents, School Year Ending July 31, 1890* (Richmond, Va.: J. H. O'Bannon, Superintendent Public Printing, 1890), 142–50; Julia H. Hayes to Elizabeth S. Smith, October 27, 1913; Richard Chiles to Elizabeth Davis, October 26, 1913, both in section 10, Daniel Webster Davis Papers, VHS.

3. Hannah E. Stevenson, April 9, 1865 letter, folder 15, box 5, Curtis–Stevenson Family Papers, 1775–1920, MHS; Bullock, *History of Negro Education in the South*, 43; James McPherson, "White Liberals and Black Power in Negro Education, 1865–1915," *American Historical Review* 64 (September 1977): 1357.

4. John W. Cromwell, "Free Labor and Schools in Virginia," *Anglo-African*, September 9, 1865, 2.

5. James Oliver Horton and Lois Horton, "Race, Occupation, and Literacy in Reconstruction Washington, D.C.," in *Free People of Color: Inside the African American Community*, ed. James O. Horton (Washington, D.C.: Smithsonian Institution Press, 1993), 193; Gen. Orlando Brown to O. O. Howard, January 22, 1867, reel 8, AMA Archives, Virginia, ARC.

6. G. L. Stockwell to Rev. Dr. Kirk, February 23, 1867, reel 8, AMA Archives, Virginia, ARC.

7. McPherson, "White Liberals and Black Power in Negro Education," 1360; Williams, *Self-Taught*, 89–92.

8. R. M. Manly to George Whipple, September 6, 1866, reel 8, AMA Archives, Virginia, ARC; Alexander, *Race Man*, 12.

9. R. M. Manly to Lyman Abbott, September 20, 1866, printed pages 86–88, reel 1, VA-BRFAL-ED; September 13,1866 Meeting Minutes, Educational Commission Records, box 1, NEFAS records, MHS.

10. R. M. Manly to O. O. Howard, August 11, 1866, printed pages 70–71; R. M. Manly to Rev. Grimes, August 28, 1866, printed pages 78–79; R. M. Manly to Robert L. Murray, August 25, 1866, printed pages 75–76; R. M. Manly to Gen. Orlando Brown, September 10, 1866, printed page 81, all in reel 1, VA-BRFAL-ED.

11. Alexander, *Race Man*, 12; "Normal Schools," *American Freedman* 2 (November 1867): 307; Elsa Barkley Brown, "Uncle Ned's Children: Negotiating Community and Freedom in Postemancipation Richmond, Virginia" (Ph.D. diss., Kent State University, 1994), 77–79.

12. John W. Cromwell, "In Memoriam (James H. Bowser), *People's Advocate*, April 30, 1881, 3; "Obituary," *Virginia Star*, April 30, 1881. Bowser noted Richmond, Virginia, as his place of birth in his 1870 application for the Freedmen's Saving Bank in Richmond. See

"Record for James H. Bowser, March 4, 1870," Freedman's Savings and Trust Company, *Registers of Signatures of Depositors in Branches of the Freedman's Savings and Trust Company, 1865–1874* (Washington, D.C.: National Archives and Records Service General Services Administration, 1970), series M816, reel 26, page 385, account 1157.

13. Letter from Bessie Canedy, March 11, 1868, entry; letter from Bessie Canedy, April 13, 1868 entry; letter to R. M. Manly, September 24, 1868 entry, all in Daily Record, 1868–69, NEFAS Records, MHS; Rabinowitz, *Race Relations in the Urban South*, 161.

14. Virginia Department of Education, *Virginia School Report, 1871: First Annual Report of the Superintendent of Public Instruction, for the Year Ending August 31, 1871* (Richmond, Va.: C. A. Schaeffter, Superintendent Public Printing, 1871), 20; Nicole Johnson, "Rosa L. Dixon Bowser," *Richmond Times-Dispatch*, February 9, 2009; "Rosa L. Dixon Bowser," in *Dictionary of Virginia Biography*, vol. 2, ed. John T. Kneebone et al. (Richmond: Library of Virginia, 2001), 160–62; Daniel Wallace Culp, "Mrs. Rosa D. Bowser," in *Twentieth Century Negro Literature; or, A Cyclopedia of Thought on the Vital Topics Relating to the American Negro, by One Hundred of America's Greatest Negros*, ed. Daniel Wallace Culp (Naperville, Ill.: J. L. Nichols, 1902), insert between 176 and 177; Richmond School Board, *Nineteenth Annual Report of the Superintendent of the Public Schools of the City of Richmond, VA., for the Scholastic Year Ending July 31st, 1888* (Richmond: Everett Waddey, City Printers, 1889), 30–33.

15. Alexander, *Race Man*, 12; "Letter from Rev. R. M. Manly concerning the Aptness of the Colored People to Learn," in Virginia Department of Education, *Virginia School Report, 1871*, 204–5.

16. Alexander, *Race Man*, 12; "Letter from Rev. R. M. Manly concerning the Aptness of the Colored People to Learn," in Virginia Department of Education, *Virginia School Report, 1871*, 204–5; Peabody Education Fund, *Proceedings of the Trustees Meeting, Held at Philadelphia 15 February 1871* (Cambridge, Mass.: Press of John Wilson and Sons, 1871), 18, file 2, Peabody Education Fund Collection, Jean and Alexander Heard Library, Vanderbilt University, Nashville.

17. Mary Patterson Manly to Virginius Douglas Johnston, May 12, 1933, VHS. Mary Patterson married R. M. Manly. She was his second wife and became his widow in 1897. For a list of graduates from 1872 to 1890, see Richmond School Board, *Sixteenth Annual Report of the Superintendent of the Public Schools of the City of Richmond, VA., for the Scholastic Year 1884–5* (Richmond, Va.: Walthall and Bowles, 1886), 31–33; and *Twenty-Fourth Annual Report of the Superintendent of the Public Schools of the City of Richmond*, 76–78.

18. Virginia Department of Education, *Virginia School Report, 1871*, 204; Virginia Department of Education, *Virginia School Report, 1872: Second Annual Report of the Superintendent of Public Instruction, for the Year Ending August 31, 1872* (Richmond, Va.: R. F. Walker, City Printer, 1872), 2–3; Virginia Department of Education, *Virginia School Report, 1874: Fourth Annual Report of the Superintendent of Public Instruction, for the Year Ending August 31, 1874 with reports of the Virginia Agricultural and Mechanical College, and Hampton Normal and Agricultural Institute* (Richmond, Va.: R. F. Walker, Superintendent Public Printing, 1874), 135–36.

19. "Colored Normal and High School," *Daily Dispatch* (Richmond, Va.), June 29, 1871, 1; quoted in Alexander, *Race Man*, 12.

20. "Eighth Annual Report of the School Board and Superintendent of Public Schools of the City of Richmond, VA., for the Scholastic Year 1875–1876," *Annual Message and Accompanying Documents of the Mayor of Richmond to the City Council for the Fiscal Year Ending January 31, 1877* (Richmond, Va.: C. C. Baughman, City Printer, 1877), 30; "Eighth Annual Report of the School Board and Superintendent of Public Schools of the City of Richmond, VA., for the Scholastic Year 1876–1877," *Annual Message and Accompanying Documents of the Mayor of Richmond to the City Council for the Fiscal Year Ending January 31, 1878* (Richmond: C. C. Baughman, City Printer, 1878), 222–23 (due to a printing error, there are two eighth annual reports).

21. Virginia Department of Education, *Virginia School Report, 1871*,, 15, 19, 106–23; and *Virginia School Report, 1874*, 116–17; Rabinowitz, *Race Relations in the Urban South*, 173–74; Table XI, in Richmond School Board, *Twenty-Fourth Annual Report of the Superintendent of the Public Schools of the City of Richmond*, 40–41.

22. "Navy Hill School," *Virginia Star*, November 18, 1882, 4; Rabinowitz, *Race Relations in the Urban South*, 174; "East End School," *Virginia Star*, December 23, 1882, 4.

23. "Daniel Webster Davis," section 8, Daniel Webster Davis Papers, VHS; Daniel Webster Davis, "Old Normal," in *Idle Moment*, 37; Daniel Webster Davis, "The Family (Domestic) Ideals," lecture, p. 3, section 1, Daniel Webster Davis Papers, VHS; Barkley Brown, "Uncle Ned's Children," 13; Alexander, *Race Man*, 15–17, 21–23. For a list of graduates, see Richmond School Board, *Sixteenth Annual Report of the Public Schools of the City of Richmond* , 31–33; and *Twenty-Fourth Annual Report of the Superintendent of the Public Schools of the City of Richmond*, 76–78.

24. Dailey, *Before Jim Crow*, 70; Richmond School Board, *Twenty-Fourth Annual Report of the Superintendent of the Public Schools of the City of Richmond*, 40–41; Rachleff, *Black Labor in Richmond*, 103–4. For a full discussion of the Readjuster Party, see chapter 7.

25. Virginia Department of Education, *Virginia School Report, 1873: Third Annual Report of the Superintendent of Public Instruction for the Year Ending August 31, 1873* (Richmond, Va.: R. F. Walker, 1873), 4–5; "Untitled," *Virginia Star*, December 23, 1882, 4.

26. "The State Colored Normal School," March 27, 1880, 2; and "The Colored Normal School at Lynchburg," March 27, 1880, 2, both in the *Virginia Star*; Virginia Department of Education, *Virginia School Report, 1880: Tenth Annual Report of the Superintendent of Public Instruction, for the Year Ending July 31, 1880* (Richmond, Va.: R. F. Walker, Superintendent Public Printing, 1880), 106–7; Lawson A. Scruggs, *Women of Distinction: Remarkable in Works and Invincible in Character* (Raleigh, N.C.: Lawson A. Scruggs, 1893), 286; Maggie N. Taylor, "Untitled," *Richmond Planet*, August 25, 1888; Virginia Department of Education, *Virginia School Report, 1888: Eighteenth Annual Report of the Superintendent of Public Instruction of the Commonwealth of Virginia with Accompanying Documents, School Year Ending July 31, 1888* (Richmond, Va.: J. H. O'Bannon, Superintendent of Public Printing, 1888), 66–75, 79–83.

27. Virginia Department of Education, *Virginia School Report, 1889*, 51–73; and *Virginia School Report, 1890*, 142–50.

28. "Navy Hill School," November 18, 1882, 4; "Colored Teachers for Colored Schools," December 9, 1882, 1; "From the People," December 16, 1882, 1, all in *Virginia Star*; R. L. Mitchell, "Colored Normal and Collegiate Institute," *People's Advocate*, March 25, 1882, 1.

29. Rabinowitz, *Race Relations in the Urban South*, 177.

30. Davis, "The Family (Domestic) Ideals"; Williams, *Freedom and Progress*, 8.

31. Quoted in Scruggs, *Women of Distinction*, 285–86.

32. "Untitled," *Virginia Star*, November 18, 1882, 1.

33. Rachleff, *Black Labor in Richmond*, 103–4; Dailey, *Before Jim Crow*, 70; Virginia Department of Education, *Virginia School Report: Annual Report of the Superintendent of Public Instruction* (published annually, 1871–91); and Richmond City Directory, 1883–84, both in LVA; Richmond School Board, *Seventeenth Annual Report of the Superintendent of the Public Schools of the City of Richmond, VA., for the Scholastic Year 1885–1886* (Richmond, Va.: Everett Waddey, City Printers, 1887), 44–45.

34. Virginia Department of Education, *Virginia School Report, 1888*, 109–17; and *Virginia School Report, 1889*, 119–29; Mary Patterson Manly to Virginius Johnston, May 12, 1933.

35. Rachleff, *Black Labor in Richmond*, 94–96; Rabinowitz, *Race Relations in the Urban South*, 238–39.

36. "Minutes of the Virginia Educational and Historical Society," *People's Advocate*, August 26, 1876, 2–3; Elizabeth McHenry, *Forgotten Readers: Recovering the Lost History of African American Literary Societies* (Durham, N.C.: Duke University Press, 2002), 141–42.

37. "Virginia Educational and Historical Association," June 17, 1876, 2; and "To the Public," August 21, 1880, 3, both in *People's Advocate*; Rachleff, *Black Labor in the Urban South*, 95; "Acme Literary Association," *Richmond Planet*, February 21, 1885, 1; Elsa Barkley Brown, "Negotiating and Transforming the Public Sphere: African American Political Life in the Transition from Slavery to Freedom," in *Jumpin' Jim Crow: Southern Politics from Civil War to Civil Rights*, ed. Jane Dailey, Glenda Elizabeth Gilmore, and Bryant Simon (Princeton, N.J.: Princeton University Press, 2000), 48–49

38. McHenry, *Forgotten Readers*, 141–42.

39. Barkley Brown, "Negotiating and Transforming," 49.

40. Williams, *Sketch of the Life and Times of Capt. R. A. Paul*, 31–41; More, "The Old Dominion," *New York Globe*, April 12, 1884, 1.

41. Williams, *Sketch of the Life and Times of Capt. R. A. Paul*, 62–67.

42. Ibid., 62.

43. Ibid., 67–68.

44. Ibid.

45. Ibid., 67–68.

46. For African American women's use of race, class, and gender to enter the public sphere for racial uplift from 1880 to 1920, see Evelyn Brooks Higginbotham, *Righteous Discontent: The Women's Movement in the Black Baptist Church, 1880–1920* (Cambridge, Mass.: Harvard University Press, 1993); and Glenda Gilmore, *Gender and Jim Crow: Women and the Politics of White Supremacy in North Carolina, 1896–1920* (Chapel Hill:

University of North Carolina Press, 1996); Williams, *Sketch of the Life and Times of Capt. R. A. Paul*, 68.

47. "Minutes of the Virginia Educational and Historical Society," 2–3; Elsa Barkley Brown, "Constructing a Life and a Community: A Partial Story of Maggie Lena Walker," *OAH Magazine of History* 7 (Summer 1993): 29; Johnson, "Rosa L. Dixon Bowser"; Culp, "Mrs. Rosa D. Bowser," insert between 176 and 177.

48. "Minutes of the Virginia Educational and Historical Society," 2–3; Johnson, "Rosa L. Dixon Bowser"; Culp, "Mrs. Rosa D. Bowser," insert between 176 and 177; Virginia State Board of Education, Teachers' Pension Disbursement Register, 1915–27, Accession 23350, LVA; Veronica A. Davis, *Here I Lay My Burdens Down: A History of the Black Cemeteries of Richmond, Virginia* (Richmond, Va.: Dietz Press, 2003), 65.

49. Richmond School Board, *Sixteenth Annual Report of the Public Schools of the City of Richmond*, 9, 20; *Seventeenth Annual Report of the Superintendent of Public Schools for the City of Richmond, Va., for the Scholastic Year, 1885–1886* (Richmond: Everett Waddey, City Printers, 1887), 8, 20, 32–34; "Eighteenth Annual Report of the Superintendent of Public Schools for the City of Richmond, VA., 1886–1887," in *Annual Message and Accompanying Documents of the Mayor of Richmond to the City Council for the Fiscal Year Ending January 31, 1888* (Richmond, Va.: C. N. Williams, City Printer, 1888), 9–10, 18–20; and *Nineteenth Annual Report of the Superintendent of the Public Schools of the City of Richmond*, 10–11, 21, 30–33; *Richmond Normal School: Twentieth Anniversary* (N. V. Randolph, City Stationer, 1887), VHS.

50. Rev. Hoge, "Negro Education in the City [of Richmond] Public Schools," 1905, section 46, Hoge Family Papers, VHS.

51. David W. Blight, *Race and Reunion: The Civil War in American Memory* (Cambridge, Mass.: Belknap Press, 2001), 1–5, 300–301.

52. "Minister Langston in Richmond," September 27, 1879, 2; "Richmond Items," April 20, 1881, 3; "Personal," June 25, 1881, 3, all in *People's Advocate*; "Have You Forgotten," *Richmond Planet*, June 12, 1885, 1; Alexander, *Race Man*, 13; Davis, *Idle Moment*, 37; Blight, *Race and Reunion*, 304.

53. Marita Sturken, *Tangled Memories: The Vietnam War, the AIDS Epidemic, and the Politics of Remembering* (Berkeley: University of California Press, 1997), 7–9.

54. Barbara Gannon, *The Won Cause: Black and White Comradeship in the Grand Army of the Republic* (Chapel Hill: University of North Carolina Press, 2011), 4–8, 74–77.

55. J. A. C. Chandler to the Principals of the Colored Schools; "Death of James H. Bowser," April 30, 1881, 1; "Funeral of James H. Bowser," April 30, 1881, 4; Robert J. Chiles, "The Cry of the Loser," April 30, 1881, 4; A Friend, "Obituary," April 30, 1881, 4, all in *Virginia Star*. Based on the writer's style and form, I believe that Daniel Webster Davis was "A Friend," but there is no conclusive evidence to corroborate this assumption. See also "Richmond Items," *People's Advocate*, May 21, 1881, 2; *In Memoriam: Ralza Morse Manly, Born January 16th, 1822, Died, September 16th, 1897. "Requiscat in pace." First Baptist Church, Wednesday Evening, November 24, 1897, eight o'clock* (Richmond, Va.: Grand Fountain Press, 1897), VHS.

56. Hoge, "Negro Education in the City."

57. "Richmond Colored High and Normal School (Armstrong)," *RPS: A Mini History: Bits and Pieces* (Richmond, Va.: Richmond Public School System, n.d.), http://web .richmond.k12.va.us/AboutRPS/RPSHistory/AE/Armstrong.aspx.

4. Remaking Old Blue College: Emerson Normal and Addressing the Need for Public Schoolteachers

1. L. B. Moore, "Address of Mr. L. B. Moore, of Alabama, on Negro Work," *American Missionary* 48 (December 1894): 459–60.

2. Ibid.

3. C. W. Buckley, "Draft Report Made to Major General Swayne Relative to Colored Schools, March 30, 1866," reel 1, AL-BRFAL-ED.

4. R. D. Harper, "Report to O. O. Howard, April 15, 1868," reel 1, AL-BRFAL-ED.

5. Bond, *Negro Education in Alabama*, 96–97; George Sisk, "Negro Education in the Alabama Black Belt, 1875–1900," *Journal of Negro Education* 22 (Spring 1953): 126–28; John Alvord, *Tenth Semi-annual Report on Schools for Freedmen, July 1, 1870* (Washington, D.C.: Government Printing Office, 1870), 5–7, in *Freedmen's Schools and Textbooks*, ed. Robert C. Morris (New York: AMS Press, 1980); Richardson, *Christian Reconstruction*, 118.

6. "Riotous," September 8, 1865, "Southern Education," February 18, 1866, 2; "A Lecture," July 1, 1871, 2; "Poisonous Doctrines," May 5, 1867, 2, all in *Mobile Daily Advertiser and Register*.

7. Richardson, *Christian Reconstruction*, 112–13; Mobile City Directories, 1871–74, Mobile Municipal Archives, Mobile, Alabama.

8. Richardson, *Christian Reconstruction*, 112–13; Mobile City Directories, 1871–87, Mobile Municipal Archives, Mobile, Alabama. For confusion over Sara Stanley's racial status and her experiences, see Ellen NicKenizie Lawson and Marlene D. Merrill, *The Three Sarahs: Documents of Antebellum Black College Women* (New York: Edwin Mellen Press, 1994), 48–50, 54–63.

9. M. H. Leatherman to E. M. Cravath, October 15, 1872, reel 3, AMA Archives, Alabama, ACT.

10. Mobile City Directories, 1870–90, Mobile Municipal Archives, Mobile, Alabama.

11. Bond, *Negro Education in Alabama*, 84; "Colored Mass Convention of the State of Alabama," May 4, 1867, 2; "Poisonous Doctrines," May 5, 1867, 2, both in *Mobile Daily Advertiser and Register*; C. A. Bradford to C. W. Buckley, August 7, 1867, reel 1, AL-BRFAL-ED.

12. Records of the Board of School Commissioners for Mobile County, Minutes, 1871–87, MCPSS. For defense of its practices, see "Public Schools," *Mobile Daily Advertiser and Register*, July 4, 1871, 3; and September 18, 1878, Meeting Minutes, Records of the Board of School Commissioners for Mobile County, Minutes, 1871–87, MCPSS; Mobile County City Directory, 1878, Mobile Municipal Archives, Mobile, Alabama.

13. Maria Waterbury to E. M. Cravath, November 6, 1871, reel 2; Maria Waterbury to E. M. Cravath, November 21, 1818, reel 2; M. H. Leatherman to E. M. Cravath, October 15, 1872, reel 3; E. P. Lord to E. M. Cravath, June 13, 1873, reel 3, all in AMA Archives,

Alabama, ARC. For examples of efforts to regain local confidence, see W. J. Squire to E. M. Cravath, July 31, 1872, reel 2; E. P. Lord to E. M. Cravath, January 11, 1873, reel 3; E. P. Lord to E. M. Cravath, May 28, 1873, reel 3, all in AMA Archives, Alabama, ARC.

14. Maria Waterbury to E. M. Cravath, November 6, 1871, reel 2; Maria Waterbury to E. M. Cravath, November 20, 1871, reel 2; Maria Waterbury to E. M. Cravath, February 17, 1872, reel 2; and E. P. Lord to E. M. Cravath, January 22, 1873, reel 3, all in AMA Archives, Alabama, ARC.

15. Clark, *History of Education in Alabama*, 280; Richardson, *Christian Reconstruction*, 119.

16. "Announcement: Opening of Emerson Institute," enclosed in E. P. Lord to E. M. Cravath, September 29, 1873, reel 3; D. L. Hickok to M. E. Strieby, December 10, 1878, reel 7, both in AMA Archives, Alabama, ARC.

17. E. P. Lord to E. M. Cravath, April 10, 1874, reel 3; E. P. Lord to M. E. Strieby, January 11, 1876, reel 5; E. P. Lord to M. E. Strieby, February 14, 1876, reel 5; E. P. Lord to M. E. Strieby, May 11, 1876, reel 5; E. P. Lord to M. E. Strieby, January 11, 1876, reel 5, all in AMA Archives, Alabama, ARC.

18. E. P. Lord to M. E. Strieby, January 11, 1876, reel 5, AMA Archives, Alabama, ARC; American Missionary Association, *Catalog of the Teachers and Student, Course of Study, Etc., of Emerson Normal Institute, Mobile, Alabama, 1900–1901* (Mobile, Ala.: A. N. Johnson, 1901), 6–9; "Population Schedule for City of Mobile, Alabama," in United States Census Bureau, *Population Schedules of the Ninth Census of the United States, 1870*, National Archives Microfilm Publication M593 (Washington, D.C.: National Archives, National Archives and Records Service, General Services Administration, 196–), reel 31.

19. Paulette Davis-Horton, *The Avenue: The Place, the People, the Memories, 1799–1986* (Mobile: Horton, 1991), 24; Kate A. Lord to E. M. Cravath, July 2, 1874, reel 4, AMA Archives, Alabama, ARC. William A. Caldwell and W. Aymar Caldwell appear interchangeably in the historical record.

20. Davis-Horton, *The Avenue*, 24.

21. Professor T. N. Chase, "Alabama: Breaking Ground for New Emerson Institute," *American Missionary* 32 (March 1878): 78; B. F. Koons, "Alabama: Dedication of Emerson Institute," *American Missionary* 32 (July 1878): 212, both in VF: Emerson Institute, University of South Alabama, Mobile, Alabama.

22. Koons, "Alabama," 212.

23. Emma Caughey, "Emerson Institute, Mobile, Ala., Burned," *American Missionary* 36 (March 1882): 80–81, VF: Emerson Institute, University of South Alabama, Mobile, Alabama.

24. Emma Caughey, "Emerson Institute," *American Missionary* 37 (June 1883): 172, VF: Emerson Institute, University of South Alabama, Mobile, Alabama; Clark, *History of Education in Alabama*, 280; American Missionary Association, *Catalog of the Teachers*, 7–8.

25. For the role of poverty on enrollment, see "Opening of Schools: Emerson Institute, Mobile, Ala.," *American Missionary* 35 (November 1881): 332–33, VF: Emerson Institute, University of South Alabama, Mobile, Alabama; American Missionary Association, *Catalog of the Teachers*, 7–8.

26. September 18, 1878, Meeting Minutes; Mobile County City Directories, 1878–90, Mobile Municipal Archives, Mobile, Alabama.

27. Records of the Board of School Commissioners for Mobile County, Minutes, 1871–87, MCPSS; Mobile City Directories, 1879–90, , Mobile Municipal Archives, Mobile, Alabama; Fitzgerald, *Urban Emancipation*, 264–65; American Missionary Association, *Catalog of the Teachers*, 6–9, 24–28; Davis-Horton, *The Avenue*, 235.

28. J. D. Smith to M. E. Strieby, September 18, 1877, reel 6, AMA Archives-Alabama, ACT.

29. National Council of the Congregational Churches of the United States, *The Congregational Yearbook, 1884* (Boston: Congregational Publishing Society, 1884), 17; Boston University, *Historical Register of Boston University, Fifth Decennial Issue, 1869–1911* (Boston: University Offices, 1911), 68.

30. W. Aymar Caldwell to M. E. Strieby, May 31, 1878, reel 6, AMA Archives-Alabama, ARC.

31. William H. Ash, "The Church and the Literary Club," *American Missionary* 32 (July 1878): 213, VF: Emerson Institute, University of South Alabama, Mobile, Alabama; McHenry, *Forgotten Readers*, 141–42; William H. Ash to M. E. Strieby, February 26, 1878; and William H. Ash to M. E. Strieby, March 13, 1878, both in reel 6, AMA Archives, Alabama, ARC.

32. William H. Ash to C. L. Woodward, June 10, 1878; and B. F. Koons to M. E. Strieby, April 13, 1878, both in reel 6, AMA Archives, Alabama; National Council of the Congregational Churches of the United States, *Congregational Yearbook, 1884*, 17.

33. W. Aymar Caldwell et al. to George Harris, June 18, 1878, reel 6, AMA Archives-Alabama, ARC. For other petitions, see Isaac Goddard et al. to M. E. Strieby, June 18, 1878; R. W. Jammitte to Pastor, June 25, 1878; Congregational Church to M. E. Strieby, June 1878; Marten Gladen et al. to M. E. Strieby, July 15, 1878; and A. F. Owens et al. to M. E. Strieby, July 17, 1878, all in reel 6, AMA Archives, Alabama.

34. Caldwell et al. to Harris, June 18, 1878; W. Aymar Caldwell to M. E. Strieby, July 10, 1878, reel 6, AMA Archives, Alabama, ARC.

35. Mobile City Directories, 1888–90, Mobile Municipal Archives, Mobile, Alabama; Davis-Horton, *The Avenue*, 24–25.

36. Davis-Horton, *The Avenue*, 39.

37. Ibid.

5. Shifting Strategies: Black Richmonders' Quest for Quality Public Schools

1. "The School Board," *Daily Dispatch* (Richmond, Va.), July 10, 1880, 1.

2. Ibid.

3. For example, see "Meeting of the City School Board," *Daily Dispatch* (Richmond, Va.), June 19, 1871, 1.

4. "Our Baltimore Visitors: The Public Schools Inspected," *Daily Dispatch* (Richmond, Va.), November 17, 1870, 1.

5. Ibid.

6. "School Officers Visiting Richmond," circa January 1872, in Virginia State Board of Education. *Official Orders of Superintendent of Public Instruction, 1870–1879: Extracted from Educational Journal of Virginia*, vol. 1 (Richmond, Va.: Educational Publishing House, 1870–79), 117, LVA; Hubbard G. Carlton, "The Evolution of the Richmond Public Schools with Reminiscences" (paper presented at the Principals' Conference, June 3, 1925), 5, Special Collections, University of Virginia, Charlottesville, Virginia.

7. "Board of Education: Selection of Teachers for Examination," September 1, 1870, 1; "Our Baltimore Visitors: The Public Schools Inspected," November 17, 1870, 1; "Colored Normal and High School," June 29, 1871, 1; and "Promotion in the Public Schools," July 4, 1871, 1, all in *Daily Dispatch* (Richmond, Va.).

8. Virginia Department of Education, *Virginia School Report, 1871*, 19–20, 106–23.

9. Rabinowitz, *Race Relations in the Urban South*, 173.

10. Smith and Dementi, *Facts and Legends of the Hills of Richmond*, 18–20; "Colored Normal and High School," June 29, 1871, 1, "The City Public Schools: Closing Exercises and Distribution of Awards in the Colored Schools," June 28, 1872, 1; and "The Public Schools: Closing Exercises and Distribution of Medals and Diplomas in the Valley and Navy Hill Colored Schools—Interesting Exercises—Addresses Made from Mayor Keiley and Rec. Dr. Dickinson—To-Day's Programme," June 12, 1876, 1, all in *Daily Dispatch* (Richmond, Va.).

11. Richmond School Board, "Eighth Annual Report of the School Board and Superintendent of Public Schools of the City of Richmond . . . 1875–1876," 30; and "Eighth Annual Report of the School Board and Superintendent of Public Schools of the City of Richmond . . . 1876–1877," 222–23.

12. "African Congregations," *Daily Dispatch* (Richmond, Va.), July 5, 1872, 1.

13. Dailey, *Before Jim Crow*, 97–98.

14. U.S. Census Bureau, *A Compendium of the Ninth Census*, 443; Table XI: Comparative Statistics, in Richmond School Board, *Twenty-Fourth Annual Report of the Superintendent of Public Schools of the City of Richmond*, 40–41.

15. Chesson, *Richmond after the War*, 166–67; Alexander, *Race Man*, 11; Williams, *Freedom and Progress*, 8.

16. Richmond School Board, "Seventh Annual Report of the School Board and Superintendent of Public Schools of the City of Richmond, VA., for the Scholastic Year 1874–1875," in *Annual Message and Accompanying Documents of the Mayor of Richmond to the City Council for the Fiscal Year Ending January 31, 1876* (Richmond, Va.: C. C. Baughman, City Printer, 1876), 261.

17. "The Necessity of Organization to Promote Our Educational Interest," *People's Advocate*, September 2, 1876, 2–3.

18. Richmond School Board, "Fourth Annual Report of the School Board and the Superintendent of Public Schools of the City of Richmond, VA., for the Scholastic Year 1871–1872," in *Annual Message and Accompanying Documents of the Mayor of Richmond to the City Council for the Fiscal Year Ending January 31, 1873* (Richmond, Va.: C. C. Baughman, City Printer, 1873), 121–23; Martha Owens, "The Development of Public Schools for Negroes in Richmond, Virginia" (M.A. diss., Virginia State College, 1947),

23–24; Rebekah Sharp, "A History of the Richmond Public School System, 1869–1958" (M.A. diss., University of Richmond, 1958), 26.

19. Sharp, "History of the Richmond Public School System," 26; Rabinowitz, *Race Relations in the Urban South*, 172.

20. Rachleff, *Black Labor in Richmond*, 36, 57–65; "Remarks of John Oliver, Esq., at the Educational Convention Held in Charlottesville, August 1877," *Virginia Star*, May 11, 1878, 2.

21. Chesson, *Richmond after the War*, 97, 160, 194–95; "Clarke et al. v. Oliver et al.," in *The Southeastern Reporter, Volume 22, Containing All the Decisions of the Supreme Courts of Appeals of Virginia and West Virginia, and Supreme Courts of North Carolina, South Carolina, Georgia: Permanent Edition, June 18–October 22, 1895* (St. Paul, Minn.: West, 1895), 175–76; Richmond City Directory, 1877, 1879–80, LVA; "An Act to Incorporate Moore Street Industrial Institution, of the City of Richmond, Approved March 6, 1882," in *Acts and Joint Resolutions Passed by the General Assembly of the State of Virginia during the Session of 1881–82* (Richmond, Va.: R. F. Walker, Superintendent Public Printing, 1882), 279–81.

22. "Minutes of the Virginia Educational and Historical Society," *People's Advocate*, August 26, 1876, 2–3; Sharp, "History of the Richmond Public School System," 26.

23. "The Public Schools," *Daily Dispatch* (Richmond, Va.), March 1, 1878, 1; Rachleff, *Black Labor in Richmond*, 103–4; Rabinowitz, *Race Relations in the Urban South*, 179.

24. Richmond School Board, "Fourth Annual Report of the School Board and the Superintendent of Public Schools of the City of Richmond," 123; and "Sixth Annual Report of the School Board and the Superintendent of Public Schools of the City of Richmond, VA., for the Scholastic Year 1873–1874," in *Annual Message and Accompanying Documents of the Mayor of Richmond to the City Council for the Fiscal Year Ending January 31, 1875* (Richmond, Va.: C. C. Baughman, City Printer, 1875), 366–67; "New Private Schools to Be Established," *Virginia Star*, September 8, 1877, 3; Rabinowitz, *Race Relations in the Urban South*, 172.

25. Owens, "Development of the Public Schools for Negroes in Richmond," 23; Rabinowitz, *Race Relations in the Urban South*, 172; Richmond School Board, "Twelfth Annual Report of the Secretary of the School Board and Supervisor of School Property for the Scholastic Year 1880–1881, Ending August 1, 1881, and Supplemental Report to February 1, 1882," in *Annual Message and Accompanying Documents of the Mayor of Richmond to the City Council for the Fiscal Year Ending January 31, 1882* (Richmond, Va.: N. V. Randolph, City Printer, 1882), 60.

26. Foner, *Reconstruction*, 512–16; Richmond School Board, "Ninth Annual Report of the School Board and Superintendent of Public Schools of the City of Richmond, VA., for the Scholastic Year 1877–1878," in *Annual Message and Accompanying Documents of the Mayor of Richmond to the City Council for the Fiscal Year Ending January 31, 1879* (Richmond, Va.: N. V. Randolph, City Printer, 1879), 54–55; Chesson, *Richmond after the War*, 118; "Public Schools in Danger," *Daily Dispatch* (Richmond, Va.), April 3, 1878, 2.

27. "New Private Schools to Be Established," September 8, 1877, 3; "The City School Board and Marshall Ward," September 8, 1877, 3; "Navy Hill School," September 8, 1877, 3, all in *Virginia Star*.

28. Richmond School Board, "Ninth Annual Report of the School Board and Superintendent of Public Schools of the City of Richmond," 54–55.

29. Ibid., 55.

30. Rabinowitz, *Race Relations in the Urban South*, 173; Richmond School Board, "Fourth Annual Report of the School Board and Superintendent of Public Schools of the City of Richmond," 121–28; "Meeting of the City School Board," *Daily Dispatch* (Richmond, Va.), September 6, 1871, 1.

31. Table XI: Comparative Statistics, in Richmond School Board, *Twenty-Fourth Annual Report of the Superintendent of Public Schools of the City of Richmond*, 40–41.

32. "The City School Board," June 25, 1875, 1; and "Applicants for Positions as Teachers in the Public Schools," June 13, 1876, 1, both in *Daily Dispatch* (Richmond, Va.); Richmond School Board, "Eighth Annual Report of the School Board and Superintendent of Public Schools of the City of Richmond . . . 1876–1877," 232; Scruggs, *Women of Distinction*, 285–86; "The Public Schools," *Daily Dispatch* (Richmond, Va.), March 1, 1878.

33. Richmond School Board, "Fourth Annual Report of the School Board and the Superintendent of Public Schools of the City of Richmond," 122; "Sixth Annual Report of the School Board and Superintendent of Public Schools of the City of Richmond," 366–89; "Seventh Annual Report of the School Board and Superintendent of Public Schools of the City of Richmond," 260, 291–95; and "Eighth Annual Report of the School Board and Superintendent of Public Schools of the City of Richmond . . . 1876–1877," 30.

34. Gertrude Woodruff Marlowe, *A Right Worthy Grand Mission: Maggie Lena Walker and the Quest for Black Economic Empowerment* (Washington, D.C.: Howard University Press, 2003), 5–7.

35. Rabinowitz, *Race Relations in the Urban South*, 173–74; Richmond School Board, "Fourth Annual Report of the School Board and the Superintendent of Public Schools of the City of Richmond," 127–28; "Sixth Annual Report of the School Board and Superintendent of Public Schools of the City of Richmond," 386–89; "Seventh Annual Report of the School Board and Superintendent of Public Schools of the City of Richmond," 291–95; and "Eighth Annual Report of the School Board and Superintendent of Public Schools of the City of Richmond . . . 1877–1878," 226.

36. Carlton, "Evolution of the Richmond Public Schools with Reminiscences," 5, 9.

37. Rabinowitz, *Race Relations in the Urban South*, 174–75; quoted in Howard Rabinowitz, "Half a Loaf: The Shift from White to Black Teachers in the Negro Schools of the Urban South, 1865–1890," *Journal of Southern History* 40 (November 1974): 579–80; "The Necessity of Organization to Promote Our Educational Interest," *People's Advocate*, September 2, 1876, 2–3.

38. "The Necessity of Organization to Promote Our Educational Interest," 2–3.

39. Virginia Department of Education. *Virginia School Report, 1871*, 15, 19, 106–23; and *Virginia School Report, 1874*, 116–17; Richmond School Board, "Eighth Annual Report of the School Board and Superintendent of Public Schools of the City of Richmond . . . 1875–1876," 30; and Table XI: Comparative Statistics, in *Twenty-Fourth Annual Report of the Superintendent of Public Schools of the City of Richmond*, 40–41.

40. Table XI: Comparative Statistics, in Richmond School Board, *Twenty-Fourth Annual Report of the Superintendent of Public Schools of the City of Richmond*, 40–41.

41. Ibid.; "The Necessity of Organization to Promote Our Educational Interest," 2–3.

42. Foner, *Reconstruction*, 512–34.

43. Sharp, "History of the Richmond Public School System," 44; Dailey, *Before Jim Crow*, 25–29; William A. Link, *A Hard Country and a Lonely Place: Schooling, Society, and Reform in Rural Virginia, 1870–1920* (Chapel Hill: University of North Carolina Press, 1986), 18–19; "The Public School in Its Relation to the Negro" was a three-part series originally published by the author "Civis" in the *Religious Herald* during the spring and summer of 1875. The *Southern Planter and Farmer*, a monthly journal published in Richmond, reprinted the articles from December 1875 to February 1876. For the text of the articles, see Civis, "The Public School in Its Relation to the Negro," *Southern Planter and Farmer* 36 (December 1875): 707–11; "The Public School in its Relation to the Negro, No. II," *Southern Planter and Farmer* 37 (January 1876): 35–42; and "The Public School in its Relation to the Negro, No. III," *Southern Planter and Farmer* 37 (February 1876): 108–16.

44. R. L. Dabney, "The Negro and the Common School," *Southern Planter and Farmer* 37 (April 1876): 252–54, 260–62.

45. L. R. Dickinson, "Dr. Dabney's on the Negro in the Public Schools," *Southern Planter and Farmer* 37 (April 1876): 317; Link, *Hard Country and a Lonely Place*, 19–20; William H. Ruffner, *Circulars (Including Addresses, Public Documents, Pamphlets, and Miscellaneous Material on Public Education in Virginia. Collected by W. H. Ruffner, Superintendent of Public Instruction)*, 1–2, LVA.

46. Ruffner, *Circulars*, 8, 10.

47. John W. Cromwell, "Dr. Dabney's Thrust at Free School," *People's Advocate*, May 13, 1876, 2; "The Necessity of Organization to Promote Our Educational Interest," 2–3.

48. James Hugo Johnston, "The Public Schools," speech, June 1876, box 3, folder 1, James Hugo Johnston, Sr. (1865–1914), Papers, Special Collections and University Archives, VSU.

49. Table XI: Comparative Statistics, in Richmond School Board, *Twenty-Fourth Annual Report of the Superintendent of Public Schools of the City of Richmond*, 40–41.

50. "City Politics," April 19, 1878, 1; "The Questions of the Day," April 20, 1878, 1; "The Local Situation," April 22, 1878, 1; "Responses from the Candidates for the Council," April 26, 1878, 1, all in *Daily Dispatch* (Richmond, Va.).

51. "Jackson Ward Republicans," *Virginia Star*, May 11, 1878, 3.

52. "The City School Board," July 3, 1878, 4; and "Public Schools," September 6, 1878, 1, both in *Daily Dispatch* (Richmond, Va.); "The Public Schools and Dr. Ruffner," *Virginia Star*, September 27, 1879, 2.

6. Rethinking Partners: Black Mobilians' Struggle for Quality Public Schools

1. "Gen. Howard and the Freedman's Bureau," *Mobile Daily Register*, July 17, 1870, 2, column 1, Interesting Transcriptions of Mobile Daily Newspapers, 1860–1901, Mobile Municipal Archives, Mobile, Alabama.

2. "Untitled," December 6, 1870, 2, column 4; "The Public Schools," January 1, 1871, 3, both in *Mobile Daily Register*.

3. Joseph Hodgson, *Laws Relating to the Public Schools of Alabama, with Remarks and Forms, 1871* (Montgomery, Ala.: W. W. Screws, 1871), 43–44, in Superintendent of Education, Reports: Annual and Other Reports, 1857–71, ADAH.

4. "Public Schools," December 25, 1870, 4; Maj. W. T. Walthall, "The School Usurpation," February 17, 1871, 4, both in *Mobile Daily Register*. For the letters officially removing Putnam and appointing Tompkins, see "County Superintendent of Education," February 24, 1871, 2; "To the Teachers," notice, February 22, 1871, 4, both in *Mobile Daily Register*.

5. "Outrage on the Public Schools," *Mobile Daily Register*, January 8, 1871, 4. For legal proceedings, see A. J. Moses, "The Public Schools," January 21, 1871, 4; "The Public Schools," January 27, 1871, 4, Pater Familias, "The Poor Teachers," February 1, 1874, 4; and Inquirer, "The Mandamus," February 21, 1871, 4, all in *Mobile Daily Register*.

6. "This Day's Election," March 4, 1871, 2; "Untitled," March 4, 1871, 2, both in *Mobile Daily Register*.

7. "Suicide of a Well-Known Colored Man, an Ex-Alderman," *Mobile Daily Register*, February 19, 1871, 4; Fitzgerald, *Urban Emancipation*, 153; "The People's Free School Ticket," March 4, 1871, 2; "The Elections," March 7, 1871, 2, both in *Mobile Daily Register*.

8. "Public School Elections," March 10, 1871, 4; "The Elections," March 7, 1871, 2, both in *Mobile Daily Register*.

9. "The Colored Public Schools," *Mobile Daily Register*, April 2, 1871, 2.

10. Ibid.

11. "Our Schools," *Mobile Daily Register*, June 29, 1871, 3; "Public Schools," *Mobile Daily Advertiser and Register*, July 1, 1871, 2; "Election of Teachers," *Mobile Daily Register*, July 3, 1872, 1.

12. Maria L. Waterbury, *Seven Years among the Freedmen* (Chicago: T. B. Arnold, 1893), 97–98; "A Lively Fight," *Mobile Daily Register*, June 30, 1871, 3.

13. For African Americans' influence over politics in Mobile, see Fitzgerald, *Urban Emancipation*, chaps. 5 and 6; Richardson, *Christian Reconstruction*, 225; Hahn, *Nation under Our Feet*, 224–26; Waterbury, *Seven Years among the Freedmen*, 90–91.

14. "Suicide of a Well-Known Colored Man, an Ex-Alderman," *Mobile Daily Register*, February 19, 1871, 4; Fitzgerald, *Urban Emancipation*, 129, 169.

15. W. Irving Squire to E. M. Cravath, December 16, 1872, reel 3, AMA Archives, Alabama, ARC.

16. "Mobile Colored Schools," *Mobile Daily Tribune*, January 22, 1873, 2, column 2, Interesting Transcriptions of *Mobile Daily Tribune*, 1870–75; and Mobile City Directories, 1873–77, both in Mobile Municipal Archives, Mobile, Alabama. For the Democrats' return to power, see Fitzgerald, *Urban Emancipation*, 198–228.

17. "Negroes Would Turn Democrats and Share Spoils, May 30, 1877," Interesting Transcriptions from the City Documents of the City of Mobile for 1861–84, 19–20, Mobile Municipal Archives, Mobile, Alabama.

18. Ibid.; Fitzgerald, *Urban Emancipation*, 226–27.

19. Fitzgerald, *Urban Emancipation*, 233–34.

20. "The Colored Public Schools," *Mobile Daily Register*, April 2, 1871, 2; Bond, *Negro Education in Alabama*, 84; "Colored Mass Convention of the State of Alabama,"

May 4, 1867, 2; and "Poisonous Doctrines," May 5, 1867, 2, both in *Mobile Daily Advertiser and Register.* The text of these petitions have been lost in the historical record, but the content can be inferred from school board minutes and local newspapers. See Records of the Board of School Commissioners for Mobile County, Minutes, 1871–87, MCPSS; "The Colored Public Schools," *Mobile Daily Register,* April 2, 1871, 2; and "Mobile Colored Schools," *Mobile Daily Tribune,* January 22, 1873, 2, column 2, Interesting Transcriptions of *Mobile Daily Tribune,* Mobile Municipal Archives, Mobile, Alabama.

21. *Report of Leroy Box, Superintendent of Education for the State of Alabama, for the Scholastic Year Ending on the 30th September 1879, with an Appendix* (Montgomery, Ala.: Barrett and Brown, 1880), in Superintendent of Education, Reports: Annual and Other Reports, 1868–79, ADAH.

22. May 15, 1871, Meeting Minutes, Records of the Board of School Commissioners for Mobile County, Minutes, 1871–87, MCPSS; *Special Report of Joseph Hodgson, Superintendent Public Instruction of the State of Alabama, to the Governor, for the Scholastic Year, January 1, 1871, to September 30, 1871* (Montgomery, Ala.: W. W. Screws, 1871), 67–69, in Superintendent of Education, Reports: Annual and Other Reports, 1868–79, ADAH; Maria L. Waterbury to E. M. Cravath, November 6, 1871, reel 3, AMA Archives, Alabama, ARC.

23. Hodgson, *Laws Relating to the Public Schools of Alabama,* 43–44, ADAH.

24. Ibid.; Rev. Spencer Snell, "A Student Letter: How I Was Educated, Led to Christ and into the Ministry," *American Missionary* 43 (May 1889): 136, VF: Emerson Institute, USA.

25. *Special Report of Joseph Hodgson,* 69–70.

26. Ibid.

27. Ibid.; Maria L. Waterbury to E. M. Cravath, November 6, 1871; and Maria L. Waterbury to E. M. Cravath, November 20, 1871, both in reel 3, AMA Archives, Alabama, ARC.

28. M. H. Leatherman to E. M. Cravath, October 15, 1872; and Edward P. Lord to E. M. Cravath, January 11, 1873, both in reel 3, AMA Archives, Alabama, ARC.

29. Maria L. Waterbury to E. M. Cravath, November 6, 1871, reel 3, AMA Archives, Alabama, ARC.

30. Maria L. Waterbury to E. M. Cravath, November 6, 1871, reel 3; Edward P. Lord to E. M. Cravath, November 28, 1873, reel 3; and Edward P. Lord to M. E. Strieby, January 11, 1876, reel 5, all in AMA Archives, Alabama, ARC.

31. W. Irving Squire to E. M. Cravath, November 25, 1872, reel 3; Edward P. Lord to E. M. Cravath, January 22, 1873, reel 3; and Albert B. Irwin to M. E. Strieby, March 7, 1877, reel 5, all in AMA Archives, Alabama, ARC.

32. Snell, "Student Letter," 136.

33. W. Irving Squire to E. M. Cravath, November 11, 1872, reel 3, AMA Archives, Alabama, ARC.

34. E. R. Dickson to E. M. Cravath, August 2, 1872, reel 2; and L. C. Steward to E. M. Cravath, September 14, 1872, reel 3, both in AMA Archives, Alabama, ARC; American Missionary Association, *The Nation Is Still in Danger; or, Ten Years after the War* (New York: American Missionary Association, 1875), 6, 8; Richardson, *Christian Reconstruc-*

tion, 118–19, 123–40; Edward P. Lord to E. M. Cravath, January 11, 1873; and Edward P. Lord to E. M. Cravath, March 29, 1873, both in reel 3, AMA Archives, Alabama, ARC; Mobile City Directories, 1870–79, Mobile Municipal Archives, Mobile, Alabama.

35. *Report of Leroy Box, Superintendent of Education for the State of Alabama, for the Scholastic Year Ending on the 30th September 1879.*

36. "The Colored Public Schools," *Mobile Daily Register*, April 2, 1871, 2; Mobile City Directories, 1870–80, Mobile Municipal Archives, Mobile, Alabama; Richardson, *Christian Reconstruction*, 112–13; Lawson and Merrill, *Three Sarahs*, 48–50, 54–63.

37. Maria J. Wilhelm to E. R. Dickson, October 13, 1874, Records of the Board of School Commissioners for Mobile County, Minutes, 1871–87, MCPSS; Mobile City Directories, 1871–75, Mobile Municipal Archives, Mobile, Alabama.

38. *Report of John M. McKleroy, Superintendent of Public Instruction for the State of Alabama, for the Scholastic Year Ending on September 30 1875* (Montgomery, Ala.: W. W. Screws, 1875), 93–94, 96–97, in Superintendent of Education, Reports: Annual and Other Reports, 1868–79, ADAH; Kaestle, *Pillars of the Republic*, 67, 76–77.

39. Rabinowitz, *Race Relations in the Urban South*, 173–74.

40. Waterbury, *Seven Years among the Freedmen*, 93–95, 97–98.

41. Mobile City Directories, 1870–77, Mobile Municipal Archives, Mobile, Alabama; "School at the College," *Nationalist* (Mobile, Ala.), June 28, 1866, 2; Fitzgerald, *Urban Emancipation*, 181; October 2, 1871, Meeting Minutes, Records of the Board of School Commissioners for Mobile County, Minutes, 1871–87, MCPSS.

42. Mobile City Directories, 1870–77, Mobile Municipal Archives, Mobile, Alabama. For the common Board of School Commissioners responses, see "The Colored Public Schools," *Mobile Daily Register*, April 2, 1871, 2; "Public Schools," *Mobile Daily Advertiser and Register*, July 4, 1871, 3; and October 2, 1871 Meeting Minutes, Records of the Board of School Commissioners for Mobile County, Minutes, 1871–87, MCPSS.

43. *Report of John M. McKleroy*, 96–97.

44. "Mobile Colored Schools," *Mobile Daily Tribune*, January 22, 1873, 2, column 2, Interesting Transcriptions of *Mobile Daily Tribune*, 1870–75, Mobile Municipal Archives, Mobile, Alabama.

45. Ibid.

46. Richardson, *Christian Reconstruction*, 118–19; American Missionary Association, *Catalog of the Teachers*, 6–9; Mobile City Directories, 1876–77, Mobile Municipal Archives, Mobile, Alabama.

47. September 18, 1878, Meeting Minutes, Records of the Board of School Commissioners for Mobile County, Minutes, 1871–87, MCPSS; American Missionary Association, *Catalog of the Teachers*, 24–28; Mobile County City Directories, 1878–90, Mobile Municipal Archives, Mobile, Alabama.

48. Peabody Education Fund, *Proceedings of the Trustees Meeting, Held at Philadelphia, 15 February 1871* (Cambridge, Mass.: Press of John Wilson and Son, 1871), 34, file 2, box 11, Peabody Education Fund Collection, Jean and Alexander Heard Library, Vanderbilt University, Nashville; Richardson, *Christian Reconstruction*, 111–13.

49. Superintendent of Education, Reports: Annual and Other Reports, 1868–79, ADAH; *Special Report of Joseph Hodgson*, 64–65.

50. Superintendent of Education, Reports: Annual and Other Reports, 1868–79, ADAH; Robert G. Sherer, *Subordination or Liberation? The Development and Conflicting Theories of Black Education in Nineteenth-Century Alabama* (Tuscaloosa: University of Alabama Press, 1977), 8; Bond, *Negro Education in Alabama*, 101–2, 104.

51. Foner, *Reconstruction*, 512; Edward P. Lord to E. M. Cravath, October 7, 1873, reel 3, AMA Archives, Alabama, ARC; Superintendent of Education, Reports: Annual and Other Reports, 1868–79, ADAH; Fitzgerald, *Urban Emancipation*, 217–20.

52. *Report of Joseph H. Speed, Superintendent of Public Instruction for the State of Alabama, for the Scholastic Year Ending on October 1, 1873* (Montgomery, Ala.: Arthur Bingham, 1874), 3, 6; *Report of Joseph H. Speed, Superintendent of Public Instruction for the State of Alabama, for the Scholastic Year Ending on October 1, 1874* (Montgomery, Ala.: W. W. Screws, 1874), 3–4, both in Superintendent of Education, Reports: Annual and Other Reports, 1868–79, ADAH; *Report of John M. McKleroy, 7, 14,* ADAH.

53. *Report of John M. McKleroy, 96; Thirty-First Annual Report of the Superintendent of Education for the State of Alabama, for the Scholastic Year Ending September 30th, 1885, Submitted by Solomon Palmer, Superintendent of Education* (Montgomery, Ala.: Barrett and Co., 1886), in Reports of the Superintendent of Education, 1880–88, ADAH.

54. Fitzgerald, *Urban Emancipation*, 199–204, 219–21.

55. "Public Schools," *Mobile Daily Tribune*, June 30, 1875, 2, column 2, Interesting Transcriptions of the *Mobile Daily Tribune*, 1870–75, Mobile Municipal Archives, Mobile, Alabama; Kaestle, *Pillars of the Republic*, 3–12, 151–55.

56. "Public Schools," 2, column 2; Kaestle, *Pillars of the Republic*, 73.

57. Bond, *Negro Education in Alabama*, 149; *Report of Leroy Box, Superintendent of Education for the State of Alabama, for the Scholastic Year Ending 30th September 1878, with Tabular Statistics of 1876–1877, Containing Also the Laws Relating to the Public School System of the State with an Appendix of Forms* (Montgomery, Ala.: Barrett and Brown, 1879), in Superintendent of Education, Reports: Annuals and Other Reports, 1868–79, ADAH.

58. *Report of Leroy Box, Superintendent of Education for the State of Alabama, for the Scholastic Year Ending 30th September 1878.*

7. Walking Slowly but Surely: The Readjusters and the Quality School Campaigns in Richmond

1. Femme, "A Prayer for Education," *New York Globe*, December 29, 1883, 4.

2. Ibid.

3. James T. Moore, "The University and Readjusters," *Virginia Magazine of History and Biography* 78 (January 1970): 87; Dailey, *Before Jim Crow*, 37–47.

4. Williams, *Sketch of the Life and Times of Capt. R. A. Paul*, 19–20; Dailey, *Before Jim Crow*, 89.

5. Williams, *Sketch of the Life and Times of Capt. R. A. Paul*, 21.

6. Ibid., 25–26.

7. Rachleff, *Black Labor in Richmond*, 103–4; Dailey, *Before Jim* Hubbard G. Carlton, "The Evolution of the Richmond Public Schools with Reminiscences" (paper presented

at the Principals' Conference, June 3, 1925), 11–12, Special Collections, University of Virginia, Charlottesville, Virginia.

8. "The Old Dominion: Masonic Celebration, Meeting of the Acme Literary, Another Victory, Colored Teachers and Principals," July 7, 1883, 1; "The Old Dominion," September 29, 1883, 4, both in *New York Globe*.

9. Carlton, "Evolution of the Richmond Public Schools with Reminiscences," 10–11.

10. Williams, *Sketch of the Life and Times of Capt. R. A. Paul*, 25–26; More, "The Old Dominion," February 9, 1884, 1; and More, "The Old Dominion," March 29, 1884, 4, both in *New York Globe*; Carlton, "Evolution of the Richmond Public Schools with Reminiscences," 10.

11. "The Old Dominion," March 29, 1884, 4; More, "The Old Dominion," May 19, 1884, 4; "More, "The Old Dominion," April 12, 1884, 1; More, "The Old Dominion," May 24, 1884, 4, all in *New York Globe*.

12. "Edwin Archer Randolph, LLC, 1880," in Yale University, *Obituary Record of Yale Graduates*, ser. 16, no. 11 (New Haven, Conn.: Yale University, 1920), 1614; Alexander, *Race Man*, 28.

13. Judith Ann Schiff, "Pioneers," *Yale Alumni Magazine* 69 (January–February 2006): 80–81; Luther Porter Jackson, *Negro Office-Holders in Virginia, 1865–1895* (Norfolk, Va.: Guide Quality Press, 1945), 58; Rachleff, *Black Labor in Richmond*, 112; "Edwin Archer Randolph," 1615.

14. "The Old Dominion," *New York Globe*, May 19, 1884, 4.

15. Table XI: Comparative Statistics, in Richmond School Board, *Twenty-Fourth Annual Report of the Superintendent of Public Schools of the City of Richmond*, 40–41.

16. Rachleff, *Black Labor in Richmond*, 103; Table XI: Comparative Statistics, in Richmond School Board, *Twenty-Fourth Annual Report of the Superintendent of Public Schools of the City of Richmond*, 40–41.

17. "The Old Dominion," October 6, 1883, 1; and More, "The Old Dominion," January 19, 1884, 1; W. R. Granger, "Richmond Colored Schools," February 23, 1884, 1, all in *New York Globe*.

18. "Meeting of the School Board," March 27, 1885, 1; "Called Council Meeting: More Schools to Be Built," June 13, 1885, 1; and "About the Public Schools," September 15, 1885, 1, all in *Daily Dispatch* (Richmond, Va.); Owens, "Development of Public Schools for Negroes in Richmond," 29–31; Richmond School Board, *Nineteenth Annual Report of the Superintendent of the Public Schools of the City of Richmond*, 7–9, 45–46.

19. Table XI: Comparative Statistics, in Richmond School Board, *Twenty-Fourth Annual Report of the Superintendent of Public Schools of the City of Richmond*, 40–41.

20. Ibid.

21. Rabinowitz, *Race Relations in the Urban South*, 174; "East End School," December 23, 1882, 4; and "Navy Hill School," November 18, 1882, 4, both in *Virginia Star*; Richmond School Board, "Twelfth Annual Report of the Secretary of the School Board," 30–31.

22. Robert J. Chiles, "The Hope of the Race," *Industrial Herald*, July 27, 1883, 2; and Daniel B. Williams, "The Education of Children," *Industrial Herald*, July 27, 1883, 3, both in folder 10, box 1, James Hugo Johnston, Sr. Papers, VSU; Williams, *Freedom and*

Progress, 46–47; Richmond School Board, "Thirteenth Annual Report of the School Board and Superintendent of Public Schools of the City of Richmond for the Scholastic Year, 1881–1882," in *Annual Message and Accompanying Documents of the Mayor of Richmond to the City Council for the Fiscal Year Ending January 31, 1883* (Richmond, Va.: Yancey, Waddey, and Co., Printers, 1883), 41; Marlowe, *Right Worthy Grand Mission*, 5–7.

23. February 26, 1883, Meeting, Minutes, printed pages 76–77; and March 5, 1883, Meeting, Minutes, printed page 87, Minutes of City School Board, box 1, Daniel Barclay William (1862–1895) Papers, Special Collections and University Archives, VSU; Williams, *Freedom and Progress*, 8.

24. "An Appeal to the White People of the South," *Virginia Star*, November 11, 1882, 1.

25. "Colored Teachers for Colored Schools," *Virginia Star*, December 9, 1882, 1.

26. "Colored Teachers for Colored Schools," December 9, 1882, 1; and "From the People," letter to the editor, December 16, 1882, 1, both in *Virginia Star*.

27. Rachleff, *Black Labor in Richmond*, 103–4; Dailey, *Before Jim Crow*, 70; Carlton, "Evolution of the Richmond Public Schools with Reminiscences," 11–12.

28. "The Old Dominion: Masonic Celebration, Meeting of the Acme Literary, Another Victory, Colored Teachers and Principals," July 7, 1883, 1; "The Old Dominion," September 29, 1883, 4, both in *New York Globe*.

29. "Old Dominion," December 1, 1883, 1; and W. R. Granger, "Richmond Colored Schools," February 23, 1884, 1, both in *New York Globe*; Carlton, "Evolution of the Richmond Public Schools with Reminiscences," 10–11.

30. More, "The Old Dominion: Ousting the Colored Teachers from Richmond Schools," *New York Globe*, July 5, 1884, 1.

31. More, "The Old Dominion," *New York Globe*, July 19, 1884, 4.

32. Carlton, "Evolution of the Richmond Public Schools with Reminiscences," 11; Richmond School Board, "Twenty-First Annual Report of the Superintendent of the Public Schools of the City of Richmond, VA., for the Scholastic Year Ending July 31st, 1890," in *Annual Message and Accompanying Documents of the Mayor of Richmond to the City Council for the Fiscal Year Ending December 31, 1890* (Richmond, Va.: C. N. Williams, City Printer, 1891), 13.

33. Williams, *Sketch of the Life and Times of Capt. R. A. Paul*, 15; Table XI: Comparative Statistics, in Richmond School Board, *Twenty-Fourth Annual Report of the Superintendent of Public Schools of the City of Richmond*, 40–41.

34. Table XI: Comparative Statistics, in Richmond School Board, *Twenty-Fourth Annual Report of the Superintendent of Public Schools of the City of Richmond*, 40–41.

35. "The City School Board," *Daily Dispatch* (Richmond, Va.), November 28, 1884, 1; Richmond School Board, "Annual Report of the Clerk of School Board and Supervisor of School Property for the Scholastic Year 1884–85," in *Annual Message and Accompanying Documents of the Mayor of Richmond to the City Council for the Fiscal Year Ending January 31, 1884* (Richmond, Va.: Walthall and Bowles, City Printer, 1885), 27–28; and *Seventeenth Annual Report of the Superintendent of Public Schools for the City of Richmond*, 9.

36. "Mr. Berry's School Bill," *Daily Dispatch* (Richmond, Va.), January 29, 1886, 1; Link, *Hard Country and a Lonely Place*, 9–10, 57.

37. More, "The Old Dominion," *New York Globe*, April 5, 1884, 4.

38. Ibid.

8. Still Crawling: Black Mobilians' Struggle for Quality Schools Continues

1. Femme, "A Prayer for Education," *New York Globe*, December 29, 1883, 4.

2. Ibid.

3. Fitzgerald, *Urban Emancipation*, 247.

4. Ibid., 247–50, 257–65; "The Election," *Mobile Daily Register*, November 10, 1888, 4, column 2, Interesting Transcriptions of Mobile Daily Newspapers, 1860–1901, Mobile Municipal Archives, Mobile, Alabama.

5. *Report of H. Clay Armstrong, Superintendent of Education for the State of Alabama, for the Scholastic Year Ending September 30th, 1884* (Montgomery, Ala.: W. D. Brown and Co., 1884), in Reports of the Superintendent of Education, 1880–88, ADAH; Mobile City Directories, 1880–81, Mobile Municipal Archives, Mobile, Alabama.

6. February 9, 1881, Meeting, Records of the Board of School Commissioners for Mobile County, Minutes, 1871–87, MCPSS; Mobile City Directories, 1880–90, Mobile Municipal Archives, Mobile, Alabama.

7. *Report of H. Clay Armstrong, Superintendent of Education for the State of Alabama, for the Scholastic Year Ending September 30th, 1884*; and *Thirty-Sixth Annual Report of the Superintendent of Education for the State of Alabama, for the Scholastic Year Ending September 30th, 1890, by Solomon Palmer, Superintendent of Education* (Montgomery, Ala.: Brown Printing Co., 1890), in Reports of the State Superintendent of Education, 1889–98, both in ADAH; Clark, *History of Education in Alabama*, 272.

8. Clark, *History of Education in Alabama*, 273.

9. Mobile City Directories, 1880–90, Mobile Municipal Archives, Mobile, Alabama; *Thirty-Fourth Annual Report of the Superintendent of Education for the State of Alabama, for the Scholastic Year Ending September 30th, 1888, by Solomon Palmer, Superintendent of Education* (Montgomery, AL: W. D. Brown and Co., 1888) in Reports of the Superintendent of Education, 1880–88, ADAH.

10. O. D. Crawford, "Anniversary Reports: Emerson Institute," *American Missionary* 35 (July 1881): 209, VF-Emerson Institute, USA Archives.

11. Emma Caughey, "Emerson Institute, Mobile, Ala., Burned," *American Missionary* 36 (March 1882): 80–81; and Emma Caughey, "Emerson Institute," *American Missionary* 37 (June 1883): 172–74, both in VF: Emerson Institute, USA.

12. September 18, 1878, Meeting Minutes; June 25, 1882, Meeting Minutes; September 14, 1885, Meeting Minutes, all in Records of the Board of School Commissioners for Mobile County, Minutes, 1871–87, MCPSS; American Missionary Association, *Catalog of the Teachers*, 24–28; Mobile City Directories, 1878–90, Mobile Municipal Archives, Mobile, Alabama; quoted in Fitzgerald, *Urban Emancipation*, 259.

13. Fitzgerald, *Urban Emancipation*, 263–64; September 14, 1885, Meeting Minutes, Records of the Board of School Commissioners for Mobile County, Minutes, 1871–87, MCPSS.

14. Fitzgerald, *Urban Emancipation*, 264–65; Mobile City Directories, 1886–87, Mobile Municipal Archives, Mobile, Alabama; Clark, *History of Education in Alabama*, 272.

15. Mobile City Directories, 1888–90, Mobile Municipal Archives, Mobile, Alabama; Davis-Horton, *The Avenue*, 24–25, 39.

16. Booker T. Washington, *Up from Slavery, with Related Documents*, ed. W. Fitzhugh Brundage (Boston: Bedford/St. Martin's Press, 2003), 52–60.

17. Ibid., 64–74.

18. Louis R. Harlan, *Booker T. Washington: The Making of a Black Leader, 1865–1901* (New York: Oxford University Press, 1972), 135–46, 161–66; Washington, *Up from Slavery*, 122–31.

19. Olivia A. Davidson to the editor of the *Southern Workman*, June 11, 1883, in *The Booker T. Washington Papers*, 14 vols., ed. Louis R. Harlan (Urbana: University of Illinois Press, 1972–1989), 1:232.

20. Booker T. Washington to Warren Logan, July 15, 1887, in ibid., 1:369.

21. Clark, *History of Education in Alabama*, 272–73; Mobile City Directories, 1885–90, Mobile Municipal Archives, Mobile, Alabama.

22. Bond, *Negro Education in Alabama*, 148–51; Reports of the Superintendent of Education, 1880–88; and *Thirty-Sixth Annual Report of the Superintendent of Education for the State of Alabama, for the Scholastic Year Ending September 30th, 1890*, both in ADAH.

23. Bond, *Negro Education in Alabama*, 135–36, 148–49; "Report of Leroy Box for the Scholastic Year Ending 30th September 1878," in Superintendent of Education, Reports: Annual and Other Reports, 1868–79, ADAH.

24. *Thirty-Fourth Annual Report of the Superintendent of Education for the State of Alabama, for the Scholastic Year Ending September 30th, 1888* in Reports of the Superintendent of Education, 1880–88; *Thirty-Sixth Annual Report of the Superintendent of Education for the State of Alabama, for the Scholastic Year Ending September 30th, 1890*, both in ADAH.

25. Quoted in Fitzgerald, *Urban Emancipation*, 251; *Thirty-Third Annual Report of the Superintendent of Education for the State of Alabama, for the Scholastic Year Ending 30th September 1887, with an Appendix of the Public School Laws and Forms for Teachers and Officers by Solomon Palmer, Superintendent of Education* (Montgomery, Ala.: W. D. Brown and Co., 1888), 17 in Reports of the Superintendent of Education, 1880–88, ADAH; More, "The Old Dominion," *New York Globe*, April 5, 1884, 4.

Epilogue: The Blair Education Bill and the Death of Educational Reconstruction, 1890

1. Waterbury, *Seven Years among the Freedmen*, 198.

2. W. E. B. Du Bois, "Of the Training of Black Men," *The Souls of Black Folk*, in *Writings*, ed. Nathan Huggins (New York: Library of America Press, 1986), 427.

3. My discussion draws on and adds to the core historiography of the Blair education bill set by Daniel Crofts, Thomas Upchurch, and Gordon McKinney. Crofts's dissertation and subsequent article discussed the legislation as one of the alternative possibilities to Jim Crow pioneered by C. Vann Woodward. Upchurch situated the legislation within the context of the 51st U.S. Congress and showed how it led to congressional acceptance of

Jim Crow. McKinney's biography provided a clearer sense of the man who championed the bill and his overall reform efforts in postwar America.

4. Foner, *Reconstruction*, 575–87; Daniel Wallace Crofts, "The Blair Bill and the Elections Bill: The Congressional Aftermath to Reconstruction" (Ph.D. diss., Yale University, 1968), iv, 176–220; Richardson, *Death of Reconstruction*, 207.

5. Gordon B. McKinney, *Henry W. Blair's Campaign to Reform America: From the Civil War to the U.S. Senate* (Lexington: University Press of Kentucky, 2013), 9–13.

6. "Blair, Henry W.," in United States National Park Services, *Civil War Soldiers and Sailors Database*, http://www.nps.gov/civilwar/soldiers-and-sailors-database.htm; "Blair, Henry William, (1834–1920)," in United States Office of Art and Archives, *Biographical Dictionary of the United States Congress, 1774–Present*, http://bioguide.congress .gov/.

7. McKinney, *Henry W. Blair's Campaign to Reform America*, 82–83; Thomas Upchurch, *Legislating Racism: The Billion-Dollar Congress and the Birth of Jim Crow* (Lexington: University Press of Kentucky, 2004), 47.

8. Daniel Wallace Crofts, "The Black Response to the Blair Education Bill," *Journal of Southern History* 37 (February 1971): 42.

9. McKinney, *Henry W. Blair's Campaign to Reform America*, 87–88.

10. Ibid., 92, 94–95; Crofts, "Black Response to the Blair Education Bill," 42; Upchurch, *Legislating Racism*, 47.

11. Thomas Henry Bayley Browne, Resolution for Special Order to Consider Bill on Federal Aid to Common Schools, Blair Educational Bill, July 9, 1888, H. Misc. Doc. 515, Serial Volume 2570, Sessional Volume 6, *LexisNexis U.S. Serial Set Digital Collection*; Resolution for Special Order to Consider Bill on Federal Aid to Common Schools, Blair Educational Bill, May 28, 1888, H. Misc. Doc. 413, Serial Volume 2570, Sessional Volume 4, *LexisNexis U.S. Serial Set Digital Collection*; Upchurch, *Legislating Racism*, 47–48.

12. "The Blair Bill Once More," *The Nation*, January 5, 1888, 5.

13. Michael E. Perman, *Struggle for Mastery: Disenfranchisement in the South, 1888–1906* (Chapel Hill: University of North Carolina Press, 2001), 260–62.

14. "The Blair Bill Once More," 6; Upchurch, *Legislating Racism*, 51. For discussion of American liberalism, see John G. Sproat, *The Best Men: Liberal Reformers in the Gilded Age* (New York: Oxford University Press, 1968); Nancy Cohen, *The Reconstruction of American Liberalism, 1865–1914* (Chapel Hill: University of North Carolina Press, 2002); and Richardson, *Death of Reconstruction*.

15. Crofts, "Black Response to the Blair Education Bill," 44–46; Geo. G. Groff, "The Blair Educational Bill," *Science* 10 (September 9, 1887): 132; "Untitled," *Christian Recorder*, January 13, 1887, 2. For additional examples, see "In Discussing His Educational Bill," April 17, 1884, 2; and "Education Discussion: The Needs of Colored People in Considered in a Public Meeting," February 7, 1889, 2, both in *Christian Recorder*.

16. Upchurch, *Legislating Racism*, 2–3, 48.

17. McKinney, *Henry W. Blair's Campaign to Reform America*, 126–30; Upchurch, *Legislating Racism*, 51–64. For negative coverage in Mobile, see "Nothing but Talk: Blair Consumes More Time Abusing the Newspapers," March 1, 1890, 1; and "A Blow for Blair," March 4, 1890, 1, both in *Mobile Daily Register*.

18. "Congress. Fortieth Day," February 8, 1890, 2; and "Untitled," March 1, 1890, 2, both in *Huntsville Gazette* (Huntsville, Ala.).

19. "Hon. Perry Carson Speaks: The Founder of the American Citizens Equal Rights Association, Expresses His Appreciation," March 8, 1890, 1; and "Various Causes of the Republic Defeat," November 16, 1889, 3, both in *Richmond Planet*.

20. "Col. Ruffin Assertions," *Richmond Planet*, March 1, 1890, 1.

21. Ibid.

22. Perman, *Struggle for Mastery*, 38–43; Upchurch, *Legislating Racism*, 64; Crofts, "Black Response to the Blair Education Bill," 59–63; Waterbury, *Seven Years among the Freedmen*.

23. "Blair Bill Dead," *Daily Dispatch* (Richmond, Va.), March 21, 1890; "The Bill Was Lost," *Mobile Daily Register*, March 21, 1890, 1.

24. "Untitled," March 22, 1890, 2; and "The Race Problem Solving Itself," May 17, 1890, 2, both in *Huntsville Gazette* (Huntsville, Ala.).

25. "Washington Letter: The Lodge Federal Election Bill," July 5, 1890, 2; and "Various Causes of the Republic Defeat," November 16, 1889, 3, both in *Richmond Planet*.

26. Slap, *Doom of Reconstruction*, 72.

27. Ibid., xii–xxv, 48, 72–89.

28. Heather Cox Richardson, "North and West of Reconstruction: Studies in Political Economy," in *Reconstructions: New Perspectives on the Postbellum United States*, ed. Thomas J. Brown (New York: Oxford University Press, 2008), 69.

29. Ibid., 83.

30. Richardson, *Death of Reconstruction*, 207–9.

31. Washington, *Up from Slavery*, 52–76.

32. Louis R. Harlan, *Booker T. Washington in Perspective: Essays of Louis R. Harlan*, ed. Raymond Smock (Jackson: University Press of Mississippi, 1988), 14.

33. Booker T. Washington to John Elbert McConnell, December 17, 1885, in Washington, *Booker T. Washington Papers*, 2:284.

34. Ibid.

35. Booker T. Washington, "A Speech before the Alabama State Teachers' Association," April 7, 1882, in ibid., 2:195.

36. Booker T. Washington to the editor of the Montgomery *Advertiser*, April 24, 1885, in ibid., 2:272.

37. Rev. J. W. Smith, "Opinions and Personalities," November 28, 1889, 1; and Rev. M. S. Steele, "The Morganton (N.C.) District Conference," March 20, 1890, 2, both in *Christian Recorder*.

38. For correspondence, see file 19, Waite–Washington, B.T. (1889–1905), and file 20, Washington, B. T. (1906–1914), box 5, Peabody Education Fund Collection, Jean and Alexander Heard Library, Vanderbilt University, Nashville Anderson, *Education of Blacks in the South*, 245–47; W. E. B. Du Bois, *Black Reconstruction in America, 1860–1880* (1935; repr., New York: Free Press, 1999), 697.

39. Henry William Blair to Booker T. Washington, February 21, 1896, in Washington, *Booker T. Washington Papers*, 4:120.

40. Booker T. Washington to Samuel Laing Williams, May 28, 1906, in ibid., 9:14.

41. "A Great Address by D. W. Davis," *The Times* (Richmond, Va.), June 24, 1900, 14.

42. Ibid.

43. Ibid.

44. Giles Beecher Jackson and Daniel Webster Davis, *Industrial History of the Negro Race of the United States* (Richmond: Virginia Press, 1908), 5.

45. Blight, *Slave No More*, 214–15.

46. Jackson and Davis, *Industrial History of the Negro Race of the United States*, 5.

47. Femme, "A Prayer for Education," *New York Globe*, December 29, 1883, 4.

Bibliography

Manuscript Collections and Archives

ALABAMA DEPARTMENT OF ARCHIVES AND HISTORY, MONTGOMERY, ALABAMA
Alabama 1867 Voter Registration Records Database
Alabama Constitution of 1867, Civil War and Reconstruction Subject Files, SG011154
Alabama Secretary of State, Ordinances and Resolutions of the Constitutional Convention of 1867, SG020651
Jabez L. M. Curry Papers, 1816–1907
Reports of the Superintendent of Education, 1880–88
Reports of the State Superintendent of Education, 1889–98
Superintendent of Education, Reports: Annual and Other Reports, 1857–71
Superintendent of Education, Reports: Annual and Other Reports, 1868–79
AMISTAD RESEARCH CENTER, TULANE UNIVERSITY, NEW ORLEANS
American Missionary Association Archives
HISTORIC MOBILE PRESERVATION SOCIETY ARCHIVES, MOBILE, ALABAMA
Black Schools, Clippings File
Schools-History, Clippings File
JEAN AND ALEXANDER HEARD LIBRARY, VANDERBILT UNIVERSITY, NASHVILLE
Peabody Education Fund Collection
LIBRARY OF VIRGINIA, RICHMOND, VIRGINIA
Henrico County: Register of Free Negroes and Mulattoes, 1852–63
Records of the Richmond Common Council, City Clerk's Office, Richmond City Hall
Richmond City Directories, 1866, 1869–89
Ruffner, William H., *Circulars (Including Addresses, Public Documents, Pamphlets, and Miscellaneous Material on Public Education in Virginia. Collected by W. H. Ruffner, Superintendent of Public Instruction)*
Virginia State Board of Education, Account Registers, 1871–1914
Virginia State Board of Education, Teachers' Pension Disbursement Register, 1915–27
MAGGIE LENA WALKER NATIONAL HISTORIC SITE, NATIONAL PARK SERVICES, RICHMOND, VIRGINIA
Maggie Lena Walker Papers
MASSACHUSETTS HISTORICAL SOCIETY, BOSTON
Caroline Dall Papers
Curtis–Stevenson Family Papers, 1775–1920
New England Freedmen's Aid Society Records
Soldiers Memorial Society Records, 1865–67
William Lloyd Garrison Papers

MOBILE COUNTY PROBATE COURT, ARCHIVES AND RECORDS DEPARTMENT, MOBILE,
   ALABAMA
Petitions to Become Slaves, 1860–62
MOBILE COUNTY PUBLIC SCHOOL SYSTEM, BARTON ACADEMY, MOBILE, ALABAMA
Records of the Board of School Commissioners for Mobile County, Minutes, 1871–87
MOBILE MUNICIPAL ARCHIVES, MOBILE, ALABAMA
Board of Alderman, Minutes, 1865–90
Interesting Transcriptions of the Mobile Daily Newspapers, 1860–1901 (WPA Project)
Interesting Transcriptions of the *Mobile Daily Republican* (WPA Project)
Interesting Transcriptions of the *Mobile Daily Tribune* (WPA Project)
Interesting Transcriptions of the *Nationalist* (WPA Project)
Mobile City Directories, 1869–90
Records of the Mayor, Board of Alderman, and Common Council
RICHMOND PUBLIC LIBRARY, RICHMOND, VIRGINIA
Ralza M. Manly Collection
SPECIAL COLLECTIONS, UNIVERSITY OF VIRGINIA, CHARLOTTESVILLE, VIRGINIA
Carlton, Hubbard G. "The Evolution of the Richmond Public Schools with Reminis-
   cences." Paper presented at the Principals' Conference, June 3, 1925.
SPECIAL COLLECTIONS AND UNIVERSITY ARCHIVES, VIRGINIA STATE UNIVERSITY,
   PETERSBURG, VIRGINIA
Daniel Barclay William (1862–1895) Papers
James Hugo Johnston, Sr. (1865–1914), Papers
SWINZELL LIBRARY, MERCER UNIVERSITY, ATLANTA
American Baptist Home Mission Society, *Baptist Home Missions in North American:
   Including a Full Report of the Proceedings and Addresses of the Jubilee Meeting, and a
   Historical Sketch of the American Baptist Home Mission Society, Historical Tables, etc.,
   1832–1882.* New York: Baptist Home Mission Rooms, 1883.
UNIVERSITY OF SOUTH ALABAMA, MOBILE, ALABAMA
Erik Overby Collection
VF: African Methodist Episcopal Zion Church
VF: Emerson Institute
VF: History of Education in Mobile
VF: Rosenwald Schools
VIRGINIA HISTORICAL SOCIETY, RICHMOND, VIRGINIA
Arthur R. Henry Report, 1865
Bagby Family Papers
Daniel Webster Davis Papers
Edward Mosley, Letters, 1863–65
Hoge Family Papers
Mary Patterson Manly to Virginius Douglas Johnston, May 12, 1933, letter
"Notice! The Colored People of the city of Richmond would most respectfully inform
   the public, that they do not intend to celebrate the failure of the Southern confed-
   eracy . . . ," broadside, Richmond, Virginia, April 2, 1866
Read Family Papers, 1828–1914
Sarah S. Carter, Diary, May 20–31, 1866

Society for the Prevention of the Absconding and Abduction of Slaves, Richmond, Va.,
    Minutes of Directors' Meetings, 1833–49
Vertical File-Richmond Slavery

Periodicals

American Freedman
American Missionary
Anglo-African
Black Republican (New Orleans)
Christian Recorder
Daily Dispatch (Richmond, Va.)
Freedmen's Record (Boston)
Huntsville Gazette (Huntsville, Ala.)
Industrial Herald
Mobile Daily Advertiser and Register (later renamed *Mobile Daily Register*)
Mobile Daily Republican
The Nation
Nationalist (Mobile, Ala.)
New York Globe
New York Times
Pennsylvania Freedmen's Bulletin
People's Advocate
Richmond Daily Examiner
Richmond Planet
Richmond Times-Dispatch
Richmond Whig
The Times (Richmond, Va.)
Science
Southern Planter and Farmer (Richmond, Va.)
Virginia Star

Published Primary Sources

American Baptist Home Mission Society. *Thirty-Third Annual Report of the American
    Baptist Home Mission Society, Convened at St. Louis, Mo., May 16–23, 1865.* New York:
    American Baptist Home Mission Rooms, 1865.
———. *Thirty-Fourth Annual Report of the American Baptist Home Mission Society,
    Convened at Boston, Mass., May 17 and 18, 1866.* New York: American Baptist Home
    Mission Rooms, 1866.
———. *Thirty-Fifth Annual Report of the American Baptist Home Mission Society,
    Convened at Chicago, Ill., May 23 and 24, 1867.* New York: American Baptist Home
    Missions Rooms, 1867.
American Freedman's Union Commission. *The Results of Emancipation in the United
    States of America by a Committee of the American Freedman's Union Commission.*
    New York: American Freedman's Union Commission, 1867.

American Missionary Association. *Catalog of the Teachers and Student, Course of Study, Etc., of Emerson Normal Institute, Mobile, Alabama, 1900–1901.* Mobile, Ala.: A. N. Johnson, 1901.

———. *History of the American Missionary Association with Illustrative Facts and Anecdotes.* New York: American Missionary Association, 1891.

———. *The Nation Is Still in Danger; or, Ten Years after the War.* New York: American Missionary Association, 1875.

Ancestry.com. *U.S. Colored Troops Military Service Records, 1863–1865.* Provo, Utah: Ancestry.com Operations Inc., 2007.

Boston University. *Historical Register of Boston University, Fifth Decennial Issue, 1869–1911.* Boston: University Offices, 1911.

Corey, Charles H. *A History of the Richmond Theological Seminary, with Reminiscences of Thirty Year's Work among the Colored People of the South.* Richmond, Va. J. W. Randolph, 1895.

Davis, Daniel Webster. *Idle Moment: Containing Emancipation and Other Poems by D. Webster Davis; with an Introduction by Hon. John H. Smythe.* Baltimore: The Educator of Morgan College, 1895.

In Memoriam: Ralza Morse Manly, Born January 16th, 1822, Died, September 16th, 1897. "Requiscat in pace." First Baptist Church, Wednesday Evening, November 24, 1897, Eight O'clock. Richmond, Va.: Grand Fountain Press, 1897.

Morrison, Andrew. *Richmond, Virginia, and the New South.* Richmond, Va.: George W. Engelhardt, ca. 1889.

National Council of the Congregational Churches of the United States. *The Congregational Yearbook, 1884.* Boston: Congregational Publishing Society, 1884.

The Southeastern Reporter, Volume 22, Containing All the Decisions of the Supreme Courts of Appeals of Virginia and West Virginia, and Supreme Courts of North Carolina, South Carolina, Georgia: Permanent Edition, June 18–October 22, 1895. St. Paul, Minn.: West, 1895.

Washington, Booker T. *The Booker T. Washington Papers.* 14 vols. Edited by Louis R. Harlan et al. Urbana: University of Illinois Press, 1972–1989.

———. *Up from Slavery, with Related Documents.* Edited by W. Fitzhugh Brundage. Boston: Bedford/St. Martin's Press, 2003.

Waterbury, Maria L. *Seven Years among the Freedmen.* Chicago: T. B. Arnold, 1893.

Williams, Daniel Barclay. *Freedom and Progress, and Other Choice Addresses on Practical, Scientific, Educational, Philosophic, Historic, and Religious Subjects.* Petersburg, Va.: Daniel B. Williams, 1890.

Yale University. *Obituary Record of Yale Graduates.* Ser. 16, no. 11. New Haven, Conn.: Yale University, 1920.

Federal Government Records and Publications

Alvord, John. *Semi-annual Report on Schools for Freedmen: Numbers 1–10, January 1866–July 1870.* 1868–70. Reprint, New York: AMS Press, c1980.

Clark, Willis G. *History of Education in Alabama, 1702–1889.* Washington, D.C.: Government Printing Office, 1889.

Freedman's Savings and Trust Company. *Registers of Signatures of Depositors in Branches of the Freedman's Savings and Trust Company, 1865–1874.* Washington, D.C.: National Archives and Records Service General Services Administration, 1970.

United States Bureau of Refugees, Freedmen, and Abandoned Lands. *Records of the Education Division of the Bureau of Refugees, Freedmen, and Abandoned Lands, 1865–1871.* National Archives Microfilm Publication M803, Record Group 105. Washington, D.C.: National Archives, National Archives and Records Service, General Services Administration, 1969.

———. *Records of the Superintendent of Education for the State of Alabama, Bureau of Refugees, Freedmen, and Abandoned Lands, 1865–1870.* National Archives Microfilm Publication M810, Record Group 105. Washington, D.C.: National Archives, National Archives and Records Service, General Services Administration, 1972.

———. *Records of the Superintendent of Education for the State of Virginia, Bureau of Refugees, Freedmen, and Abandoned Lands, 1865–1870.* National Archives Microfilm Publication M1053, Record Group 105. Washington, D.C.: National Archives, National Archives and Records Service, General Services Administration, 1977.

United States Census Bureau. *A Compendium of the Ninth Census (June 1, 1870,): Compiled Pursuant to a Concurrent Resolution of Congress, and under the Direction of the Secretary of the Interior.* Washington, D.C.: Government Printing Office: 1872.

———. *Population of the United States in 1860: Compiled from the Original Returns of the Eighth Census, under the Direction of the Secretary of the Interior.* Washington, D.C.: Government Printing Office, 1864.

———. *Population Schedules of the Ninth Census of the United States, 1870.* National Archives Microfilm Publication M593. Washington, D.C.: National Archives, National Archives and Records Service, General Services Administration, 196–.

———. *Report on Population of the United States at the Eleventh Census: 1890, Part I.* Washington, D.C.: Government Printing Office, 1895.

———. *Statistics of the Population of the United States at the Tenth Census.* Washington, D.C.: Government Printing Office, 1883.

———. *Statistics of the United States (Including Mortality, Property, &c.) in 1860: Compiled from the Original Returns and Being Final Exhibit of the Eighth Census, under the Direction of the Secretary of the Interior.* Washington, D.C.: Government Printing Office, 1866.

United States Congress, House. *Affairs in the Late Insurrectionary States.* 42nd Cong., 2nd Sess., H. Rep. 22, Pt. 1.

———. *Annual Report of the Secretary of War, 1868, Pt. 1.* 40th Cong., 3rd Sess., H. Ex. Doc. 1/14.

———. Resolution for Special Order to Consider Bill on Federal Aid to Common Schools, Blair Educational Bill, May 28, 1888. H. Misc. Doc. 413. Serial Volume 2570. Sessional Volume 4. LexisNexis. U.S. Serial Set Digital Collection.

———. Resolution for Special Order to Consider Bill on Federal Aid to Common Schools, Blair Educational Bill, July 9, 1888. H. Misc. Doc. 515. Serial Volume 2570, Sessional Volume 6. LexisNexis U.S. Serial Set Digital Collection.

United States Congress, House Committee on Rules. *Blair Educational Bill.* 50th Cong., 1st Sess., H. Misc. Doc 413.

———. *Blair Educational Bill.* 50th Cong., 1st Sess., H. Misc. Doc 515.

United States Congress, Joint Committee on Reconstruction. *Report of the Joint Committee on Reconstruction, at the First Session, Thirty-Ninth Congress.* Washington, D.C.: Government Printing Office, 1866.

United States Congress, Senate. *Address of the Republican State Convention.* 41st Cong., 2nd Sess., S. Misc. Doc. 3.

United States National Park Services. *Civil War Soldiers and Sailors Database.* http://www.nps.gov/civilwar/soldiers-and-sailors-database.htm.

United States Office of Art and Archives. *Biographical Dictionary of the United States Congress, 1774–Present.* http://bioguide.congress.gov/.

State Government Records and Publications

Alabama State Board of Education. *Report of the Superintendent of Public Instruction of the State of Alabama to the Governor for the Year 1868–9 Ending 30 September 1869.* Montgomery, Ala.: John G. Stokes and Company, State Printers, 1869.

New Hampshire. *Journal of the Honorable Senate of the State of New Hampshire.* June Session, 1864. Concord: Amos Hadley, State Printer, 1864.

Virginia Department of Education. *Virginia School Report, 1871: First Annual Report of the Superintendent of Public Instruction, for the Year Ending August 31, 1871.* Richmond, Va.: C. A. Schaeffter, Superintendent Public Printing, 1871.

———. *Virginia School Report, 1872: Second Annual Report of the Superintendent of Public Instruction, for the Year Ending August 31, 1872.* Richmond, Va.: R. F. Walker, City Printer, 1872.

———. *Virginia School Report, 1873: Third Annual Report of the Superintendent of Public Instruction for the Year Ending August 31, 1873.* Richmond, Va.: R. F. Walker, 1873.

———. *Virginia School Report, 1874: Fourth Annual Report of the Superintendent of Public Instruction, for the Year Ending August 31, 1874, with Reports of the Virginia Agricultural and Mechanical College, and Hampton Normal and Agricultural Institute.* Richmond, Va.: R. F. Walker, Superintendent Public Printing, 1874.

———. *Virginia School Report, 1877: Seventh Annual Report of the Superintendent of Public Instruction, for the Year Ending July 31, 1877.* Richmond, Va.: R. F. Walker, Superintendent Public Printing, 1877.

———. *Virginia School Report, 1878: Eighth Annual Report of the Superintendent of Public Instruction, for the Year Ending July 31, 1878.* Richmond, Va.: R. E. Frayser, Superintendent Public Printing, 1878.

———. *Virginia School Report, 1880: Tenth Annual Report of the Superintendent of Public Instruction, For the Year Ending July 31, 1880.* Richmond, Va.: R. F. Walker, Superintendent Public Printing, 1880.

———. *Virginia School Report, 1882: Twelfth Annual Report of the Superintendent of Public Instruction, for the Year Ending July 31, 1882.* Richmond, Va.: R. F. Walker, Superintendent Public Printing, 1882.

———. *Virginia School Report, 1883: Thirteenth Annual Report of the Superintendent of Public Instruction, for the Year Ending July 31, 1883.* Richmond, Va.: R. F. Walker, Superintendent Public Printing, 1883.

———. *Virginia School Report, 1885: Fifteenth Annual Report of the Superintendent of Public Instruction of the Commonwealth of Virginia with Accompanying Documents, School Year Ending July 31, 1885.* Richmond, Va.: J. H. O'Bannon, Superintendent Public Printing, 1885.

———. *Virginia School Report, 1886: Sixteenth Annual Report of the Superintendent of Public Instruction of the Commonwealth of Virginia with Accompanying Documents, School Year Ending July 31, 1886.* Richmond, Va.: J. H. O'Bannon, Superintendent Public Printing, 1886.

———. *Virginia School Report, 1888: Eighteenth Annual Report of the Superintendent of Public Instruction of the Commonwealth of Virginia with Accompanying Documents, School Year Ending July 31, 1888.* Richmond, Va.: J. H. O'Bannon, Superintendent Public Printing, 1888.

———. *Virginia School Report, 1889: Nineteenth Annual Report of the Superintendent of Public Instruction of the Commonwealth of Virginia with Accompanying Documents, School Year Ending July 31, 1889.* Richmond, Va.: J. H. O'Bannon, Superintendent Public Printing, 1889.

———. *Virginia School Report, 1890: Twentieth Annual Report of the Superintendent of Public Instruction of Public Instruction of the Commonwealth of Virginia with Accompanying Documents, School Year Ending July 31, 1890.* Richmond, Va.: J. H. O'Bannon, Superintendent Public Printing, 1890.

Virginia General Assembly. *Acts and Joint Resolutions Passed by the General Assembly of the State of Virginia during the Session of 1881–82.* Richmond, Va.: R. F. Walker, Superintendent Public Printing, 1882.

Virginia State Board of Education. *Official Orders of Superintendent of Public Instruction, 1870–1879: Extracted from Educational Journal of Virginia.* Vol. 1. Richmond, Va.: Educational Publishing House, 1870–79.

City Government Publications

Richmond School Board. "Fourth Annual Report of the School Board and Superintendent of Public Schools of the City of Richmond, VA., for the Scholastic Year 1871–1872." In *Annual Message and Accompanying Documents of the Mayor of Richmond to the City Council for the Fiscal Year Ending January 31, 1873.* Richmond, Va.: C. C. Baughman, City Printer, 1873.

———. "Sixth Annual Report of the School Board and Superintendent of Public Schools of the City of Richmond, VA., for the Scholastic Year 1873–1874." In *Annual Message and Accompanying Documents of the Mayor of Richmond to the City Council for the Fiscal Year Ending January 31, 1875.* Richmond, Va.: C. C. Baughman, City Printer, 1875.

———. "Seventh Annual Report of the School Board and Superintendent of Public Schools of the City of Richmond, VA., for the Scholastic Year 1874–1875." In *Annual Message and Accompanying Documents of the Mayor of Richmond to the City Council for the Fiscal Year Ending January 31, 1876.* Richmond, Va.: C. C. Baughman, City Printer, 1876.

———. "Eighth Annual Report of the School Board and Superintendent of Public Schools of the City of Richmond, VA., for the Scholastic Year 1875–1876." In *Annual Message and Accompanying Documents of the Mayor of Richmond to the City Council for the Fiscal Year Ending January 31, 1877.* Richmond, Va.: C. C. Baughman, City Printer, 1877.

———. "Eighth Annual Report of the School Board and Superintendent of Public Schools of the City of Richmond, VA., for the Scholastic Year 1876–1877." In *Annual Message and Accompanying Documents of the Mayor of Richmond to the City Council for the Fiscal Year Ending January 31, 1878.* Richmond, Va.: C. C. Baughman, City Printer, 1878.

———. "Ninth Annual Report of the School Board and Superintendent of Public Schools of the City of Richmond, VA., for the Scholastic Year 1877–1878." In *Annual Message and Accompanying Documents of the Mayor of Richmond to the City Council for the Fiscal Year Ending January 31, 1879.* Richmond, Va.: N. V. Randolph, City Printer, 1879.

———. "Eleventh Annual Report of the School Board and Superintendent of Public Schools of the City of Richmond, VA., for the Scholastic Year 1879–1880." In *Annual Message and Accompanying Documents of the Mayor of Richmond to the City Council for the Fiscal Year Ending January 31, 1881.* Richmond, Va.: N. V. Randolph, City Printer, 1881.

———. "Twelfth Annual Report of the Secretary of the School Board and Supervisor of School Property for the Scholastic Year 1880–1881, Ending August 1, 1881, and Supplemental Report to February 1, 1882." In *Annual Message and Accompanying Documents of the Mayor of Richmond to the City Council for the Fiscal Year Ending January 31, 1882.* Richmond, Va.: N. V. Randolph, City Printer, 1882.

———. "Thirteenth Annual Report of the School Board and Superintendent of Public Schools of the City of Richmond for the Scholastic Year, 1881–1882." In *Annual Message and Accompanying Documents of the Mayor of Richmond to the City Council for the Fiscal Year Ending January 31, 1883.* Richmond, Va.: Yancey, Waddey, and Co., Printers, 1883.

———. "Annual Report of the Clerk of School Board and Supervisor of School Property for the Scholastic Year 1884–85." In *Annual Message and Accompanying Documents of the Mayor of Richmond to the City Council for the Fiscal Year Ending January 31, 1886.* Richmond, Va.: Everett Walthall and Bowles, City Printer, 1886.

———. *Sixteenth Annual Report of the Public Schools of the City of Richmond, VA., for the Scholastic Year 1884–5.* Richmond, Va.: Walthall and Bowles, Printers, 1886.

———. *Seventeenth Annual Report of the Superintendent of Public Schools for the City of Richmond, VA., for the Scholastic Year, 1885–1886.* Richmond, Va.: Everett Waddey, City Printers, 1887.

———. "Eighteenth Annual Report of the Superintendent of the Public Schools of the City of Richmond, VA., for the Scholastic Year 1886–87." In *Annual Message and Accompanying Documents of the Mayor of Richmond to the City Council for the Fiscal Year Ending January 31, 1888.* Richmond, Va.: C. N. Williams, City Printer, 1888.

———. *Nineteenth Annual Report of the Superintendent of the Public Schools of the City of Richmond, VA., for the Scholastic Year Ending July 31st, 1888.* Richmond, Va.: Everett Waddey, City Printers, 1889.

———. "Twentieth Annual Report of the Superintendent of the Public Schools of the City of Richmond, VA., for the Scholastic Year Ending July 31st, 1889." In *Annual Message and Accompanying Documents of the Mayor of Richmond to the City Council for the Fiscal Year Ending December 31, 1889*. Richmond, Va.: C. N. Williams, City Printer, 1890.

———. "Twenty-First Annual Report of the Superintendent of the Public Schools of the City of Richmond, VA., for the Scholastic Year Ending July 31st, 1890." In *Annual Message and Accompanying Documents of the Mayor of Richmond to the City Council for the Fiscal Year Ending December 31, 1890*. Richmond, Va.: C. N. Williams, City Printer, 1891.

———. *Twenty-Fourth Annual Report of the Superintendent of the Public Schools of the City of Richmond, VA., for the Scholastic Year Ending 1893*. Richmond, Va.: C. N. Williams, City Printer, 1894.

Richmond Public Schools. *Richmond Public Schools: A Mini History*. Richmond, Va.: Richmond Public School System, 1992.

Secondary Books

Alexander, Ann Field. *Race Man: The Rise and Fall of the "Fighting Editor," John Mitchell, Jr.* Charlottesville: University of Virginia Press, 2002.

Amos, Harriett, *Cotton City: Urban Development in Antebellum Mobile*. Birmingham: University of Alabama Press, 1985.

Anderson, James D. *The Education of Blacks in the South, 1860–1935*. Chapel Hill: University of North Carolina Press, 1988.

Appiah, Kwame Anthony, and Henry Louis Gates, eds. *Africana*. New York: Basic Civitas, 1999.

Barney, William L. *Battleground for the Union: The Era of the Civil War and Reconstruction, 1848–1877*. Englewood Cliffs, N.J.: Prentice Hall, 1990.

Bergeron, Arthur W., Jr. *Confederate Mobile*. Jackson: University Press of Mississippi, 1991.

Berlin, Ira. *Slaves without Masters: The Free Negro in the Antebellum South*. New York: Vintage, 1976.

Blight, David W. *Race and Reunion: The Civil War in American Memory*. Cambridge, Mass.: Belknap Press, 2001.

———, ed. *A Slave No More: Two Men Who Escaped to Freedom, Including Their Own Narratives*. Orlando, Fla.: Harcourt, 2007.

Bond, Horace Mann. *Negro Education in Alabama: A Study in Cotton and Steel*. 1939. Reprint, Tuscaloosa: University of Alabama Press, 1994.

Brenaman, J. N. *A History of Virginia Conventions*. Richmond, Va.: J. L Hill, 1902.

Brown, Thomas J, ed. *Reconstructions: New Perspectives on the Postbellum United States*. New York: Oxford University Press, 2006.

Buck, J. L. Blair. *The Development of Public Schools in Virginia, 1607–1952*. Richmond: Commonwealth of Virginia State Board of Education, 1952.

Bullock, Henry A. *A History of Negro Education in the South: From 1619 to the Present*. Cambridge, Mass.: Harvard University Press, 1967.

Butchart, Ronald. *Northern Schools, Southern Blacks, and Reconstruction: Freedmen's Education, 1862–1875*. Westport, Conn.: Greenwood Press, 1980.

———. *Schooling the Freed People: Teaching, Learning, and the Struggle for Black Freedom, 1861–1876*. Chapel Hill: University of North Carolina Press, 2010.

Carpenter, John A. *Sword and Olive Branch: Oliver Otis Howard*. New York: Fordham University Press, 1999.

Chesson, Michael. *Richmond after the War, 1865–1890*. Richmond: Virginia State Library, 1981.

Church, Charles A. *History of Rockford and Winnebago County Illinois: From Settlement in 1834 to the Civil War*. Rockford: New England Society of Rockford, Illinois, 1900.

Cimbala, Paul A., and Randall M. Miller, eds. *The Freedmen's Bureau and Reconstruction: Reconsiderations*. New York: Fordham University Press, 1999.

Cocks, Catherine. *Doing the Town: The Rise of Urban Tourism in the United States, 1850–1915*. Berkeley: University of California Press, 2001.

Cohen, Nancy. *The Reconstruction of American Liberalism, 1865–1914*. Chapel Hill: University of North Carolina, 2002.

Cox, Karen L. *Dixie Daughters: The United Daughters of the Confederacy and the Preservation of Confederate Culture*. Gainesville: University Press of Florida, 2004.

Culp, Daniel Wallace, ed. *Twentieth Century Negro Literature; or, A Cyclopedia of Thought on the Vital Topics Relating to the American Negro, by One Hundred of America's Greatest Negros*. Naperville, Ill.: J. L. Nichols, 1902.

Dabney, Charles William. *Universal Education in the South*. Vol. 1. Chapel Hill: University of North Carolina Press, 1936.

Dailey, Jane Elizabeth. *Before Jim Crow: The Politics of Race in Postemancipation Virginia*. Chapel Hill: University of North Carolina Press, 2000.

Dailey, Jane Elizabeth, Glenda Gilmore, and Bryant Simon, eds. *Jumpin' Jim Crow: Southern Politics from Civil War to Civil Rights*. Princeton, N.J.: Princeton University Press, 2000.

Davis, Veronica A. *Here I Lay My Burdens Down: A History of the Black Cemeteries of Richmond, Virginia*. Richmond, Va.: Dietz Press, 2003.

Davis-Horton, Paulette. *The Avenue: the Place, the People, the Memories, 1799–1986*. Mobile, Ala.: Horton, 1991.

Diggs, Margaret A. *Catholic Negro Education in the United States*. Washington, D.C.: Margaret A. Diggs, 1936.

Dorman, James, H, ed. *Creoles of Color in the Gulf South*. Knoxville: University of Tennessee Press, 1996.

Doyle, Don H. *New Men, New Cities, New South: Atlanta, Nashville, Charleston, Mobile, 1860–1910*. Chapel Hill: University of North Carolina Press, 1990.

Drewry, Henry N., and Humphrey Doermann. *Stand and Prosper: Private Black Colleges and Their Students*. Princeton, N.J.: Princeton University Press, 2001.

Du Bois, W. E. B. *Black Reconstruction in America, 1860–1880*. 1935. Reprint, New York: Free Press, 1999.

———. *Writings*. Edited by Nathan Huggins. New York: Library of America Press, 1986.

Dunning, William A. *Reconstruction, Political and Economic, 1865–1877*. New York: Harper and Brothers, 1907.

Eng, Robert Francis. *Freedom's First Generation: Black Hampton Virginia, 1861–1890.* Philadelphia: University of Pennsylvania Press, 1979.

Faulkner, Carol. *Women's Radical Reconstruction: The Freedmen's Aid Movement.* Philadelphia: University of Pennsylvania Press, 2006.

Fitzgerald, Michael. *Urban Emancipation: Popular Politics in Reconstruction Mobile, 1860–1890.* Baton Rouge: Louisiana State University Press, 2002.

Foner, Eric. *Reconstruction: America's Unfinished Revolution, 1863–1877.* New York: Harper and Row, 1988.

Franklin, John Hope. *Reconstruction after the Civil War.* Chicago: University of Chicago Press, 1961.

Franklin, John Hope, and Alfred A. Moss, Jr. *From Slavery to Freedom: A History of African Americans.* New York: Alfred A. Knopf, 2000.

Frantel, Nancy C. *Richmond Virginia Uncovered: The Records of Slaves and Free Blacks Listed in the City Sergeant Jail Register, 1841–1846.* Westminster, Md.: Heritage Books, 2010.

Gaines, Foster. *Ghosts of the Confederacy: Defeat, the Lost Cause, and the Emergence of the New South, 1865–1913.* New York: Oxford University Press, 1987.

Gannon, Barbara A. *The Won Cause: Black and White Comradeship in the Grand Army of the Republic.* Chapel Hill: University of North Carolina Press, 2011.

Gassan, Richard H. *The Birth of American Tourism: New York, the Hudson Valley, and American Culture, 1790–1830.* Amherst: University of Massachusetts Press, 2008.

Giddings, Paula. *When and Where I Enter: The Impact of Black Women on Race and Sex in America.* New York: William Morrow, 1984.

Gillard, John T. *The Catholic Church and the American Negro; Being an Investigation of the Past and Present Activities of the Catholic Church in Behalf of the 12,000,000 Negroes in the United States, with an Examination of the Difficulties Which Affect the Work of the Colored Missions.* 1929. Reprint, New York: Johnson Reprint Corporation, 1968.

Gilmore, Glenda. *Gender and Jim Crow: Women and the Politics of White Supremacy in North Carolina, 1896–1920.* Chapel Hill: University of North Carolina Press, 1996.

Goldfield, David R. *Cotton Fields and Skyscrapers: Southern City and Region, 1607–1980.* Baton Rouge: Louisiana State University Press, 1982.

Hahn, Steven. *A Nation under Our Feet: Black Political Struggles in the Rural South from Slavery to the Great Migration.* Cambridge, Mass.: Belknap Press, 2003.

Hanchett, Thomas W. *Sorting Out the New South City: Race, Class, and Urban Development, 1875–1975.* Chapel Hill: University of North Carolina Press, 1998.

Harlan, Louis R. *Booker T. Washington: The Making of a Black Leader, 1865–1901.* New York: Oxford University Press, 1972.

———. *Booker T. Washington in Perspective: Essays of Louis R. Harlan.* Edited by Raymond Smock. Jackson: University Press of Mississippi, 1988.

Higginbotham, Evelyn Brooks. *Righteous Discontent: The Women's Movement in the Black Baptist Church, 1880–1920.* Cambridge, Mass.: Harvard University Press, 1993.

Hodes, Martha. *White Women, Black Men: Illicit Sex in the Nineteenth-Century South.* New Haven, Conn.: Yale University Press, 1997.

Holt, Thomas. *Black over White: Negro Political Leadership in South Carolina during Reconstruction*. Urbana: University of Illinois Press, 1977.

Horsman, Reginald. *Josiah Nott of Mobile: Southerner, Physician, and Racial Theorist*. Baton Rouge: Louisiana State University Press, 1987.

Horton, James Oliver, ed. *Free People of Color: Inside the African American Community*. Washington, D.C.: Smithsonian Institution Press, 1993.

Horton, James Oliver, and Lois E. Horton, ed. *Slavery and Public History: The Tough Stuff of American Memory*. New York: New Press, 2006.

Jackson, Giles Beecher, and Daniel Webster Davis, *Industrial History of the Negro Race of the United States*. Richmond, Va.: Virginia Press, 1908.

Jackson, Luther Porter. *Negro Office-Holders in Virginia, 1865–1895*. Norfolk, Va.: Guide Quality Press, 1945.

Jones, Jacqueline. *Saving Savannah: The City and the Civil War*. New York: Alfred A. Knopf, 2008.

———. *Soldiers of Light and Love: Northern Teachers and Georgia Blacks, 1865–1873*. Chapel Hill: University of North Carolina Press, 1980.

Jones, Maxine D. *Talladega: The First Century*. Tuscaloosa: University of Alabama Press, 1990.

Kaestle, Carl F. *Pillars of the Republic: Common Schools and American Society, 1780–1860*. New York: Hill and Wang, 1983.

Kelly, Howard A., and Walter L. Burrage, eds. *A Cyclopedia of American Medical Biography*. Baltimore: Norman Remington, 1920.

Kimball, Gregg D. *American City, Southern Place: A Cultural History of Antebellum Richmond*. Athens: University of Georgia Press, 2000.

Knight, Edgar W. *Reconstruction and Education in Virginia*. Syracuse, N.Y.: Gaylord Brothers, 1916.

Kolchin, Peter. *First Freedom: The Responses of Alabama's Blacks to Emancipation and Reconstruction*. Westport, Conn.: Greenwood Press, 1972.

Kneebone, John T., et al., eds. *Dictionary of Virginia Biography*. Richmond: Library of Virginia, 2001.

Lamb, Daniel Smith, ed. *Howard University Medical Department, Washington, D.C.: A Historical Biographical and Statistical Souvenir*. 1900. Reprint, Freeport, N.Y.: Ayers Publishing, 1971.

Lawson, Ellen NicKenizie, and Marlene D. Merrill. *The Three Sarahs: Documents of Antebellum Black College Women*. New York: Edwin Mellen Press, 1994.

Link, William A. *A Hard Country and a Lonely Place: Schooling, Society, and Reform in Rural Virginia, 1870–1920*. Chapel Hill: University of North Carolina Press, 1986.

Litwack, Leon, and August Meier, eds. *Black Leaders of the Nineteenth Century*. Urbana: University of Illinois Press, 1991.

Maddox, William Arthur. *The Free School Idea in Virginia before the Civil War: A Phase of Political and Social Evolution*. New York: Teachers College, Columbia University, 1918.

Marlowe, Gertrude Woodruff. *A Right Worthy Grand Mission: Maggie Lena Walker and the Quest for Black Economic Empowerment*. Washington, D.C.: Howard University Press, 2003.

McAfee, Ward M. *Race, Religion, and Reconstruction: The Public School in the Politics of the 1870s*. Albany: State University of New York Press, 1998.

McHenry, Elizabeth. *Forgotten Readers: Recovering the Lost History of African American Literary Societies*. Durham, N.C.: Duke University Press, 2002.

McKinney, Gordon B. *Henry W. Blair's Campaign to Reform America: From the Civil War to the U.S. Senate*. Lexington: University Press of Kentucky, 2013.

Meagher, Margaret. *History of Education in Richmond*. Richmond: Virginia Division of the Works Progress Administration, 1939.

Morris, Robert C., ed. *Freedmen's Schools and Textbooks*. New York: AMS Press, 1980.

———. *Reading, 'Riting, and Reconstruction: The Education of Freedmen in the South, 1861–1870*. Chicago: University Chicago Press, 1981.

Perman, Michael E. *Struggle for Mastery: Disenfranchisement in the South, 1888–1906*. Chapel Hill: University of North Carolina Press, 2001.

Rabinowitz, Howard N. *Race Relations in the Urban South, 1865–1890*. 1978. Reprint, Athens: University of Georgia Press, 1996.

Raboteau, Albert J. *Slave Religion: The Invisible Institution in the Antebellum South*. New York: Oxford University Press, 1978.

Rachleff, Peter. *Black Labor in Richmond, 1865–1890*. Philadelphia: Temple University Press, 1984.

Richardson, Heather Cox. *The Death of Reconstruction: Race, Labor, and Politics in the Post–Civil War North, 1865–1901*. Cambridge, Mass.: Harvard University Press, 2001.

Richardson, Joe M. *Christian Reconstruction: The American Missionary Association and Southern Blacks, 1861–1890*. Athens: University of Georgia Press, 1986.

Richings, G. F. *Evidence of Progress among Colored People*. 12th ed. Philadelphia: Geo. S. Ferguson, 1905.

Rose, Willie Lee. *Rehearsal for Reconstruction: The Port Royal Experiment*. New York: Bobbs-Merrill, 1964.

Samito, Christian G. *Becoming American under Fire: Irish Americans, African Americans, and the Politics of Citizenship during the Civil War Era*. Ithaca, N.Y.: Cornell University Press, 2009.

Scruggs, Lawson A. *Women of Distinction: Remarkable in Works and Invincible in Character*. Raleigh: L. A. Scruggs, 1893.

Sherer, Robert G. *Subordination or Liberation? The Development and Conflicting Theories of Black Education in Nineteenth-Century Alabama*. Tuscaloosa: University of Alabama Press, 1977.

Slap, Andrew L. *The Doom of Reconstruction: The Liberal Republicans in the Civil War Era*. New York: Fordham University Press, 2006.

Smith, Brooks, and Wayne Dementi. *Facts and Legends of the Hills of Richmond*. Manakin-Sabot, Va.: Dementi, 2008.

Smith, J. Douglas. *Managing White Supremacy: Race, Politics, and Citizenship in Jim Crow Virginia*. Chapel Hill: University of North Carolina Press, 2002.

Smith, Jessie Carney, and Shirelle Phelps, eds. *Notable Black Women*. Detroit: Gale Research, 1992.

Sproat, John G. *The Best Men: Liberal Reformers in the Gilded Age.* New York: Oxford University Press, 1968.

Stanonis, Anthony J., ed. *Dixie Emporium: Tourism, Foodways, and Consumer Culture in the American South.* Athens: University of Georgia Press, 2008.

Sturken, Marita. *Tangled Memories: The Vietnam War, the AIDS Epidemic, and the Politics of Remembering.* Berkeley: University of California Press, 1997.

Swint, Henry. *The Northern Teacher in the South, 1862–1870.* 1941. Reprint, New York: Octagon Books, 1967.

Takagi, Midori. *Rearing Wolves to Our Destruction: Slavery in Richmond, Virginia, 1782–1865.* Charlottesville: University Press of Virginia, 1999.

Townsend, Luther Tracy. *History of the Sixteenth Regiment, New Hampshire Volunteers.* Washington, D.C.: Norman T. Elliott, 1897.

Upchurch, Thomas. *Legislating Racism: The Billion-Dollar Congress and the Birth of Jim Crow.* Lexington: University Press of Kentucky, 2004.

Vaughn, William Preston. *Schools for All: The Blacks and Public Education in the South, 1865–1877.* Lexington: University of Kentucky Press, 1974.

Wertheimer, Leo Weldon, ed. *The Twelfth General Catalogue of the Psi Upsilon Fraternity.* New York: Executive Council of Psi Upsilon Fraternity, 1917.

Williams, Daniel Barclay. *A Sketch of the Life and Times of Capt. R. A. Paul: An Authentic and Abbreviated History of His Career from Boyhood to the Present Time; Containing a Reliable Account of the Politics of Virginia from 1874 to the Present Time.* Richmond, Va.: Johns and Goolsby, 1885.

Williams, Heather A. *Self-Taught: African American Education in Slavery and Freedom.* Chapel Hill: University of North Carolina Press, 2005.

Williams, Juan, and Dwayne Ashley. *I'll Find a Way or Make One.* New York: Amistad, 2001.

Woodson, Carter G., ed. *The Mind of the Negro as Reflected in Letters Written during the Crisis, 1800–1860.* Washington, D.C.: Association for the Study of Negro Life and History, 1926.

Scholarly Articles

Barkley Brown, Elsa. "Constructing a Life and a Community: A Partial Story of Maggie Lena Walker." *OAH Magazine of History* 7 (Summer 1993): 28–31.

Cartland, Elizabeth. "Chimborazo School." *Virginia History Society: An Occasional Bulletin* 43 (December 1981): 7–11.

Cox, John, and LaWanda Cox. "General O. O. Howard and the 'Misrepresented Bureau.'" *Journal of Southern History* 19 (November 1953): 427–56.

Crofts, Daniel Wallace. "The Black Response to the Blair Education Bill." *Journal of Southern History* 37 (February 1971): 41–65.

Dana, Henry Wadsworth Longfellow. "'Sail on O Ship of State!': How Longfellow Came to Write These Lines 100 Years Ago." *Colby Quarterly* 2 (February 1950): 209–14.

Grundman, Adolph H. "Northern Baptists and the Founding of Virginia Union University: The Perils of Paternalism." *Journal of Negro History* 63 (January 1978): 26–41.

Hume, Richard L. "Carpetbaggers in the Reconstruction South: A Group Portrait of Outside Whites in the 'Black and Tan' Constitutional Conventions." *Journal of American History* 64 (September 1977): 313–30.

McPherson, James. "White Liberals and Black Power in Negro Education, 1865–1915." *American Historical Review* 75 (June 1970): 1357–86.

Moore, James T. "The University and Readjusters." *Virginia Magazine of History and Biography* 78 (January 1970): 87–101.

Myers, John B. "The Education of the Alabama Freedmen during Presidential Reconstruction, 1865–1867." *Journal of Negro History* 40, no. 2 (1971): 163–71.

Nott, Josiah C. "The Negro Race." *Popular Magazine of Anthropology* 1 (July 1866): 102–18.

Rabinowitz, Howard. "Half a Loaf: The Shift from White to Black Teachers in Negro Schools of the Urban South, 1865–1890." *Journal of Southern History* 40 (November 1974): 565–94.

Rousey, Dennis C. "Friends and Foes of Slavery: Foreigners and Northerners in the Old South." *Journal of Social History* 35 (Winter 2002): 373–96.

Schiff, Judith Ann. "Pioneers." *Yale Alumni Magazine* 69 (January–February 2006): 80–81.

Taylor, A. A. "Giving Virginia a Democratic Constitution." *Journal of Negro History* 11 (July 1926): 478–93.

———. "Progress in Mental Development." *Journal of Negro History* 11 (April 1926): 395–415.

———. "Religious Efforts among the Negro." *Journal of Negro History* 11 (July 1926): 425–44.

———. "Solving the Problem of Education." *Journal of Negro History* 11 (April 1926): 379–94.

West, Earle H. "The Harris Brothers: Black Northern Teachers in the Reconstruction South." *Journal of Negro History* 48 (Spring 1979): 126–38.

White, Kenneth B. "The Alabama Freedmen's Bureau and Black Education: The Myth of Opportunity." *Alabama Review* 34 (April 1981): 107–24.

———. "Wager Swayne: Racist or Realist?" *Alabama Review* 31 (April 1978): 92–109.

Williams, Heather Andrea. "'Clothing Themselves in Intelligence': The Freedpeople, Schooling, and Northern Teachers, 1861–1871." *Journal of African American History* 87 (Fall 2002): 372–73

Work, Monroe N., Thomas S. Staples, H. A. Wallace, Kelly Miller, Whitefield McKinlay, Samuel E. Lacy, R. L. Smith, and H. R. McIlwaine. "Some Negro Members of Reconstruction Conventions and Legislatures and of Congress." *Journal of Negro History* 5 (January 1920): 63–119.

Zipf, Karin L. "'The Whites Shall Rule the Land or Die': Gender, Race, and Class in North Carolina Reconstruction Politics." *Journal of Southern History* 65 (August 1999): 499–534.

Dissertations

Barkley Brown, Elsa. "Uncle Ned's Children: Negotiating Community and Freedom in Postemancipation Richmond, Virginia." Ph.D. diss., Kent State University, 1994.

Cantrell, Kimberly Bess. "A Voice for the Freedmen: The Mobile *Nationalist*, 1865–1869." M.A. diss., Auburn University, 1989.

Crofts, Daniel Wallace. "The Blair Bill and the Election Bill: The Congressional Aftermath to Reconstruction." Ph.D. diss., Yale University, 1968.

Mansfield, Betty. "That Fateful Class: Black Teachers of Virginia's Freedmen, 1861–1882." Ph.D. diss., Catholic University of America, 1980.

Nordmann, Christopher Andrew. "Free Negroes in Mobile County, Alabama." Ph.D. diss., University of Alabama, 1990.

Owens, Martha. "The Development of Public Schools for Negroes in Richmond, Virginia." M.A. diss., Virginia State College, 1947.

Sharp, Rebekah. "A History of the Richmond Public School System, 1869–1985." M.A. diss., University of Richmond, 1958.

Shelley, Dian Lee. "The Effects of Increasing Racism on the Creole Colored in Three Gulf Coast Cities between 1803 and 1860." M.A. diss., University of West Florida, 1971.

Index

Edmund L. Drago, *Confederate Phoenix: Rebel Children and Their Families in South Carolina.*

Mary Farmer-Kaiser, *Freedwomen and the Freedmen's Bureau: Race, Gender, and Public Policy in the Age of Emancipation.*

Paul A. Cimbala and Randall Miller, eds., *The Great Task Remaining Before Us: Reconstruction as America's Continuing Civil War.*

John A. Casey Jr., *New Men: Reconstructing the Image of the Veteran in Late-Nineteenth-Century American Literature and Culture.*

Hilary Green, *Educational Reconstruction: African American Schools in the Urban South, 1865–1890.*

Christopher B. Bean, *Too Great a Burden to Bear: The Struggle and Failure of the Freedmen's Bureau in Texas.*